DISASTER CANADA

by JANET LOOKER

PROJECT PRODUCERS

ANDREA GUTSCHE
RUSSELL FLOREN

To the victims, to the survivors, and to the families and friends...

...the truly noble and resolved spirit raises
itself, and becomes more conspicuous in
times of disaster and ill-fortune.

Plutarch (AD 46-120)
Lives, Eumenes

IN ONLY SECONDS THE QUEBEC BRIDGE COLLAPSED, AUGUST 29, 1907

At 5:30 p.m., while the New York City architect discussed newly-discovered weaknesses in the Bridge's design, a normal workday was ending in Quebec. The 86 workmen had tromped all day over the stressed components of the bridge that rose 49 metres (160 ft.) over the St. Lawrence River. It only took ten seconds for the bridge to buckle and collapse, dragging workmen down with it.

QUEBEC CITY FIRE, 1866

Two major fires destroyed the newer sections of Quebec in 1845. The city was rebuilt, using more stone, but money was saved by skimping on firefighting equipment and personnel. In 1866, a third blaze whipped through the upper city, taking five lives and leaving 20 000 homeless.

TABLE OF CONTENTS

216   PART FIVE: TECHNOLOGY AND HUMAN ERROR

Our hour is marked, and no one can claim a moment of life beyond what fate has predestined.

Napolean Bonaparte, 1821

**UNKNOWN MINER
SPRINGHILL,
NOVA SCOTIA
1956 OR 1958**

Worry, tension and exhaustion expressed through a mask of coal grime. The mining community was striken several times by disaster.

INTRODUCTION

The human face of disaster... what does it reveal about our past? Each event has been an amplified moment in history, when the nation has stopped to watch and listen, absorbed by its headlines. Awakening us from routine, these violent confrontations compel us to pause and re-evaluate our society: how much did we risk, and why? What have we learnt? Pieced together, the fragments give insight into our country at a particular time—its technological progress, its customs and laws, and its values and beliefs.

These are the stories of the uncommon acts of ordinary people who have faced the worst, and of the humbling self-sacrifice of those individuals coming to their aid. Stripping us, suddenly and viciously, of all security, disasters expose the inner being to tell us who we really are, while leaving us, with our lists of dead, wondering who we might have been.

Many of the stories show recurring patterns. There are always people who forfeit their instinct for self-preservation to help others, like Arnold Burden, who was overcome with carbon monoxide poisoning while trying to save miners after the 1956 Springhill mine accident. There are frequently strange waves of luck. It is possible for a man to be blown across a neighbourhood in an explosion, losing every thread of clothing in his flight, and suffer only bruises.

Historically under-protected by legislation, labourers in the major industries have frequently been vulnerable to disasters. Newfoundland's sealers, for example, spent long shifts far from their ships on unstable ice. They were poorly paid, poorly fed, and lived in squalor on ill-equipped vessels. Before the captains and merchants would agree to any changes, there would be many needless deaths reported in the papers.

The media has long been key in understanding events as they unfolded. In Canada's early papers—the *Canadian Illustrated News* and its French counterpart, *L'Opinion publique*, founded in 1869-70—dramatic wood engravings depicted many details taken from survivors' accounts, feeding readers across the country descriptive images of the horrifying scenes. Even after photography became more popularized in the late 1800s, these engravings were often preferred as they could tell a more dramatic narrative than could the early photographs, limited by their cumbersome technology. But by the turn of the 20th century, with improvements to the photographic process, photoreportage was born. Suddenly, papers began filling with real and graphic images of disasters.

FATHER CLUTCHING YOUNG VICTIM, *VICTORIA* CAPSIZAL, 1881
Before photography, the news was interpreted visually by artists. This image was featured in Canada's first national newspaper, the Canadian Illustrated News.

**J. FRANK WILLIS GAVE THE FIRST LIVE
RADIO COVERAGE OF A CANADIAN DISASTER**
*(Above) 1936: the tense hours after the collapse of the
mine at Moose River, Nova Scotia, were broadcast
throughout Canada, the United States and Britain.
(Right) At the Moose River mine disaster, a radio transmitter dropped down a drill tube allowed people at the
pithead to listen underground to the rescue in progress.*

With Canada's first live radio coverage of a disaster, the speed of relaying the story accelerated. It was Nova Scotia's Moose River mine collapse in 1936, a story which enthralled thousands both in North America and across the Atlantic. The first live rescue shown on television was after Nova Scotia's Springhill mine collapse in 1958. Miners and rescuers, shy before the cameras, became North American heroes. Forty years later, after Swissair Flight 111's disappearance into the Atlantic Ocean, it took less than half an hour for calls to flood the Rescue Co-ordination Centre in Halifax—even on its unlisted numbers. And when airline officials said that survivors were unlikely, TVs across the globe made the announcement almost simultaneously.

No matter how communities hear the story, their natural instinct is to pull together, overlooking regional differences and international boundaries. Through the decade of Prairie droughts, clothes, shoes, Ontario's fruit and Newfoundland's salt cod found its way into the dust bowl. And Manitoba's 1997 flood relief funds were inundated with donations from the people of Saguenay, Quebec, who'd suffered their own deluge the previous year.

Sometimes what is revealed is disquieting to our current sensibilities and values. Bigoted and belittling newspaper reports were once generally acceptable. Immigrant victims of the Frank Slide in Alberta, 1903, were not named in the papers. They were simply "Poles" or "Czechs," with or without their "concubines." Japanese labourers, killed in the Rogers Pass avalanche of 1910, suffered the same anonymity, listed as a group of "Japs." This was nothing unusual—the tone of the era.

Looking back, one of the most interesting aspects of disasters is the impact they have had on the evolution of the country. The social, economic

The Gazette.

WEATHER FORECAST:
FAIR AND COLD

TEMPERATURE YESTERDAY
Max 20 above m 10 above

VOL. CXLVI. NO. 295

MONTREAL, MONDAY, DECEMBER 10, 1917—TWENTY PAGES

PRICE TWO CENTS

Elements Still Scourge Desolated City of Halifax
1050 Bodies at Morgues; All Germans Being Arrested

DELUGE HINDERS SEARCH OF DEBRIS;   **EVIL SPELL OF**   **COSSACK CHIEFS**   **INCREDIBLE HAPPENINGS**

and political movements that emerged from the West during the Great Depression may well have been galvanized by those years of hardship in the droughts. A disaster's influence on the country's psychology fades with the passing generations, but technological and regulatory changes remain. Each investigation yields recommendations for improvement. With groups like the National Search and Rescue Program and Emergency Preparedness Canada our response to crisis has become a well-organized network of shared information and skills. RADARSAT-1—a Canadian observation satellite capable of imaging the earth through clouds and darkness—is already in orbit. It was used to predict weaknesses in defense against Quebec's floods in 1996 and Manitoba's in 1997.

We have learnt from our catastrophes. Safety procedures and precautions continue to be improved and re-evaluated. Yet as recently as 1992, miners in Westray, Nova Scotia, worked in poorly-ventilated conditions, breathing in methane gas and dodging frequent roof collapses until a spark ignited a pocket of methane gas, killing 26 miners. The lessons continue to be learned.

This rugged and expansive land, with its far-reaching boundaries and extremes of climate, has produced disasters of tremendous scope and severity. Among Canada's oldest and most devastating, nautical disasters comprise the first chapter of this book. In a country edged on three sides by imposing oceans and webbed by inland lakes and rivers—a country in which our waterways

"ALL GERMANS BEING ARRESTED"
(Above) When the Parliament Buildings in Ottawa burned and Halifax was levelled by a massive explosion during WWI, Germans were suspected of sabotage.

were our early highways—the frequency of marine tragedies is not surprising. Those disasters of our convulsive earth are grouped together, as are those caused by fire. Wind, water and ice often team up to wreak havoc, and their stories are largely inseparable. The final chapter tells of technological and human error. Many events are quite recent, and lead us to reflect on our ability to anticipate, and our commitment to minimizing, the inherent risks of rapidly developing technologies.

DRAEGERMEN FROM THE BELLEVUE MINE DISASTER CROWSNEST PASS, ALBERTA, 1910

The design principles of rescue equipment used by early draegermen are still being employed today.

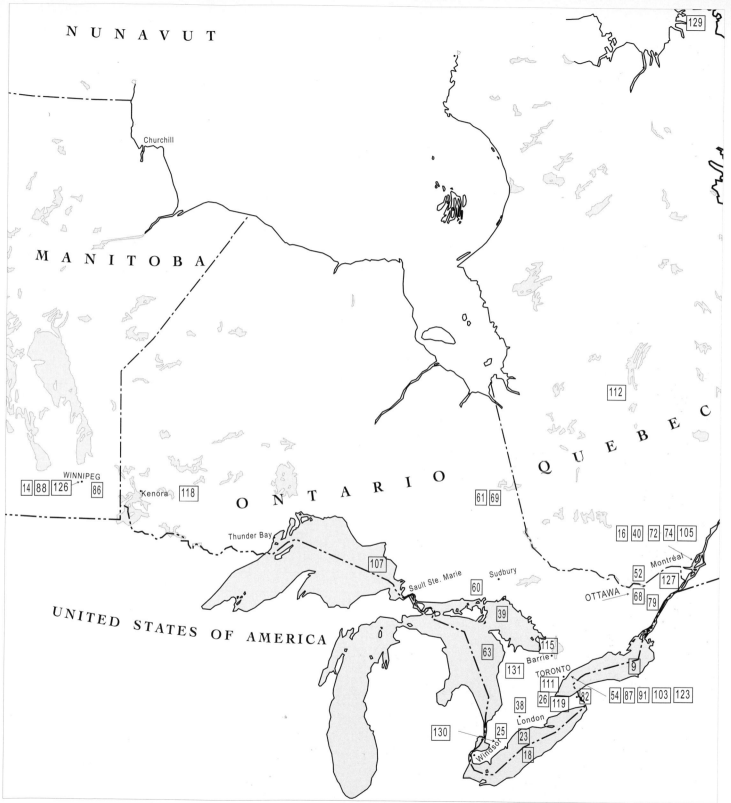

N U N A V U T

Churchill

M A N I T O B A

WINNIPEG
14 88 126 86

Kenora 118

Thunder Bay

O N T A R I O

112

Q U E B E C

61 69

16 40 72 74 105

Montréal

52

127

OTTAWA 68 79

U N I T E D   S T A T E S   O F   A M E R I C A

Sault Ste. Marie   Sudbury

60

39

107

63

115

Barrie

TORONTO

131

111

9

54 87 91 103 123

38

26 119 82

London

130

25

23

Windsor

18

xv

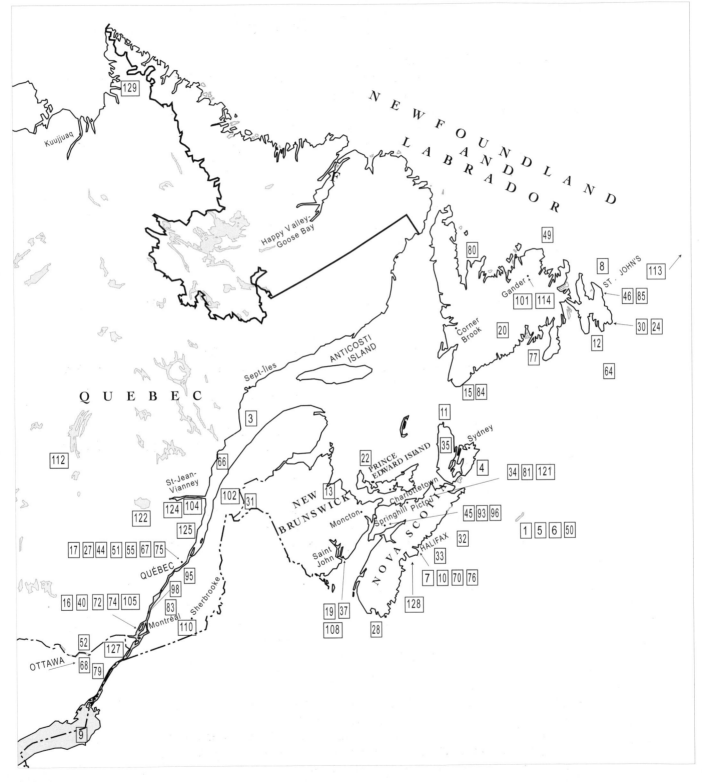

NEWFOUNDLAND

LABRADOR

129

Kuujjuaq

Happy Valley-
Goose Bay

49

80

8

Gander

ST. JOHN'S

113

101 114

46 85

Corner
Brook

20

30 24

12

77

64

Sept-Îles

ANTICOSTI
ISLAND

15 84

QUEBEC

3

11

Sydney

112

66

35

St-Jean-
Vianney

22

PRINCE
EDWARD
ISLAND

4

34 81 121

102 31

124 104

NEW

Charlottetown

122

BRUNSWICK

13

Moncton

45 93 96

1 5 6 50

125

Springhill Pictou

17 27 44 51 55 67 75

32

16 40 72 74 105

QUÉBEC

95

Saint
John

HALIFAX

33

98

Sherbrooke

NOVA SCOTIA

7 10 70 76

83

Montréal

110

19 37

128

52

108

28

OTTAWA

127

68 79

9

LIST OF DISASTERS

1   Wreck of the *Delight*, Sable Island, Nova Scotia; 1583. Deaths: 85
2   Tsunami caused by Earthquake, Vancouver Island, British Columbia; 1700. Deaths: unknown
3   Ile-aux-Oeufs Disaster, Quebec; 1711. Deaths: 950
4   *Le Chameau* Wrecked in Storm, near Louisbourg, Nova Scotia; 1725. Deaths: 316
5   *Catherine* Wrecked, off Sable Island, Nova Scotia; 1737. Deaths: 98
6   Four French Warships Sank, due to Storm off Sable Island, Nova Scotia; 1746. Deaths: 200-300
7   Pestilence Aboard 8 French Armada Ships after surviving Storm off Sable Island, Anchored in Bedford Basin, Nova Scotia; 1746. Deaths: over 1000
8   Storm off Grand Banks, Newfoundland; 1775. Deaths: 2-4000
9   *Ontario* sinks in Eastern Lake Ontario; 1783. Deaths: 190
10   HMS *La Tribune* Ran Aground, Halifax, Nova Scotia; 1797. Deaths: 238
11   *Sovereign* Wrecked, St. Paul's Island, Nova Scotia; 1814. Deaths: 799
12   *Harpooner* Ran Aground, St. Shotts, Newfoundland; 1816. Deaths: 206
13   Miramichi Fire, New Brunswick; 1825. Deaths: 200-500
14   Red River Flood, Winnipeg, Manitoba; 1826. Deaths: 5
15   *Lady Sherbrook* Lost, near Port Aux Basques, Newfoundland; 1831. Deaths: 273
16   Montreal Cholera Epidemic, Quebec; 1832. Deaths: 947
17   Cap Diamant Slide, Quebec City, Quebec; 1841. Deaths: 32
18   Hurricane-force Winds, Lake Ontario and Lake Erie; 1844. Deaths: 200
19   Typhus Epidemic, Partridge Island Quarantine Station near Saint John, N.B.; 1847. Deaths: '000s
20   Hurricane, Newfoundland; 1847. Deaths: 300
21   Loss of the Franklin Expedition, Canadian Arctic; 1847-48. Deaths: 129
22   The Yankee Gale, P.E.I.; 1851. Deaths: 150
23   *Atlantic* Collides with *Ogdensburgh*, Lake Erie; 1852. Deaths: 130
24   *Arctic* collides with French schooner, *Vesta*, Grand Banks, off Cape Race, Nfld.; 1854. Deaths: 322
25   Baptiste Creek Train Crash, near Chatham, Ontario; 1854. Deaths: 52
26   Des Jardines Train Wreck, Hamilton, Ontario; 1857. Deaths: 60
27   Fire Aboard Steamer Montreal, near Quebec City, Quebec; 1857. Deaths: 253
28   *Hungarian* Wrecked, off Cape Sable, Nova Scotia; 1860. Deaths: 205
29   Smallpox Epidemic, Canada-wide; 1862. Deaths: 20 000
30   *Anglo-Saxon* Wrecked, near Clam Cove, Cape Race, Newfoundland; 1863. Deaths: 238
31   St. Hilaire Train Wreck, St. Hilaire, Quebec; 1864. Deaths: 99
32   *City of Boston* Lost, Storm off Nova Scotia; 1870. Deaths: 191
33   Sinking of the *Atlantic*, waters off Nova Scotia; 1873. Deaths: 560
34   Drummond Colliery Disaster, Pictou, Nova Scotia; 1873. Deaths: 70
35   The Great Nova Scotia Cyclone, Cape Breton Island, Nova Scotia; 1873. Deaths: 500
36   Sinking of the S.S. *Pacific*, near Victoria, British Columbia; 1875. Deaths: 236
37   Saint John Fire, New Brunswick; 1877. Deaths: 11
38   The *Victoria* Capsizes, London, Ontario; 1881. Deaths: 182
39   Sinking of the *Asia*, Lake Huron's Georgian Bay, Ontario; 1882. Deaths: 120
40   Smallpox Outbreak, Montreal, Quebec; 1885. Deaths: 5864
41   Vancouver Fire, British Columbia; 1886. Deaths: 30-40
42   Nanaimo Mine Disaster, Nanaimo, British Columbia; 1887. Deaths: 153
43   Number Five Mine Fire, Wellington, British Columbia; 1888. Deaths: 75
44   Rockfall of Quebec City, Quebec; 1889. Deaths: 47

89 U.S. Military Transport Plane Crash, Yukon; 1950. Deaths: 44
90 Polio Outbreaks Prior to Salk Vaccine, Canada-wide; 1953-54. Deaths: 638
91 Hurricane Hazel, Toronto, Ontario; 1954. Deaths: 81
92 Trans-Canada Airlines Crash, Moose Jaw, Saskatchewan; 1954. Deaths: 34
93 Springhill Mine Explosion, Springhill, Nova Scotia; 1956. Deaths: 39
94 Trans-Canada Airlines Mount Slesse Crash, Chilliwack, British Columbia; 1956. Deaths: 62
95 Central Airways Crash, Issoudun, Quebec; 1957. Deaths: 77
96 Springhill Bump, Springhill, Nova Scotia; 1958. Deaths: 75
97 Second Narrows Bridge Collapse, Vancouver, British Columbia; 1958. Deaths: 18
98 Ste. Thérèse Air Crash, Ste. Thérèse, Quebec; 1963. Deaths: 118
99 Granduc Mine Avalanche, Stewart, British Columbia; 1965. Deaths: 27
100 CP Air Crash, 100 Mile House, British Columbia; 1965. Deaths: 52
101 Czechoslovakia State Airlines Crash, Gander, Newfoundland; 1967. Deaths: 37
102 Fire in Notre Dame du Lac, Quebec; 1969. Deaths: 40
103 Toronto International Air Disaster, Toronto, 1970. Deaths: 109
104 Quebec Landside, St.-Jean-Vianney, Quebec; 1971. Deaths: 31
105 Bluebird Café Fire, Montreal, Quebec; 1972. Deaths: 37
106 Pan Arctic Electra Crash, Rea Point, Northwest Territories; 1974. Deaths: 32
107 Wreck of the *Edmund Fitzgerald*, Lake Superior, off Whitefish Point, Ontario; 1975. Deaths: 29
108 Cell Block Fire at Saint John Police Headquarters, New Brunswick; 1977. Deaths: 20
109 Pacific Western Airlines Crash, Cranbrook, British Columbia; 1978. Deaths: 43
110 Bus Brake Failure, near Eastman, Quebec; 1978. Deaths: 43
111 Mississauga Train Disaster, Mississauga, Ontario; 1979. Deaths: 0
112 New Year's Eve Fire, Chapais, Quebec; 1979. Deaths: 44
113 The Sinking of the *Ocean Ranger*, waters off Newfoundland; 1982. Deaths: 84
114 Gander Air Disaster, Gander, Newfoundland; 1985. Deaths: 256
115 Barrie Tornado, Barrie, Ontario; 1985. Deaths: 12
116 Hinton Train Disaster, Hinton, Alberta; 1986. Deaths: 23
117 Edmonton Tornado, Edmonton, Alberta; 1987. Deaths: 26
118 Air Ontario Crash, Dryden, Ontario; 1989. Deaths: 24
119 Hagersville Tire Fire, Ontario; 1990. Deaths: 0
120 Calgary Hailstorm, Alberta; 1991 and 1992. Deaths: 0
121 Westray Mine Disaster, Pictou, Nova Scotia; 1992. Deaths: 26
122 Lac-Bouchette Automobile Crash, Quebec; 1993. Deaths: 19
123 Toronto Subway Crash; Toronto, Ontario; 1995. Deaths: 3
124 Saguenay Floods, Saguenay River, Quebec; 1996. Deaths: 10
125 Bus Brake Failure, Les Eboulements, Quebec; 1997. Deaths: 44
126 Red River Flood, Winnipeg, Manitoba; 1997. Deaths: 0
127 Ice Storm, Ontario, Quebec and Maritimes; 1998. Deaths: 25
128 Swiss Air Flight 111 Crash, 1998. Deaths: 229
129 Northern Quebec Avalanche, Kangiqsualujjuaq, Quebec; 1999. Deaths: 9
130 Highway 401 between London and Windsor, Ontario; Deaths: 40 between March 1999-July 2000
131 E-coli Outbreak, Walkerton, Ontario; 2000. Deaths: 6
132 Pine Lake Tornado, Alberta; 2000. Deaths: 11

***ATLANTIC* FOUNDERS, PEGGY'S POINT, NOVA SCOTIA, 1877**
Only 415 of 975 on board the Atlantic survived when the ship struck the treacherous reefs off Peggy's Point.

NAUTICAL DISASTERS

Build then a ship of death, for you
must take the longest
journey to oblivion

D.H. Lawrence
The Ship of Death

**BOUND FOR NEW YORK, THE *ARCADIA* FOUNDERS OFF
SABLE ISLAND, NOVA SCOTIA, JANUARY 1857**

*170 people on board were rescued thanks to the lifesaving crew stationed on Sable Island.
According to the* London Illustrated News, *the horses featured in this engraving were tamed to be
used in rescue operations. The island is still renowned for its wild horses.*

NAUTICAL DISASTERS

Part One

Canada's nautical liaisons have been long, rich and turbulent. Surrounded on three fronts by ocean, and with a landscape webbed with fresh water, the waters of the North—their beauty, moods, terrifying cold and depths—envelop untold mysteries and romance. Natural hazards abound: ice, fog, storms and blizzards, rogue waves and shoals.

Southeast of Nova Scotia is Sable Island, the "Graveyard of the Atlantic," having claimed three hundred ships or more. Obscured either by fog or storms most of the year, by 1801, the island had surprised so many vessels that the Government of Nova Scotia urged that a "Sable Island Establishment" be settled on the sand. Forerunner of the Coast Guard, the Establishment built lighthouses and lifesaving stations, its settlers racing through pounding surf toward doomed vessels.

It is not surprising that thousands of wrecks dot the rugged East Coast shores. But the Great Lakes, safely surrounded by land mass, have dragged down at least 3000 vessels of their own. Long Point, the peninsula reaching out into Lake Erie, is littered with shipping remains.

The sealing industry and Arctic adventures pushed men and vessels into unstable fields of ice, and dire consequences. In 1847, the Franklin expedition resulted in 129 deaths aboard the HMS *Erebus* and HMS *Terror*.

The West Coast has also had its share of drama. Ripple Rock in the Seymour Narrows was deadly to heavy shipping traffic, gutting up to thirty ships before the navigational hazard was blown sky high in 1958.

Beyond even geography and intemperate weather, the most dangerous maritime element is human error. Several of the worst nautical catastrophes in Canada have occurred in sheltered waterways, caused solely by arrogance, navigational bumbling, or a lack of respect for water and its power.

In 1836, a Select Committee investigating the world's shipwrecks for the British House of Commons unearthed a long list of human causes. Among them were defective ship construction, inadequate equipment, incompetency of master and officers, insobriety of crews, and errors in charting.

The basics—sustaining life until help arrives—were frequently overlooked. When the American luxury steam liner, the *Arctic*, collided in the fog with a French schooner on the Grand Banks in 1854, there were only lifeboats for fewer than half the passengers. Three hundred and twenty-two died. Soon

CAPTAIN SAVAGE BLAMED FOR THE DEATHS OF 122 PASSENGERS ON BOARD THE *ASIA* WHICH FOUNDERED ON LAKE HURON, 1882

Why would a Captain sail his ship into a storm? In the case of Capt. Savage, the question goes unanswered. He died of exposure after floating for days in a lifeboat (see page 13). Ship's captains faced unyielding pressure to meet quotas and delivery dates— fertile ground for risk taking.

THE *EMPRESS OF IRELAND'S* FINAL MINUTES PAINTED BY A SURVIVOR

1914, 1057 people were on board the luxury liner heading for Liverpool, England, when it struck another ship in the frigid St. Lawrence River. 1012 people perished. 700 of the dead were not recovered.

afterwards, the use of steam whistles in fog became mandatory, and shipping lanes were designated for incoming and outgoing vessels, but the scarcity of lifeboats was still an issue when the *Titanic* went down in 1912. Sealing vessel, the SS *Newfoundland*, with no radio for clear communication, abandoned 135 men on the ice packs of the frigid Atlantic in 1914. The oil rig, *Ocean Ranger*, destroyed in a storm off Newfoundland in 1982, had not supplied its men with survival suits that would have prevented hypothermia.

MONKSHAVEN FOUNDERED ON LAKE SUPERIOR NOVEMBER 1905

The Great Lakes have been ravaged by three Great Storms: 1905 (70 vessels foundered, 70 killed); 1913 (21 ships lost, 52 damaged, over 248 sailors killed); 1942 (50 ships lost, 50 lives lost). The Monkshaven was one of 14 ships taken by a three-day storm on Lake Superior in 1905. Lifted high on a monstrous wave, the Monkshaven was cut open by the rocks of Angus Island. Her 21-man crew clambered onto the rocks where they struggled to endure three terrifying days of extreme weather.

A vessel with the best equipment still primarily relies on the judgment of the captain, the person who is in ultimate control. According to writer Cassie Brown, captains of the sealing industry were regarded as heroes, in great demand as pilots for polar expeditions, and renowned for their ice field skills. Despite the horrendous working conditions, sealers vied for berths on their ships. But the captains were frequently unworthy of their exalted status, being over-confident in their knowledge of the sea.

When the worst occurred, and the vessel began to break apart, there was an unwritten code: women and children into the lifeboats first; and the captain goes down with his ship. Yet the 1854 collision of the *Arctic* saw senior officers commandeer a lifeboat, while women and children were left slipping over the deck. The one remaining officer tried to make a raft to save them without success. In 1873,

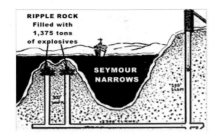

the passenger liner *Atlantic* drove straight into the reefs off Peggy's Point, Nova Scotia, taking 560 lives. Four hundred and fifteen people were saved, none of them women, and only one child. Similarly, when the French passenger ship *La Bourgoyne* went down off Sable Island in 1898, only 173 of more than 700 people survived. The survivors were mainly crew, and included only one woman.

Technology has reduced the number of shipping catastrophes, as has flight as an alternative form of transportation. Marine disasters, though rare now, will likely continue as long as the dangers causing them remain: the elements, geography, and human fallibility.

PATHFINDER BATTLES A STORM ON LAKE HURON

(Below) Thousands of ships have foundered on the Great Lakes. The Lakes' sheer size is enough to create their own weather systems and storms as terrifying as any on the oceans.

SUBDUING THE UNDERSEA MENACE RIPPLE ROCK, BRITISH COLUMBIA

(Above) From 1875 to 1958, 125 vessels struck Ripple Rock. After two earlier failed attempts to blow up the rock, engineers finally succeeded in 1958. (Above left) A network of tunnels was packed with explosives, and the blast was witnessed by thousands across the country on television. The explosion sent rock and debris 305 metres (1000 ft.) in the air, and created a 7.5-metre (25-ft.) tidal wave.

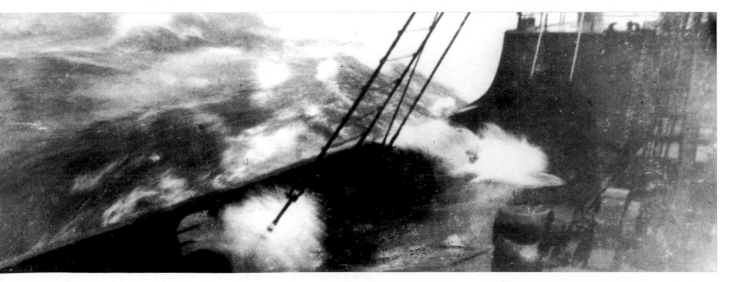

7

CANADIAN Illustrated News

ol. XXIII.—No. 24   MONTREAL, SATURDAY, JUNE 11, 1881

"A FATHER AND HIS DARLING"
Such was the title of this illustration of a father clutching his dead daughter when it was originally printed in the Canadian Illustrated News, *seventeen days after the disaster on the Thames River, 1881.*

A VICTORIAN CAPSIZAL

Thames River, London, Ontario

MAY 24, 1881

It was the first holiday of Spring, 1881. And in London, Ontario, Queen Victoria's birthday was celebrated with jubilance. It was a day of happy rebellion against the repression of the era, a day that would breed its own dark lunacy.

A riot of picnics, games and excursions had broken out with many Londoners ending up at the Springbank parkland, a thirty-minute ride up the river from the central Sulphur Springs docks. Three steamboats—the *Princess Victoria* among them—began their boating season that day, ferrying holidayers up and down the river. The crowds—and the revenue—were substantial.

At about four o'clock that afternoon, the steamer *Forest City* was grounded on one of many sandbars on the Thames. Coming to the rescue, the *Victoria* transferred the *Forest City's* passengers to the docks, and then collected a load of returning picnickers. By now, the *Victoria* had fallen behind schedule. Soon the youthful crowds were tired of waiting on the docks. When the *Victoria* finally pulled up, they rushed her, vaulting the railings, and bounding up the stairs to the top deck. The young purser, Herbert Parish, was completely overpowered by the mob. With great difficulty, Captain Rankin forced several families off the boat, but some 600 people refused to move. The boat was now dangerously top heavy, loaded at two to three times her safe capacity.

Rankin shouted warnings to the crowd and still no one disembarked. Near exasperation, the Captain swung the steamer around, and so began the *Victoria's* last mad voyage.

Rankin noticed that the boat was riding low and responding sluggishly. He felt something briefly snag the hull. Meanwhile the young passengers raced up and down the stairs, delirious from the day, crowding to one side, then the other. The steamer began to see-saw and to sink lower.

OVERWHELMED CREW

Captain Rankin (top) who lost control of his ship, and deckhand Nick Forkey who tried to keep people on the lower deck.

9

SHALLOW AFTERMATH

The capsized ship in tranquil waters. On it, an estimated 182 passengers died. Bodies were loaded onto the Princess Louise *and transported back to London.*

While Rankin focused on completing the journey, his novice crew tried unsuccessfully to calm the passengers. Boys on the top deck ran from one railing to another, trying literally to rock the boat. Water doused the feet of passengers on the lower deck. A few leapt off the decks and swam to shore. Still, the prevailing mood among the passengers was delight.

Then, as the boat began to list too far, fun turned into panic. People clutched each other on the steeply sloping decks, either clinging to the stanchions or being thrown into the water. The boiler crashed through the supports, crushing some and scalding others with its broken steam lines. With some supports gone, and the stress from clinging bodies, the upper deck collapsed, crushing everyone beneath it.

A savage fight followed under water, as passengers kicked, pulled and trampled each other in frantic attempts to surface. People climbed up other people, only to be pulled under as others climbed on them. Although the true number of fatalities was not confirmed, an estimated 182 passengers died. About 125 were women and children. Many of the women were dragged beneath the surface by the weighty dresses of the time. Some of the victims tried to swim, but were too stunned or exhausted to make the short distance to shore. One survivor, Samuel Glass, later told how he stood in water only up to his shoulders and saved many lives.

Some passengers of a passing steamer, the *Princess Louise*, plunged into the water to help the *Victoria*. As people tried to get the badly injured to the banks, there remained a pervading strangeness. Writer Ken McTaggart in his book, *The Victoria Day Disaster*, tells:

The first survivors who managed to stagger ashore were met by the angry farmer whose field they'd landed on. Without any sympathy he ordered them from his property. However, his tirade of words soon vanished when big John Mitcheltree, a butcher with a physique of a football player coolly looked him up and down, called for a coil of rope, and searched around with his eyes for a convenient branch to loop it over. When he proceeded to knot a noose in the end, the farmer quickly offered to give assistance.

As daylight faded, large bonfires lit along the banks cast a flickering glow on the bodies being loaded aboard the *Princess Louise*. Volunteers worked well into the night. A man called Mose Cox pulled 65 people from the water in five hours, and Lambert Payne, a reporter with the *London Free Press*, stood in the water for six hours, bringing up more than twenty bodies with his pike pole. Thieves also laboured through the early hours of the morning, frisking bodies on the shore when no one was watching.

The holiday steamer, *Princess Louise*, took a load of 152 bodies to the Sulpher Springs docks where they were laid out in the sheds for identification. Hearses and wagons transported the dead to their families, some drivers cashing in on the tragedy by doubling and tripling their prices. One driver and his assistant, arriving at one house when no one was home, simply opened a

TICKET-TAKER
Young Alfred Wastie was unable to calm the crowds. He drowned in the accident.

RECOVERING THE DEAD
The city of London mobilized, searching for victims into the night.

window and slid the corpse inside, then dashed back for more. Another left the dead relative propped up in a chair on the porch with a note to the family attached.

The city of London was devastated. Black armbands were worn for the entire month, and a citizen's committee—including brewers John Carling and John Labatt—started a relief fund. Condolences streamed in from across the continent, from Britain, and from Queen Victoria herself.

Inspection of the boat revealed a small gash in its underbelly, which may have been exacerbated by its tremendous load that day. An inquest was held which seemed only to conclude that somebody, somewhere had been negligent. The public, meanwhile, cast blame on the captain, the owner, the inspector and the crew, and they, in turn, rebuked the reckless passengers.

In the end, no charges were laid. The *Canadian Illustrated News* pointed an accusing finger at two renowned culprits: "*Hurry and money-making, the twin curses of an age of over-excitement.*"

TRANSPORTING COFFINS THE MONDAY AFTER THE DISASTER

Hearses and wagons transported the dead to their families. Some drivers cashed in on the tragedy by doubling their prices.

THE TWO SURVIVORS

Wreck of the *Asia*, Lake Huron, Ontario

SEPTEMBER 14, 1882

The steamer, *Asia*, pushed northward across Georgian Bay from Owen Sound. Loaded with logging equipment, provisions, livestock and 97 passengers, she battled a rough first night in mounting winds, only to find herself, the next morning, in the full fury of a hurricane that was ripping across Lake Huron's Georgian Bay.

The ship was tossed in menacing seas, the passengers terrified and seasick. Captain Savage, in a last, desperate effort to save the ship veered west toward Lonely Island. In that moment, two enormous waves tipped the ship, pulling it downwards. Passengers leapt into the water, grabbing at anything afloat. Seventeen-year-old Christy Anne Morrison, hurled from the railings by the wind, clung to a lifeboat with her cousin, the First Mate, bracing against each wave, and gasping for air.

When the waves finally calmed, Christy drifted for three days, far from shore, watching as six out of seven other survivors in the lifeboat died from exposure. Christy and fellow teenaged passenger, Dunkan Tinkiss, would be the only two survivors of the *Asia*'s 122 passengers and crew. The *Asia*'s demise spurred the government to chart thoroughly Georgian Bay's treacherous waters.

CHRISTY ANNE MORRISON
Christy Anne survived three days adrift in a lifeboat following the hurricane of September 15, 1882 (below). The wreck of the steamer Asia *has never been located (below left).*

13

ATLANTIC FOUNDERING ON THE REEFS OFF PEGGY'S POINT, APRIL 1, 1873

Five hundred and sixty people perished as the Atlantic *foundered on the reefs off Peggy's Point. The booming voice of Captain J. Williams (top right inset) could be heard even above the crashing waves. He offered $500 to local fishermen for every boatload of his passengers they rescued. The Captain survived the ordeal, but was relieved of his command by his employers, the British White Star Line. The Reverend William Ancient (middle inset) performed a dramatic rescue, leaping aboard the ship as it broke apart, and carrying the First Officer—with his two broken legs—to safety. John Hindley (bottom inset) was the sole child who survived.*

14

Five Hundred And Sixty Perished

Wreck of the *Atlantic* off Peggy's Point, Nova Scotia

APRIL 1, 1873

It was late March, 1873, when the SS *Atlantic* sailed from Queenstown, England, bound for New York. The image of elegance and strength, she had three iron decks, seven watertight bulkheads, and four powerful engines. Her 975 passengers and crew enjoyed a few days of tranquil sailing before vicious North Atlantic weather slowed the ship. With coal and food supplies dwindling, Captain John A. Williams gave orders to divert to Halifax, Nova Scotia. It was a port he didn't know. Before retiring for bed, Williams gave a cursory glance at the charts, believing he was heading for Sambro Light at Halifax Harbour's entrance. He was, in fact, headed straight for Peggy's Point, and the treacherous reefs in between.

Quartermaster Raylance first saw the white froth of waves hitting rock. He ran screaming to the bridge, "*BREAKERS TO PORT!*" But the *Atlantic* drove full speed into the reefs, her belly tearing open at once. Pandemonium erupted. Overloaded lifeboats tipped and crashed into the frigid waves. Boilers exploded. Steerage passengers flooded from portholes. The captain rushed around, tying unconscious passengers to the rigging, out of the water's reach.

Three heroic crewmen swam to a nearby islet. They hoped to secure ropes to serve as an escape route from the ship's bow. As the ship thrashed on the rocks, those who tried the ropes were submerged one minute, and then thrown high into the air the next. The ship's flares attracted local fishermen, but few would brave the boiling waters. Reverend William Ancient, resident clergyman of Terence Bay, ventured close to the ship with some fishermen. Climbing on board he pried a numb First Officer from the rigging, and hauled him into the rescue boat.

There were ultimately 415 survivors, none of them women. John Hindley was the only child saved.

NO WOMEN SURVIVORS
Illustrators for newspapers often drew on information from survivor accounts. This image may have originated from Reverend Ancient's description of a woman in white night clothes who was clinging to the rigging beside the First Officer. Although Ancient rescued the First Officer, the woman was considered beyond help and was left to die at sea.

SEARCHING THE HORIZON FOR "SWILES" (SEALS)

Though many men flocked to Newfoundland's ports to find sealing work, life was harsh aboard the sealing vessels.

16

HUMAN FAILINGS

The *Newfoundland* Sealing Disaster and the loss of the *Southern Cross*

MARCH 31-APRIL 2, 1914

Captain Abraham Kean was a proud man with an iron will and a narrow and suspicious mind. Decades of commanding sealing vessels had preserved his reputation in brine: "slave-driver," "opportunist." For Captain Kean would not abide softness in his crew, and no efforts by The Fisherman's Protective Union to improve the sailors' lot could withstand Kean's opposition. He believed crews cosseted by the luxuries of sufficient food and comfortable lodging were apt to become insubordinate and lazy. And Captain Kean, as his sailors knew, was not beyond helping himself to the occasional pile of fresh pelts and blubber, if they appeared too lonely on the ice, no matter whose crew had worked them.

His comrades in greed were the ship owners and merchants of Newfoundland, men who ranked commercial gain higher than the safety of their crews. When the seal herds began to dwindle late in the nineteenth century, the aging ships were simply sent out further, the hunters pushed to work even harder. And when war was rumoured in the spring of 1914, Kean and his opportunistic friends were determined to exploit the potential rise in oil prices. Even the oldest, most decrepit, wooden galleys were sent, leaking and listing, into the Gulf of St. Lawrence, where the ice was less daunting. Meanwhile, the newer steamships and sturdier old whaling boats were dispatched to the shifting ice fields of the North Atlantic.

Kean, commodore of the latter fleet, was in charge of the *Stephano*. He procured positions for his sons, too. The eldest, Joseph, was to command the steamer *Florizel*, while a younger son, Westbury, was captain of the wooden *Newfoundland*.

SEALERS STRUGGLING ACROSS ICE FLOES

With a staple diet of only hard tack and tea, sealers then spent long, physically-demanding shifts on the ice.

Westbury Kean, at 29 years old, had almost no experience as a sealing captain. His ship, the *Newfoundland*, although the most solid of the wooden vessels, had been stripped of her wireless and deck thermometer, to better equip one of the newer steel ships. Because young Westbury did not yet have his master's certificate, he was required to have a navigating officer aboard, Captain Charles Green, to give advice. Green was rich with Arctic experience, but Westbury practically ignored him.

As the fleet set out, the young captain struggled to keep up with the other vessels, but was trapped immediately in an infuriating ice jam. Unable to release his ship, and far from any sign of seals, Westbury watched the other vessels, scarcely visible through his binoculars, racing off to harvest the biggest catch. By the early morning of March 31, Westbury was completely maddened by his own inaction. He ordered all of his men—sealers and officers—off the ship and across the ice to the *Stephano*, approximately six miles away. Once they reached the *Stephano* they were to take orders from its captain, Westbury's father.

The day was extraordinarily mild, the sun veiled in a hazy sky, and the crew climbed down from the steaming deck dressed in light clothing to keep from becoming overheated on the walk. The barometer was reading high, though without a thermometer, Kean couldn't know if the temperature was rising or falling. His men set off, their spirits high.

After several hours clambering over the rugged ice, some of the experienced sealers became suspicious of the wind, now easterly, and the red-tinged, heavy sky. They insisted on returning to the *Newfoundland*. The laughter and derision of their fellow sailors pursued these 34 as they retreated across the ice. Wes Kean watched angrily through his binoculars.

He also saw the remaining 132 men reaching the *Stephano* on the horizon. It was shortly before midday and the first flakes of snow were beginning to fall. Captain Abraham Kean was surprised by the arrival of his son's crew. He hustled them down below for a rest and some bowls of tea while the *Stephano* steamed southwest towards a patch of seals Kean seemed to know about. Arriving at the spot, Kean ordered the men back onto the ice, instructing them to slaughter the seals and return to their own vessel. He'd done his bit to help. He'd found them some seals, given them something hot to drink. And now it was time to pick up his own men.

The crew of the *Newfoundland* stood on the ice, silently exhaling the vapour of their mounting fear as they watched the *Stephano* steam away. They were already tired from the morning's trek, and had fully expected to spend the night aboard Abraham Kean's ship. They were without provisions and miles from their ship, beneath a gathering storm that would prove one of the most furious in history.

Tuesday, March 31, the storm hit the island of Newfoundland with deep snow and violent winds, surprising the old wooden galleys returning from the Gulf, their decks greased with seal blood and blubber. Most sought shelter in the bays along Newfoundland's south shore, but the SS *Southern Cross* chose instead to battle open water. She never made it home. The *Southern Cross* and her crew of 174 vanished that night, into the squalls. As the storm moved north, it intensified.

SEALERS OF THE DAY
In 1914, rumours of war and a rise in oil prices sent men scrambling over precarious ice in search of seals. Dwindling herds forced captains to sail their ships too far out to sea.

ADRIFT ON THE ATLANTIC
At the edge of the ice fields, the ice pans rose and fell with the seas. Obscured by mushy ice, fissures between the pans became death traps.

19

Back aboard the *Newfoundland*, young Captain Westbury Kean listened to the raging weather from the warmth of his cabin, ignorant of his crew's misfortune. Surely his men would be safely on his father's ship by now. Westbury's men marched lost through the knee-deep snowdrifts into the raging blizzard. The pans of ice wheeled and dipped as the sealers trudged across them. Art Mouland, a teenager from Doting Cove, fell into water to his waist. Other sealers hauled him out, but drenched and exhausted, he fell behind the group and disappeared.

Daylight nearly gone, the men staggered with fatigue. Then they heard their ship's whistle. Two shrill blasts. The lost sealers waited desperately for more sounds but there were none. Kean had blown the whistle only to humour his bo'sun who was anxious for the men, but confident his sealers were aboard the *Stephano*, Kean refused to continue.

The sealers pushed a little further into the snow, unsure of their direction, unsure of everything. Finally it was impossible to continue. They would have to spend the night on the ice. Chipping at blocks of ice with their gaffs, they struggled to build shelter.

Speculation on the fate of the *Newfoundland*'s men rippled through the other sealing ships. By then, everyone had heard that the men had been put back on the ice. Some mustered the courage to speak out to their bo'suns or even Abraham Kean's relatives on board, but none had the courage to approach the Old Man himself. Only Joseph Kean, captain of the *Florizel*, broached the question with his father. He sent a wireless message: *"Have you the* Newfoundland's *men on board?"* The response came: *"Carried the* Newfoundland's *crew within three miles of ship before noon, have no doubt they are aboard their own ship."* Westbury, with no wireless, could not be asked.

By midnight the changing winds brought torrential rain, soaking the sealers to the skin. The shelters were of little help. Then, as the morning crept on, a freezing gale blew in from the Arctic, soaking their hair and clothing. The men tried to keep moving. Their hands were numb in frozen mittens, and ice gripped the roots of their eyelashes, fusing their eyelids. Sealer Jessie Collins froze his lips, going

**CAPTAIN
ABRAHAM KEAN**

He was generally considered to have been morally responsible for the sealers' deaths.

from man to man, trying to bite the ice off. By morning, two sealers who had given up lay sprawled on the ice. Edward Tippet and his two sons stood frozen together in a firm embrace.

Mid-afternoon brought a small reprieve. Officer George Tuff, climbing a mound of ice, spotted the *Bellaventure* about two miles to the northwest. Those who had retained the spark to live started stumbling towards it. Climbing the ice, they motioned wildly, waving their gaffs, but the *Bellaventure* was loading pelts on the opposite side and then steamed away.

The *Newfoundland* was about four miles to the south and the same brave group headed that way. For two hours they fought the bone-chilling winds to reach her. But the ship finally broke free from the ice and a triumphant Westbury headed off to find the fleet. When daylight vanished this time, it took with it the forgotten sealers' last hopes for salvation.

A second night out on the ice was torture, with wind chills of -30C. Without food for thirty-six hours, many of the men were hallucinating. Some walked off the pans into the sea, while others just lay down to die. One slashed his own hand to drink his blood. The bodies were frozen sculptures in the clear light of the stars.

Dawn brought calmer winds and better visibility. Captain Westbury Kean set off to retrieve his crew from his father's ship, his binoculars trained out to the water. By chance he turned to look back at the ice, and there the men were, some staggering, some crawling, some clawing forward on their bellies.

SS *SOUTHERN CROSS*
The Southern Cross *was lost in the same storm with 174 men on board.*

The rescue began as the entire sealing fleet rushed to save the stranded men. The crews of the *Stephano*, the *Bellaventure*, and the *Florizel*, were out on the ice, building fires, pouring brandy into the survivors and nursing blackened limbs. Many died in the arms of their rescuers. Wes Kean, in no state to think, handed command of the *Newfoundland* over to his navigating officer, Green. If only he'd had a radio. But more than that: if only he'd continued to blow the whistle during the storm; if only he'd given clearer orders; if only he'd relied less on his single-minded father.

Seventy-seven men died on the ice, and one after reaching port. The *Bellaventure* carried the corpses, stacked on her deck, into port. The spectacle horrified St. John's. By now, the *Southern Cross* had been missing for two days, but Newfoundlanders chose to hope rather than contemplate more loss. Perhaps the storm had pushed the *Southern Cross* far out to sea. Her full load would likely have slowed her down. The ship's fate was only discovered in August of that year. Some planks from her prow bearing the remnants of her name washed up on the Irish coast. The same storm that had maimed and killed the *Newfoundland*'s crew, had dragged another 174 men out to sea.

This had been the most disastrous season on record. And in early April, when, in a scandalous display of greed, the merchants ordered the rest of the fleets to stay near the ice and continue the seal hunt, the community was galvanized behind a public inquiry. No longer would it tolerate such disregard for human life. The inquiry resulted in positive change. Wireless equipment with an operator became mandatory on all sealing ships. And two years later, new legislation prohibited men from being on the ice after dark, required official certification for mates and masters, and provided search parties, rocket signals, medical officers, better food for the men and other basic compensations.

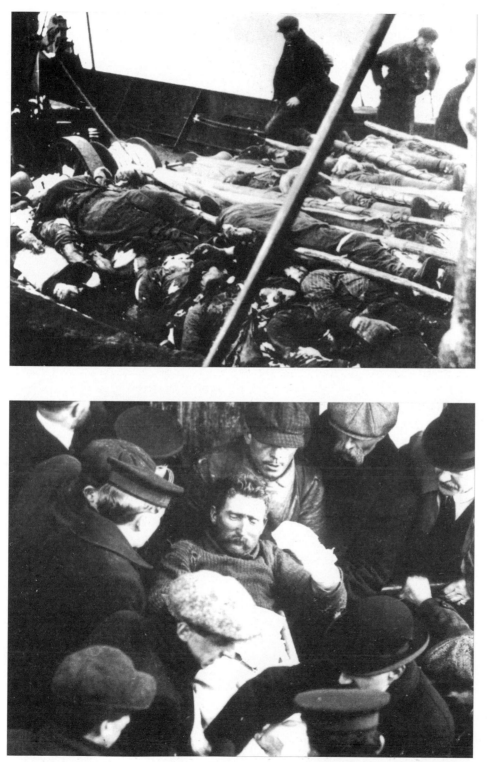

STACKED BODIES

Frozen sealers are pried loose from the decks of the Bellaventure. Not all of the men were recovered. In May 1914, a fisherman reported passing the body of a sealer, frozen in an ice floe.

SURVIVOR THOMAS DAWSON

Dawson holds up his frost-bitten hands as he is carried off the ship. He lost both his feet to exposure.

DREAD IN ST. JOHN'S

A solemn crowd awaits the arrival of the Bellaventure. Mass demonstrations later broke out when the Captain of the Newfoundland *was acquitted of responsibility for the tragedy.*

24

The inquiry did not find Westbury Kean to be at blame. As for his father, Abraham Kean, his emphatic, detailed and self-righteous testimony confused the commissioners, and they laid no official charges. Abraham Kean returned to sealing the following year as commander of the *Florizel*. As he was considered morally responsible for the deaths of the *Newfoundland's* crew, public indignation boiled into a mass demonstration on the streets of St. John's. Hundreds of sealers barred his approach to the ship, but as writer Cassie Brown describes: "...*he walked straight through them in his long sealskin coat and fur hat, nodding as he went to those he knew. They made way and touched their caps in salute. Not a hand, not even a voice, was raised against him.*" Kean continued sealing for another twenty years, eventually receiving the Order of the British Empire for his accomplishments on the ice.

ST. JOHN'S, NEWFOUNDLAND MOURNS 78 DEAD, APRIL 1914
The sealers froze to death on the ice because of wrong assumptions made by the ships' captains.

GREENLAND DISASTER

Off Cape Freels, Newfoundland

MARCH 20, 1898

SS *GREENLAND*

The death of 48 crew from the SS Greenland *gave birth to the Fishermen's Protective Union. Staunchly opposed to unionization was Captain Abraham Kean (see p.20), whose men were accused of stealing the* Greenland's *pelts.*

Sealing season was almost over, the holds already filled with pelts, when the SS *Greenland* put her men out for one last patch of seals. The *Greenland*'s captain, having lost some pelts to theft on the ice, was determined to return to St. John's with the winning cargo.

The spring-like weather took a sudden turn so the captain steamed south to pick up one watch. As he swung around to get the other men, he found the ship was trapped in an ice-bound lake, and more than a hundred of his men, still on the ice, were well out of reach.

The next morning, about fifty half-frozen sealers appeared on the horizon. They were hauled to the ship where the pharmacist crudely amputated their blackened limbs. Two days later, the bodies of the remaining 48 men were found on the ice in small and scattered frozen groups. The crew used block and tackle to lift them onto the ship. Four more men died before they reached St. John's.

TORPEDOED BY A U-BOAT

Sinking of the *Caribou*
off Port aux Basques, Newfoundland

OCTOBER 14, 1942

The *Caribou* was not so much a vessel of war as a regular ferry between North Sydney, Nova Scotia and Port aux Basques, Newfoundland. But owing to the war, she often ferried military personnel along with civilian passengers. And because the *Caribou's* route was so close to the Atlantic, an escort vessel was assigned to her and blackout regulations were enforced on board.

It was in the early hours of October 14. The ferry was 64 kilometres (40 mi.) southwest of Port aux Basques when a torpedo ripped into her starboard side. She instantly began to list. Passengers hurried for the lifeboats, two of which had been destroyed by the blast. The angle of the ship made it impossible to lower other lifeboats. In their panic, people were yelling, leaping into the water, grabbing at capsizing liferafts. Then the *Caribou* exploded, caught fire, split in half and sank.

The escort vessel gave chase to the U-boat that had fired on the ferry. She returned to find that 136 of the *Caribou's* 237 passengers had drowned.

THE SS *CARIBOU* AND KILLED CREW
For decades there was no proof that a German U-boat was to blame for the Caribou's demise. Then the ferry's name was found listed as a target in the log book of U-boat 69.

REMEMBER THE "CARIBOU" AND HER GALLANT CREW

COLLISION

This illustration from the June 11, 1914 Christian Herald *depicts the collier* Storstad *colliding with passenger liner,* Empress of Ireland. *Blind in a sudden bank of dense fog, the* Storstad *sliced an enormous hole in the* Empress' *starboard.*

"DEAD IN THE WATER"

The Sinking of the *Empress of Ireland*

FRIDAY MAY 29, 1914

It seems to me that the resentful sea gods never do sleep, and as long as men will travel on the water, the sea gods will take their toll.

Joseph Conrad
commenting on the tragedy
of the *Empress of Ireland*

The sea gods took their toll, and with profound cruelty, on the beautiful ocean liner the *Empress of Ireland*, leaving her where she lies today—52 metres (170 ft.) deep in the frigid swells of the throat of the St. Lawrence seaway. She is filled with sediment, gnawed by rust, and shrouded by web-like filaments of old fishing nets. Bubbles no longer burst their stale contents onto the water's surface, nor are the currents stained, as they once were, by seeping contents of things foreign to the sea. The ship has been claimed. Yet, entombed within the decaying mass, remain the shadowy remnants of more than a thousand, once-promising, human lives.

They boarded on the afternoon of May 28, 1914, amidst the chaos of last-minute preparations. The week before, while berthed at Quebec City, Canadian Pacific's *Empress of Ireland* was packed with 1000 tonnes (1100 tons) of cargo, huge quantities of produce, and 3000 kilograms (7000 lbs.) of fresh meat, including 1200 prepared chickens. Mountains of coal were handed one bucket at a time into the boiler room. Baggage was loaded, and a cargo of 212 silver bars from Ontario's Nipissing Mine was safely secured in the ship's treasury.

Now it was time for the 1057 passengers to be brought aboard and shown to their quarters. A large contingent—167—was from the Salvation Army. They were thrilled to be attending the third Salvation Army Congress in London, and their excitement was infectious. Their voyage had begun with a well-attended march down Yonge Street in Toronto to Union Station, where boisterous crowds sent them off. Now the Salvationists gathered on the *Empress's* decks wearing new red tunics and

CANADIAN PACIFIC'S EMPRESS OF IRELAND

Launched in 1906, the elegant liner was popular for her steady high seas performance. Bad luck came in 1909 when she hit an uncharted rock in the St. Lawrence.

Mountie-style Stetson hats. The staff band pulled instruments from baggage and started to play "O Canada" and "Auld Lang Syne." Hundreds gathered on the quay, waving Union Jacks and shouting their good-byes. As the ship cast off at 4:30 p.m., the cheering and flag waving came to a crescendo. The band was playing "God Be With You Till We Meet Again."

The *Empress of Ireland's* destination was Liverpool, England. She spent the first night of her journey passing through the sheltered St. Lawrence waters. It was a benevolent night; cool but calm, with a clear, starlit sky. Since her maiden voyage eight years before, the stately liner had earned a reputation for stability and comfort. True, the *Titanic* had gone down on a similar crossing just two years before, but the lessons had been learned and passengers were assured that the lifeboats and the crew aboard the *Empress* would keep them safe.

Dashing English actor, Laurence Irving with his wife and stage partner, Mabel Hackney, dined in the first-class dining room. They chose a private

LIFE ABOARD SHIP

First-class passengers relax in the plush alcoves of the music room.

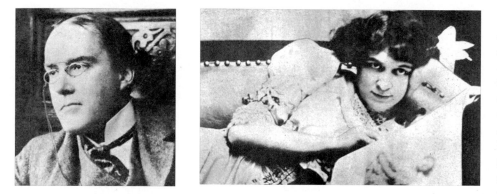

FAMOUS PASSENGERS
Actor Laurence Irving (left) and his wife, Mabel Hackney. The acting team was returning home to England after touring Canada with their stage productions of The Unwritten Law *and* Typhoon. *Irving tried to rescue his wife from the sinking ship. His hand was still clutching a fragment of her nightdress when his body was discovered.*

alcove of Spanish mahogany, beneath sculpted moldings and stained glass portholes. Closer to the five-piece orchestra, engaged in small talk, sat robust big-game hunter and explorer, Sir Henry Seton-Karr and Sherbrooke socialite Mrs. Ethel Paton, bedecked in diamonds.

After dinner, the ship's doctor, young James Grant, a recent graduate of McGill University, followed the strains of the orchestra up through the café. The library in first-class—with its glowing Tiffany lamps and Ambonia-paneled walls—was empty, so he gravitated to the first-class smoking room. While the men savoured cigars, or nightcaps in the bar, ladies in first-class relaxed in the music room on the Upper Promenade Deck, grouped at the piano or nestled into rose taffeta sofas near the fireplace.

Second-class swelled with Salvationists, including their Canadian commander, Commissioner David Rees, his wife and children. Some Salvationists,

AMUSEMENT FOR THE VOYAGE
Passengers pass the time with a cramped game of cricket on deck.

31

enjoying the new moon on the Lower Promenade Deck, started an impromptu sing-a-long, in four-part harmony, lifting their voices with soul-stirring hymns.

Third-class was filled to overflowing with people from many cultural backgrounds. These working-class families were making a special trip or going home to stay. Most of the children on board the *Empress* were on these lower decks.

Captain Henry Kendall stood on the bridge. All was as it should be on his floating palace. He looked forward to an entertaining journey. At 39, Kendall was a seaman of broad experience and fascinating stories. He had been instrumental in the capture of famous British murderer, Dr. Hawley Crippen. Four years earlier, Dr. Crippen, fresh from dismembering his wife, had boarded a transatlantic vessel under Kendall's command. The captain had seen through a weak disguise and alerted Scotland Yard by wireless.

Kendall at the helm, the *Empress* settled at a steady, seaward, 18 knots. Sporadic fog banks drifted over, a common hazard on this waterway. But when a dense fog enveloped the ship, blotting out another steamer, Captain Kendall grew worried. The approaching ship had been a few points off the starboard bow before it disappeared. Now Kendall could see nothing but the fog. He ordered both engines full astern, and when the forward momentum of the *Empress* slowed, Kendall ordered an all-stop. The *Empress* was "dead in the water," and whistled a warning to the inbound steamer. The responding whistle seemed safely to starboard. It was 1:50 a.m., and the blinded *Empress* sat tensely silent.

A few minutes later, a Norwegian collier, the *Storstad*, materialized in the fog off the *Empress*' starboard bow. It was making straight for the

Empress' hull. *"FULL AHEAD,"* screamed Kendall, while the *Storstad,* equally surprised, flung herself into full reverse. But it was too late. The *Storstad's* chiseled bow sliced neatly into the *Empress,* opening a wound seven metres high and five metres wide (23x16 ft.). As the river water gushed into the ship, the whole vessel listed towards her injury.

Kendall tried to move the *Empress* toward the shore, but the engine room was quickly flooded and momentum died. Radio operators Edward Bamford and Ronald Ferguson gasped incredulously as the lights of the *Storstad* disappeared down the starboard side. They tapped out a message—*"May have struck ship..."*—then frantically added an S.O.S. call, *"listing terribly."*

The *Empress of Ireland* was consumed by water in fourteen desperate minutes. Devastating though it was, some likened the collision to a gentle bump against a quay. Many died while they were still in their bunks. Kendall ordered all lifeboats lowered. Yes, there were enough to save every passenger, if only there had been more time, and if only the ship hadn't heeled so acutely to the side. Only five or six lifeboats were successfully launched.

Of all the poignant stories told by the survivors, most overwhelming are the tales of gallantry and sacrifice. Frederick Abbot of Toronto encountered actor Laurence Irving and his wife at a stairway in their nightclothes. Laurence had been thrown against his cabin door and was injured, but he had managed to carry his sobbing wife up the tilting stairs to the deck. Abbot offered him assistance, but Irving replied *"Look after yourself first, old man. But God bless you all the same."* He managed to get a life-belt around his wife, and as Abbot leapt into the water, he saw the Irvings locked in an embrace. Laurence Irving's body was later found, his hand still clutching a fragment of his wife's nightdress.

THE SALVATION ARMY STAFF BAND
En route to their Third International Congress in London, the large contingent of Salvationists included the Canadian Staff Band. Only nine band members survived the voyage.

Sir Seton-Karr stumbled from his cabin and straight into Mr. Darling, his young English neighbour. Seton-Karr carried a lifebelt while Darling was empty-handed. Seton-Karr thrust his lifebelt at the stranger, insisting that he could get another, then disappeared inside his cabin. He didn't make it out alive. Darling ran up to the deck and climbed over the railings onto the port side hull, now almost horizontal. There he found the young ship's doctor lodged halfway out of a port hole, and managed to pull him free.

By now, the port hull sloped gently down into the water and people were able to walk down it. The ship had lost all power and the dark passages inside were filled with blind terror. That didn't stop Salvation Army Captain Rufus Spooner from venturing below deck to gather blankets and lifebelts for the ladies. The stairs were so steeply angled, he claimed, "*An angel of mercy must have lifted me up them.*" Spooner survived in the water, and was pulled onto a rescue boat.

George Crellin, a farmer from British Columbia, carried a struggling little girl on his back as he swam through the bodies, even though he nearly drowned from exhaustion. (The two were eventually pulled out of the water into a boat. Crellin, on learning that the child had lost her family, convinced his wife to take her in.)

The black waters frothed with chaos. As the ship heeled over, it crushed a full lifeboat just escaping from its side. The *Empress* started

34

sucking water, debris and victims into stacks and ventilation ports, then something in the belly of the ship exploded, spewing forth its mangled contents.

RESCUED CREW
Empress crewmembers aboard the Storstad— *lucky to be alive.*

The fog dissipated as quickly as it had rolled in, leaving the Norwegian collier, the *Storstad*, wrapped in confusion. Captain Thomas Anderson had readied his lifeboats for evacuation, but soon discovered his own ship was not taking on water. That's when he first heard the cries of distress. He immediately sent his crew to help. One of the first aboard was the *Empress*' Dr. Grant who set to work reviving his shipmates. Although weak with shock, he treated case after case of exposure, lacerations and fractures. One of his patients was distraught and barely coherent, *"Doctor,"* he said, *"there is only one thing I am sorry for... that they did not*

THE CROWD MOURNS
Coffins are unloaded at Pier 27 in Quebec, where a large shed became the temporary morgue.

IN A COAL SHED ON RIMOUSKI'S WHARF

The bodies are laid out awaiting coffins. This photograph was used on a postcard shortly after the tragedy. More passengers were lost on the Empress of Ireland *than on either the* Titanic *or the* Lusitania.

let me drown." It was Captain Kendall. He had jumped from his doomed bridge and been hauled into a lifeboat.

The *Storstad* Captain's wife, Mrs. Anderson, leapt into action. She searched the *Storstad* for garments and coverings for her three hundred, shivering guests, and plied them with whiskey and coffee. Wireless operator Ferguson, naked and in shock, encountered Mrs. Anderson as he made his way to the warmth of the *Storstad's* engine room. "*She said something in Norwegian that sounded sympathetic, and took off her long blue scarf and gave it to me. I tied it around my neck and carried on!*"

Class divisions dissipated as factory workers huddled with socialites, bellhops with officers, trying to warm their numb frames. Mrs. Anderson did notice one passenger, however, who was immaculately turned out and dripping only with diamonds. When Ethel Paton was awakened by the whistles, she had taken time to dress, with the help of her assistant, and, on reaching the upper deck, had tumbled gracefully into a waiting lifeboat. (To Mrs. Paton's great relief, the class system was restored in Quebec City, where first-class survivors were accommodated at the Château Frontenac. The lady herself was whisked back to Sherbrooke in the comfort of her private railway car.)

The tug *Eureka* and the government ship, *Lady Evelyn*, alerted by Ferguson's first S.O.S., rushed to the scene from Point-au-Père, but most of the bodies pulled out of the water were lifeless. They transported all survivors and 213 bodies to the little town of Rimouski, whose citizens went to great lengths to offer help. They took in the 465 survivors, fitted them with new clothes, and built coffins for the bodies. One survivor said of Rimouski, "*It was the most wonderful place in the world.*"

The bodies were shipped back to Quebec City and lowered to the docks as a single bugle played. More than ten thousand people watched in silence, their emotions rising with each passing coffin. When the sailors passed, each carrying one, tiny, white coffin, the crowd openly sobbed. Of 148 children aboard the *Empress of Ireland*, only four survived.

In June, an inquiry was held in Quebec City. Each captain acidly blamed the other: Kendall claiming that the *Storstad* should have tried to block the gash, to physically stay the rush of water; Anderson arguing, impossible! the *Empress* had been in forward motion. Kendall was absolved of blame by the Canadian inquiry. Likewise, Anderson was found guiltless by a similar inquest held in Norway. A few months later, the newspapers turned their voracious appetites to the outbreak of The Great War. Both captains enlisted. Both served on ships that were torpedoed, and both survived.

Events in bloodied Europe all but obliterated the *Empress of Ireland* from public memory, even though she took 1012 lives. Her remains still lie in murky water, her story obscure in the pages of history. A difficult salvage operation in July of 1914 recovered most of the mail, money and silver, and added one more fatality to the tragedy. Some bodies were retrieved, but more than 700 victims still lie in the depths of the St. Lawrence.

DAMAGE TO THE *STORSTAD*

The Storstad's bow cut into the liner's side.

LA BOURGOYNE FOUNDERING
Harper's Weekly *commissioned painters to illustrate the disaster. Artists used survivors'*
testimonies to create their renderings.

DISGRACE

Sinking of *La Bourgoyne* off Sable Island, Nova Scotia

JULY 4, 1898

The Canadian schooner *Cromartyshire* was south of Sable Island, creeping through dense fog, when the magnificent French transatlantic liner, *La Bourgoyne*, suddenly appeared to port. Travelling full speed, the liner collided with the schooner then disappeared. The schooner's Captain Henderson assessed his ship's significant damage, and set about some repairs.

As the fog lifted, two lifeboats could be seen flying French flags. They carried survivors of the liner which had apparently gone down. Henderson at once sent his crew in search of others. *La Bourgoyne*, bound for Le Havre from New York, had carried over 700 people. Only 173 survived.

Henderson noted that the first boatload of survivors were all sailors, and all completely dry. As the *Cromartyshire* limped into Halifax, further shocking details were divulged by the few passengers who were saved. Not only had the French crew largely refused to assist in the rescue, but passenger C. Brunno claimed he had witnessed a sailor strike and kill a passenger who was attempting to climb into a lifeboat. The *Halifax Herald* reported that: "*Knives were flourished in every direction and used with deadly effect,*" and that "*women were stabbed like so many sheep.*" Only one female survived.

The stories so enraged the public that the surviving passengers and crew required police protection on their arrival in New York.

VICTORIE LACASSE
The only female survivor of La Bourgoyne

THE PRINCESS SOPHIA AT DOCK

The Canadian Pacific Railway's steamship provided a service to those seeking their fortunes in Alaska and the Yukon.

LOSS OF THE *PRINCESS SOPHIA*

Vanderbilt Reef, Alaska

OCTOBER 25, 1918

The *Princess Sophia* was stuck. Immobile. Lodged securely on the Vanderbilt Reef, just off Alaska's coast. Shallow, icy waves slapped at the stout steamer, and a cold northerly wind cut through the jackets of her crew, but Captain Locke, a veteran of the seas, strolled the deck calmly, allaying the fears of his 350 passengers. The tragic loss of the *Titanic*, not six years before, meant that attention had been paid to safety on board ships like the Canadian Pacific's *Sophia*. She had been built with a double hull, and well-supplied with lifeboats and rafts. Although the jagged reef might have damaged the *Sophia's* outer hull, Captain Locke was confident his ship was taking in no water.

Circling the *Sophia* were some small American vessels, their crews anxious to help evacuate the grounded ship. But Locke waved them off. In this wind his passengers might be safer staying put—waiting out the rough weather—than transferring to other boats. Undisturbed, the captain leant against the *Sophia's* railings, shouting through his megaphone to the smaller boats to watch out for the rocks.

Inside, the *Princess Sophia* sheltered a lively cast of passengers and crew. They were part of the annual October exodus from the Yukon and Alaska: adventurous souls escaping a severe winter in the north, some to retire, some to find work further south, and some to join forces in the trenches of Europe. The Great War was in its final few weeks.

Also aboard were American, Canadian, and British entrepreneurs, Chinese porters, and a Japanese prospector. One passenger was mining millionaire, Walter Barnes, with his faithful mining horse, Billy. Locals rumoured that "the lady known as Lou" from Robert Service's poem, "The Shooting of Dan

CAREER SEAMAN, CAPTAIN LEONARD LOCKE

While his ship sat on the Vanderbilt Reef, the trusted and experienced Captain Locke chose to gamble that the wind would die.

THE DAILY COLONIST, VICTORIA, B.C., TUESDAY, OCTOBER 29, 1918

CAPTAIN LOCKE VETERAN SEAMAN

Master of Ill-Fated Princess Sophia Had Long Experience in Coast Waters — Well-Known Victorians Victims.

The Princess Sophia, now resting at the bottom of Lynn Canal, was manned by men, the greater number of whom had been many years in the employ of the C.P.R. and who were known among their fellow mariners as efficient and experienced.

The skipper, Captain Locke, had been an officer on boats running out of this port for twenty-seven years, first as skipper of the tug Lorne and later in the employ of the C.P.R., by which he was employed for seventeen years. He has commanded most of the boats of the Canadian Pacific

river steamer Casca for some Mr. Davies was born in Winni 1888, being 30 years of ag came out to this coast in 1907. Davies was 25 years old. Mr. had one brother, John, killed front; Arthur is now in F Stanley is in England with th perial Forces; Evan is on fu from the West Indies, where been on duty for three years William is with the V. M. D. are also two younger brother also leaves four sisters, one Mrs. F. W. Battrick, of 702 D Street. Mr. Davies leaves three siste two brothers, one of whom is seas.

Mr. and Mrs. Bridges

Coming south on a pleasur for the Winter, Mr. and Mrs. mer Bridges went to their de the wrecked vessel. The paren and Mrs. George Bridges, res 155 Croft Street. Mr. Bridge the proprietor of the Yukon C Dawson and had not been o about five years. Born in V 40 years ago he had been up Yukon at Fairbanks and Daws about 18 years engaged in th business. He leaves three br Stanley, on the Prince Rupert. a moving picture operator. o

CAPT. LEONARD LOCKE

McGrew" was also on board. Lulu Mae had sought the lucrative entertainment opportunities of the Klondike gold rush in the 1890s. Marrying her employer, hotel owner Murray Eads, she shocked her new social class with her "bright dressing" and saloon expressions. Lulu's phobia of sea voyages had kept the couple in the north for twenty years, but an impending economic crisis was now driving them out on the *Princess Sophia*.

Also on board was Edmund Ironside and his mother setting off for their winter holiday. Ironside was a Yukon customs collector with a passion for poetry. Heading south with his wife and five children was Bill O'Brien, a Dawson businessman, well-loved by locals along the coast for his beautiful baritone voice.

The *Sophia's* departure from Scagway had been delayed in part by straggling passengers with their many belongings, and in part by the search for replacements for six of Locke's men stricken with Spanish Influenza. The ship eventually set off at 10:00 p.m., three hours later than planned, which may explain why Locke kept up such speed. His route was through Lynn Canal, a long fjord of steep, glacier-draped shores which funnel storm winds, infusing them with freezing spray. That night it began to snow, reducing visibility even further. Vanderbilt Reef lies about two-thirds of the way down the canal. It is the top of an underwater mountain, the summit of which lies just beneath the water at high tide and, at that time, was graced with just one buoy. In rough seas, the reef was menacingly obscure. But Captain Locke had charmed this coast for decades. He confidently maintained a pace of about eleven knots, using the echoes of the ship's whistle bouncing off the rock walls to "feel his way" as he'd done countless times before. Captain Locke didn't realize that in the turbulent, snowy blackness, he'd veered one and a quarter miles off course.

At one o'clock in the morning, with a tremendous scraping sound, the *Sophia* ground onto the reef. There was immediate panic, a fumbling for life jackets, a scramble for the upper deck. But Locke must have assessed the damage quickly and ordered calm, assuring his passengers that help was on its way and that they were perfectly safe in their warm cabins.

A bleak morning brought with it several small American rescue boats, shouting suggestions over the wind to Captain Locke. At this point, as the crew of the smaller boats would later testify, all of the passengers could have been removed safely from the *Sophia*. But Locke refused. The barometer was rising, heralding calmer weather, and perhaps the tide would be enough to lift the ship back into the deep. Those in his charge could do nothing but adopt the Captain's optimism. They could be seen strolling on the deck, or casually leaning on the railings, piano music drifting out into the dusk. But by nightfall a storm was setting in and the tide had done nothing to budge the ship.

Two larger vessels, sent out from the Juneau docks by a frantic Canadian Pacific agent, arrived at the reef to offer help: the *King and Winge*, a powerful fishing boat with a crew of 22 under Captain Miller, and the *Cedar*, a large lighthouse tender under Captain Leadbetter. Both ships were American, both captains had decades of rough water experience, but the weather was so bad that neither could approach the reef. The *Cedar* was equipped with a radiotelegraph and had already been communicating with the *Sophia's* operator, twenty-year-old David Robinson. They told him the *Cedar* would drop anchor for the night in the lee of Sentinel Island. If the *Sophia* remained stable on the rock, the passengers would be fine until morning. Locke agreed. The *King and Winge* opted to ride out the waves and squalls next to the treacherous reef so that the *Sophia's* passengers could take comfort in the nearby lights. It was a brave and thoughtful act for which Captain Miller would never be thanked.

Friday, October 25. The second day on the reef dawned with no further hope of rescue. Thick snow fell into the heaving waters of the Lynn Canal. Only the two large boats stood by the *Sophia*, their crews creating wild rescue schemes with ropes and dories, schemes too dangerous to attempt. By early afternoon, both the *King and Winge* and the *Cedar* were forced to find another place to shelter. The *Princess Sophia* stood in the storm, lonely and forlorn.

It is conjecture to suggest that Captain Locke's composure faltered, that the relentless beating on his bruised ship rattled his nerves. But fear did enter

43

the vessel, as passengers' letters, found later, would attest. John Maskell, a 32-year-old Englishman returning home to marry, wrote on October 24:

> *My Dear Own Sweetheart, I am writing this dear girl while the boat is in grave danger. We struck a rock last night which threw many from their berths, women rushed out in their night attire, some were crying, some too weak to move, but the life boats were soon swung out in readiness, but owing to the storm would be madness to launch until there was [no] hope for the ship.... I made my will this morning, leaving everything to you, my own true love and I want you to give a hundred pounds to my dear mother, a hundred pounds to my dear Dad, a hundred pounds to dear wee Jack and the balance of my estate (about three hundred pounds) to you, Dorrie dear. The Eagle Lodge will take care of my remains.*

Auris McQueen, a 35-year-old American soldier en route to France, told his mother in a letter dated October 25: "*She [the* Sophia*] pounds some on a rising tide and it is slow writing but our only inconvenience is, so far, lack of water.*" He describes the eighty-kilometre (50 mi.) winds and negligible visibility on account of snow and spray, ending his letter: "*We are mighty lucky we were not all buried in the sea water.*"

All that very afternoon, the storm gathered momentum. As the scraping and pounding worsened, so must have the fear. Then, at 4:40 p.m., a frantic wireless message from young Robinson crackled through the snowy dusk to the *Cedar*: "*Taking water and foundering. For God's sake come and save us.*"

HER FINAL HOURS

A blurry photograph of the Sophia, *stranded on the reef in the mounting storm. The captain considered it too risky to remove the passengers to other boats.*

Captain Leadbetter of the *Cedar* weighed anchor at once and began to fight through the furious weather. Robinson radioed again: "*For God's sake hurry... the water is coming in my room.*" The *Sophia's* battery was weakening and the operator on the *Cedar* advised his friend to save its power in order to guide them in when they were closer. "*All right, all right, but you talk to me so I know you're coming,*" responded Robinson. But the *Cedar* could not defeat the storm, and had to retreat to shelter. The heroism of Leadbetter and his crew would never be officially recognized. After their retreat, they tried to maintain contact with the doomed *Princess Sophia*, but her radio had become ominously silent.

The storm finally calmed the next morning, and crews arriving at the reef were frozen by the sight: just the tip of the *Sophia's* mast showed above water. Three hundred and fifty people had perished. There were no survivors. An extensive search turned up only bodies, floating in the water or washed up on the beaches. Eighty bodies were later found within the wreck, some still in their cabins. The *Sophia's* oil tanks were ripped open and many of the dead had choked to death on the oil. Thousands of sea birds also died from the oil which smeared the beaches and rocks of the islands in the canal.

As the bodies began to pile up on the docks at Juneau, and the citizens of that town bent to the gruesome task of washing off the oil and trying to identify the dead, the *Vancouver Sun*, still buoyant with Captain Locke's self-assurance, ran the headline: "Princess Sophia *reported safe—she rests easily on rocks with four U.S. government boats standing by.*"

Locke's reputation also rested easily throughout the inquiry that followed. Held in Victoria, British Columbia, the inquiry included testimonies from all captains of the responding vessels, both large and small. Despite the sense that the total loss had been avoidable, no one cast aspersions on Locke. A selection of skippers from other coastal vessels told of his respected skills as a mariner, and confirmed that Locke had made the best decisions available. Before the short inquiry was over, local newspapers had already printed exonerations of the captain and his crew.

The Canadian Pacific's *Princess Alice* brought the bodies back to Vancouver. Loaded with coffins, she was nicknamed "The Ship of Sorrow." Vancouver's shores were dotted with bonfires, every flag in the city's possession flapped madly in the night, and groups of revellers shouted and danced. It was Armistice Day and the Great War had just ended. At 11:00 p.m. on November 11, 1918, the *Alice* slid quietly up to the only dock draped in black. A group of bereaved relatives awaited her arrival, their grief drowning in the city's joy.

OMINOUS FINDINGS
Forced to abandon the Sophia *and seek shelter from the storm, rescue boats returned the next morning to discover the tragedy.*

SAGONA LIFEBOAT ARRIVES TO RESCUE MEN CLINGING TO WRECKAGE OF THE VIKING'S STERN

Three men, King, Kennedy and Sargeant clung to a fragment of the ship's stern, held afloat by an ice-pan. They drifted all that day and through the night, 22 miles into the Atlantic.

WHAT THE SHIP SAGONA SAW

What the crew of the Sagona thought to be seals floating on a pan of ice (middle) turned out to be the survivors of the Viking including King, Kennedy and Sargeant shown being lifted to safety (bottom).

THE *VIKING* DISASTER

Off the Horse Islands, Newfoundland

MARCH 14, 1931

In early March, Harry Sargeant and Varrick Frissell premiered their movie, *White Thunder*, to a packed and prestigious St. John's audience. The film depicted the hardships of sealing on ice. It was a great success with local audiences, but did not have wide enough appeal to land international distribution with Paramount Pictures. A week later, the film crew set out for the ice again aboard the *Viking*, this time with a revised script and plans to film a capsizing iceberg. They brought along a load of extra gun powder for the journey.

As the sealing vessel snuggled into the ice for the night, just 20 kilometres (12 mi.) east of the Horse Islands, the crew spoke of the dangers of carrying explosives at sea. They were acutely aware of the kerosene lamps and the cigarettes in close proximity to the cargo.

At 9:00 p.m., their fears were confirmed. A huge explosion tore through the *Viking*'s stern. Frissell was tossed backwards and never seen again. Sargeant, burnt and injured, leapt to the ice and huddled there with the ship's navigator, Kennedy, and another man named King. The *Viking* was now burning furiously and rocking with sporadic, small explosions.

On the ice, the badly-injured Captain realized that the surviving men would suffer from exposure. Some of the men boarded the burning ship to throw down supplies and lower the remaining dories. The injured men were loaded into the small boats and at daybreak, the bedraggled party began a difficult trek across the ice pans towards the islands.

Sargeant, Kennedy and King somehow missed the expedition and found themselves afloat on a small pan of ice, heading out to sea. Despite a fractured skull, Kennedy kept their spirits up, bandaging their wounds, building small fires, and working to make them all more comfortable. Meanwhile, the pan of ice was disintegrating in the sea. It was 36 hours before a rescue vessel spotted the men. Kennedy died from his injuries and pneumonia before he reached the mainland.

Those who walked the 16 hours to the islands survived the harrowing journey, but 58 men died in the explosion.

Paramount Pictures asked Sargeant to give his account of the disaster for a filmed news feature. Shown at the Hotel Newfoundland, it was filled with real and tragic spectacle.

WRACKED BY EXPLOSIONS

Extra gunpowder brought aboard by the film crew turned the Viking *into a fireworks display, with debris and bodies flying across the ice.*

THE *OCEAN RANGER*

Eighty-four men died when the enormous oil rig was consumed by a North Atlantic storm on February 15, 1982.

THE LOSS OF THE *OCEAN RANGER*

Hibernia Oil Fields, North Atlantic

FEBRUARY 15, 1982

February 6, 1982: The *Ocean Ranger*, a 16 500-ton (15 000-tonne) steel oil rig sat like a giant spider on the black seas of Hibernia. Eight enormous legs extended from submerged pontoons to support an upper platform. The largest of three rigs in the area, the *Ocean Ranger* was operated by ODECO, a Louisiana engineering firm, under contract to Mobil Oil of Canada (MOBIL). The rig had weathered wild conditions in the Bering Sea, the Gulf of Alaska and at two other sites in the Northern Atlantic. She was a fortress. Until February 6.

Captain Clarence Hauss was relieving an operator in the ballast control room—the brain of the rig—housed close to the water in a starboard leg. Hauss was a worthy marine captain, but having taken command just eight days before, he had little knowledge of the *Ocean Ranger*'s ballast control system. Hauss looked at the two inclinometers mounted on the wall. The rig was listing slightly. He approached the control panel. To correct the list all he had to do was pump some air out of a ballast tank. It was all clearly marked. How hard could it be? Hauss pushed the right green button, without first closing the sea-chest valve. Instead of pumping out, water gushed into the tank, quickly worsening the list.

Meanwhile on deck, drilling expert Kent Thompson sounded the alarm to ready the crew for evacuation, while the senior ballast controller raced to the control room. Crew members hovered in the passages, sleepy and undressed. There had been two false alarms in the past 48 hours. So when Thompson ordered all hands to lifeboat stations, his voice blasting from the speakers, the men barely picked up speed. It took a full twenty minutes before the whole crew was on deck, shuffling around in confusion.

Sixty-five men arrived at *Lifeboat No. 1*, a boat designed for 50. A few men gathered around *Lifeboat No. 4*, but it was new, with an unfamiliar lowering system. The seat belts in some lifeboats were corroded, and if the men were not secured, the craft would not right itself once in the water. One lifeboat motor wouldn't start at all, and there weren't enough lifejackets to go around. Luckily, the control room problem was solved and the evacuation was cancelled.

The crew returned to their quarters, relieved and joking. Their weekly Sunday drills—in which no one actually lowered a lifeboat—had been of little use. Meanwhile, the drilling expert warned the Captain never to touch the ballast panel again.

February 14, 1982: A ferocious storm whipped the North Atlantic into a maelstrom. The icy swells were so large beneath the *Ocean Ranger* that Thompson stopped the drilling and "sheared" the *Ocean Ranger*'s pipe, cutting the rig free for safety. So did two other rigs in the oil fields, the *Zapata Ugland* and the *SEDCO 706*.

Kent Thompson contacted the MOBIL office in St. John's to explain his actions. It was 7:00 p.m., and as he chatted to the mainland, a gigantic wave thundered past the *Ocean Ranger*. The *SEDCO*'s buoys measured it at 24 metres (78 ft.), higher than that rig's deck. The *SEDCO* was unharmed, but got word from the *Ocean Ranger* that the wave had smashed a porthole in the ballast control room, causing significant damage: the public address and gas detection systems were down; dangerous charges arched out from the panel; and valves in the ballast system seemed to be opening and closing erratically. But Donald Rathburn, the senior ballast controller, sounded calm. He had closed the brass porthole covers and was drying the panel and replacing bulbs.

At 9:45 p.m. the *Ocean Ranger* reassured St. John's that the electrical problems were all but solved. The rig should soon be up to her "survival draft," and was coping well in the 90-knot winds.

For the next three hours, the storm dominated the airwaves. The crew of the *SEDCO* sat in their coffee room, hoping for news from other rigs. The *Seaforth Highlander*, standby ship for the *Ocean Ranger*, was mired in difficulties of her own. The tremendous seas crashed onto the *Highlander*'s aft deck. Several crew members were inexperienced and worried by the storm. And Captain Ronald Duncan struggled with the ever-changing wind. At 11:30, the *Ocean Ranger* contacted the *Highlander* to check on her position. Standby vessels were supposed to stay within 3.2 kilometres (2 mi.) of their oil rigs at all times, but battered in the storm, the *Highlander* was eleven to thirteen kilometres (7-8 mi.) due south of the *Ocean Ranger*.

At 1:05 a.m., February 15, Captain Duncan received an urgent radio request from the *Ocean Ranger*: "*Please come in as close as you can make it.*" The rig had a list of 12 to 15 degrees and progressing, all counter-measures ineffective. Duncan swung his vessel around and charged, full-blast, through the treacherous waves towards the *Ocean Ranger*. The oil rig sent a message to other rigs and ships within range: "*We are experiencing a list of 10 to 15 degrees, and we are in the middle of a severe storm... requesting assistance ASAP.*" The *Highlander*, unequipped for serious rescue work, was by far the closest.

At 1:30 a.m. the *Ocean Ranger* dispatched her last communication to St. John's: "*Crew going to lifeboat stations. Repeat, crew going to lifeboat stations.*" Far away from safety, the *Ocean Ranger*'s crew—oil rig drillers, not marine men—were fumbling now with lifeboats they knew to be unsafe, high above the churning black Atlantic.

Shortly after 2:00 a.m. the *Highlander* neared the site. The *Ocean Ranger* was a pointed, dark hulk, dipping into the swells. Pushing closer, the *Highlander* lit a flare into the night. Thrashing through the waves towards the ship was a lifeboat under power. Duncan could see men inside bailing madly. The lifeboat had been battered and was taking water. The *Highlander's* crew threw out lines that were caked immediately in ice and then caught by the men in the lifeboat. They abandoned the bailing, climbing out onto the side of the lifeboat. Then tragedy struck. The little boat capsized, tossing the men into the freezing water. The *Highlander's* crew threw a life-raft and more lines but the men in the water, immobilized by the cold, couldn't grasp them. They were dead within minutes.

At 3:38 a.m. the *Ocean Ranger* disappeared from the radar screen. All hands were lost. Of the 84 victims, 69 were Canadian, and 54 of those, Newfoundlanders. Despite days of scouring the North Atlantic, rescue teams found only 22 bodies.

A joint commission from Ottawa and Newfoundland used submersible crafts to retrieve and examine fragments of the rig. It came to light that the men in the ballast control room had used brass rods to override the actions of the erratic tank valves. The men may have believed they were locking the valves closed, when in fact the brass rods would have locked them open, allowing them to take on more water. The operators had misunderstood the fine details of the operation, but then, there had been no formal education, no written policies or manuals to refer to. The men had learned from others on the job.

After seventeen months of testimonies, investigations and brainstorming, the commission passed a number of recommendations, some of which were followed. Ballast systems were redesigned, and operators given extensive, formalized training. Emergency teams were introduced, trained to handle ballast problems, fire fighting and evacuation. In future, oil rig crews were to receive rigorous marine training. All rigs under Canadian jurisdiction have since been equipped with personal survival suits for every man on board. The changes notwithstanding, there continues to be concern by some that the issue of evacuation procedures on some rigs needs further attention.

In the days that ensued the loss of the rig, the families of those who were feared to be lost or missing were unable to obtain confirmations as to the souls that were lost until media reports became available. It was reported that the insurance payout for the lost *Ocean Ranger* was $86 million, and that this amount significantly exceeded the depreciated value of the rig. The loss of the rig did not prompt charges of criminal negligence.

PONTOON OF OVERTURNED *OCEAN RANGER*

When the Ocean Ranger's standby vessel, the Seaforth Highlander reached the site of the giant oil rig, all that could be seen was a piece of its hull.

EARTH

...and the earth did quake, and the rocks rent.
Matthew 27:51
The Holy Bible

SAINT-JEAN-VIANNEY, QUEBEC,
MAY 5, 1971
In five terrifying minutes thirty-four houses were swallowed by a massive slide of mud.

EARLY DRAEGERMEN WITH THEIR RESCUE GEAR

While digging, crawling through tight spaces, and hauling out bodies from the mine, these rescuers had to be careful not to overexert themselves due to their limited oxygen supply.

EARTH

Part Two

We try to shape it, blasting and scraping its surface, pulling out its veins of wealth, covering it with concrete cities. Still we have never conquered this earth nor been able to predict its startling dynamism.

With barely a foothold on this continent, the Europeans started mining for coal. Around the rudimentary holes dug out of the earth's crust, communities grew. Battling isolation and harsh weather and living conditions, the miners and their families forged modest lives, wholly dependent on what the earth would offer.

There was magic in the coal. Pressed into its shiny black folds were the memories of fossilized forests, the gifts of heat and light, the fuel to move ships and trains over continents and oceans. And the proceeds from coal fed, clothed and housed countless families.

Miners' sons entered the pits as children, some so small that the lamps on their belts dragged along the floor. The Nova Scotia Mines Act of 1873 restricted boy labour to a minimum age of ten years, their work-week limited to 54 hours. At the time, mine managers protested such intervention. The minimum age was raised to twelve in 1891, the year of the first major tragedy in Springhill.

Immigrant labour suffered as well. In British Columbia, where laws were stricter (though seldom enforced) the large Chinese work-force was relied on to perform similar tasks to the boy-workers in other provinces. And for as little, or sometimes less, pay. As boys were slowly legislated out of the pits, the Chinese continued to fill the low-paid jobs until the Depression of the 1930s forced them out in favour of unemployed white men.

Despite the hardships, most youths were eager to earn their 65

DRAEGERMEN AT SPRINGHILL MINE EXPLOSION, 1958

Exhausted draegermen (miners specially trained for rescue) wait to return to the collapsed mine.

BUT FATE OF 55 MEN UNKNOWN

cents a day in the mine. They could escape the boredom of school, add to family income and launch themselves into the adult world. Their simple duties were crucial to the safe operation of the works.

The risks were well-known and ever present, and no amount of inspection or obsession with safety could prevent the danger. The roofs of coal mines were littered with natural structures that were difficult to detect and prone to collapse. Sudden falls of stone were not uncommon, crushing a miner or severing a foot or limb. Runaway trips and falling cages broke many backs. The everyday accidents were so brutal and so frequent that, over the years, they claimed more lives than the great mining disasters.

But the larger tragedies brought greater horror, felling a whole community in a single blow. Mine fires were a constant worry. They would rip through tunnels, sometimes taking weeks to extinguish. Methane, a highly flammable gas, seeped out of coal and gathered in unstable, toxic pockets in poorly-ventilated mines. The coal in Stellarton, Nova Scotia, was so gassy that cracks in the mine face hissed and popped. Coal dust suspended in the air added to the danger. One spark, one shift of the earth's layers, and entire tunnels filled with men were gone.

Relatives were sometimes left wondering about their loved ones' fates. During the 1944 expansion of the Allan shaft, in Nova Scotia's Pictou County, workers broke into the old workings of the Foord pit. They found the belts, boots and skeletons of nine victims of an explosion 46 years earlier. More than thirty years later, more remains were found.

TURTLE MOUNTAIN COLLAPSES ON THE TOWN OF FRANK, APRIL 29, 1903

Weakened by coal mining, the mountain collapsed, burying mining cottages at the the edge of town. Over 65 people were killed under the mass of boulders.

Mothers, wives and children lived with a daily fear of loss. The sound of a distant report or a disturbing vibration was enough to send them running to the entrance of the mine.

If this extraordinary, multi-layered earth can offer up ancient carbon forests, while pushing mountains to the sky, it should be no surprise that our foundations shift from time to time, or that a mountain shrugs off a piece of its rocky burden.

MANGLED WESTRAY MINE EQUIPMENT NOVA SCOTIA, 1992

(above) Exploding coal dust spewed poisonous gas and was powerful enough to bend equipment. Twenty-six men were killed.

PARKING LOT DROPPED INTO ABANDONED MINE TIMMINS, ONTARIO

(left) Developers are often unaware of the hazards of abandoned mine sites (especially the old closures). In 1967, Cobalt, Ontario was cut off when Highway 11B collapsed into a mine shaft.

THE FACE OF CHILD LABOUR

Deep within the mines, young boys loaded coal, drove horses and operated ventilation doors. Once they were old and strong enough, they joined their brothers and fathers at the coal face.

CHILD VICTIMS

Springhill Mine Explosion, Nova Scotia

FEBRUARY 21, 1891

A bruised and sullen pre-dawn sky cast its greys on Springhill, Nova Scotia. The town slept on, but at the mouth of the mine, where steamy air belched up from the earth's belly, Willard Carter was already struggling into his pit clothes. He tied his trousers, mostly black and shiny at the knees, at his waist with rope. His coat, encrusted with soot, was two sizes too large. The creases of his hands held the bluish tinge of coal. Willard strapped his tea and dinner cans securely to his back. Today, like every day, he would earn 65 cents for his family. He would laugh with the miners as he descended the dim slope, and share the fatigue of physical labour. But today, more than ever, he felt like a man, for this was Willard Carter's thirteenth birthday.

Willard was not the youngest boy to descend the pit on February 21, 1891. There were many other thirteen-year-olds, while Joseph Dupuis and Willie Terris were still only twelve. In fact, of the five thousand miners in Nova Scotia that year, more than eleven hundred were under eighteen years of age. Young sons in mining families often left school as soon as they were able to earn money. Many of their fathers had started work at the age of eight. Above ground, the boys filled gunpowder cans, cleaned lamps, fed horses and washed coal. Deep within the labyrinth of tunnels, they loaded coal, drove horses to the slopes, and operated ventilation doors. When the boys were strong enough, they joined their brothers and their fathers at the coal face.

At thirteen, Willard was already familiar with the underground routines of the Cumberland Railway and Coal Company mine. He understood that the young trappers like Willie Terris—who opened and shut trap doors—performed a vital safety function. Willard enjoyed an adult camaraderie

with fellow miners, but he also shared their dark knowledge that a sudden shifting of the earth's forces could crush them without mercy. One wayward spark catching on some mine dust could char a human body within seconds.

The company officials were aware of the potential risks and the mines were regularly and meticulously inspected. Underground manager, James Conway, had checked the mine that morning. The air was circulating freely, the pumps keeping it dry. Conway had also been present for a six-hour examination two days before by the Miner's Union. The report concluded that the mine was in peak condition, one of the safer mines in the province.

Carter, Terris, and the other boys broke with the men at noon for half an hour and, as always, the rats gathered to watch them eat. Willard savoured his birthday dinner. At 12:30 the young miners went back to work. Just three minutes later, their world convulsed with a tremendous explosion.
It came from somewhere near the 580-metre (1900-ft.) level on the busy east slope, and it brought the mine to a standstill. The long tunnels served as the many barrels of an enormous underground gun. In all directions, burning gas, dust and debris blasted through. Wooden props supporting the roofs were blown to splinters, trapdoor shrapnel burned as it flew, and humans and horses were left in mangled heaps.

Immediately, Killer Damp—a lethal wash of carbon monoxide—crept through the tunnels. As they gasped for air in the dust-filled shafts, the stunned survivors in the Springhill mine understood one thing: get out, and get out now. Most were in darkness, their lamps damaged or extinguished, and they ran blindly, feeling the broken walls, stumbling over bodies, relying on their senses to lead them up. Alexander Blue, a young man working near the blast, heard the boom and squeezed between the timber props and the coal face. When a bolt of fiery lightning flashed down the tunnel, it ripped the safety lamp from his hand. Unhurt, Blue grabbed some cotton waste from his pocket, dipped it in a nearby puddle of water and stuffed it into his mouth as a filter. Panting through the cotton, he fled through the poisoned mine, finally reaching daylight. He passed many bodies along his frightening course. Others, such as John Bentcliffe, were overtaken by the "damp" within twenty feet of safety. Bentcliffe's uninjured body was one of the first recovered from near the mouth of the mine.

Willie Terris, hearing the thunder deep within the mine, dropped to the floor and crawled beneath his chair beside the trap door, covering his face with his hands. The flames and debris passed him, scorching only his ears and fingertips.

Danny Robertson, a fourteen-year-old miner, was blown backwards when the blast occurred. His light fizzled to blackness as around him, timbers crashed through dust and rocks fell from the roof, illuminated only by the flames of his clothing. In a panic, he tore off his fiery coat and vest, badly burning his arms and hands. Danny was picking his way out of the mine when he heard somebody whimper. In acute pain, he groped through the darkness towards the sound, and discovered young Terris still beneath his chair, paralyzed with fear. Danny encouraged the little trapper to climb onto his back, then carried the boy through the tunnels all the way to the surface. The boys were wrapped in blankets and taken to their homes on sleds, but Danny Robertson insisted on walking in unaided. He did not want to worry his mother.

Back at the mouth of the mine, chaos reigned as men and boys staggered into a growing crowd of worried relatives. Although many had made it to safety, about one hundred and fifty remained below. Within fifteen minutes of the explosion rescue operations were in full swing. A handful of miners and volunteers entered the smoke and suffocating heat and began bringing out survivors. With wet cloths across their faces, they crawled and clambered into recesses, lamps in their teeth, bodies on their backs.

Manager Conway had been on the surface at a meeting. He raced back to the mine to learn his thirteen-year-old son, John, was still among the missing. More than an hour later, rescuers would hear the boy's faint cries from beneath the body of a horse, where he'd been pinned but not gravely injured.

Springhill's Reverend David Wright descended several hundred feet, standing at a tunnel crossroads. As rescuers struggled through many black hours, Rev. Wright served them hot coffee, laced with ecclesiastical support. They

UNKNOWN PIT BOY
Children laboured in mines throughout Canada. In 1873, Nova Scotia limited the workweek of ten-year-old children to 54 hours.

61

needed it. Some of the bodies were unhurt and leaning, life-like, against coal walls, or with an arm around a prop. Other bodies were unrecognizable. The birthday boy, Willard Carter, was rescued from the mine alive. He'd sustained a deep gash below his left eye and serious burns to his hands and face. He was treated by doctors at the mouth of the mine but died at ten o'clock that night. The search for bodies continued for five days until the last man, a manager, Henry Swift, was discovered beneath three feet of stone. 125 men and boys were dead.

An inquiry determined that no one person was at fault. The method used to loosen coal from the face of the seam involved boring a small hole into the wall, filling it with explosives, and then packing it to keep the flame from entering the mine. In this instance, an unusual crack in the stone had allowed the flame to escape, igniting gas and dust that was present. The company was absolved, although several recommendations were made to improve safety: the purchase of a Shaw machine to test for gases; in gaseous portions of the mine, a short inspection to be made after dinner breaks; and in the dustier areas, a ban on the use of powder.

Three years later, a monument to the lost miners was erected in Springhill, a white marble statue of a full-grown miner. Inscribed at his feet are the names of the coal-blackened victims.

CHILD MINERS POSING AT THE MOUTH OF A B.C. COAL MINE

Fewer children were employed in British Columbia mines because adult Chinese labourers could perform the same tasks for the same or less pay.

SECOND DEADLY EXPLOSION

Springhill, Nova Scotia

NOVEMBER 1, 1956

In the seconds leading up to the catastrophe six out of seven empty coal cars broke free from their rake and ran backwards down the slope of Springhill's No. 4 mine. When some of the runaway cars jumped the tracks, they slammed into a power cable, causing it to arc. Dust ignited, exploding upwards to the surface. Five workers at the entrance of the mine were killed instantly, and the bankhead was destroyed. Flames roared from the mouth of the mine. Inside there were more than 100 men.

As soon as the fire was under control, volunteers went in to try and save the men, but poisonous gases pushed them back. Even the draegermen, equipped with masks, were overcome and dragged back to the surface.

Deep in the mine, at 1650 metres (5400 ft.), an extraordinary drama was unfolding. A group of 47 men, aware that their air was being poisoned, used the tar-covered brattice cloth to seal themselves into a tunnel. When even the air in their chamber became unsafe to breathe, manager Con Embree cut holes into the tunnel's compressed-air hose—one hole for each man to breathe from. As time wore on, small groups of men left the chamber—soaked rags covering their mouths—to pull other miners to the air hose, or to seek help. Two were never seen again. When miner Douglas Beaton was found nearby, barely alive, the men dragged him into their shelter. It took four hours of artificial respiration to revive him.

At the surface, rescuers noticed that the compressed air gauges were fluctuating, and took this as a sign of life below. Their hopes were confirmed when a small group of weakened miners found the fresh air station set up at the 670-metre (2200-ft.) level, and told of the group that was trapped below.

With the mine still dangerously volatile, rescuers poured in. They were teams of draegermen, hundreds of barefaced men, and several doctors, many of whom had never before entered a mine. Their bravery and determination helped to rescue 88 men from the mine. In total, 39 men lost their lives.

DEVASTATION
(Below) View down the collapsed mine. Draegermen somberly enter the mine (at bottom).

DRAEGERMEN HEAD TOWARDS CUMBERLAND PIT NO. 2

One hundred and seventy-four miners were trapped in collapsed Cumberland Pit No. 2.
Over fifty hours later, 121 of the trapped men had been brought to the surface.

THE BUMP

Springhill's Third Deadly Disaster
Springhill, Nova Scotia

OCTOBER 23, 1958

The No. 2 in Springhill, Nova Scotia, was the deepest coal mine on the continent. Opened in 1873, by 1958 its maze of tunnels burrowed to a vertical depth of 1322 metres (4340 ft.). Apart from occasional accidents and many "bumps," the mine, like the nearby town of 8000 residents, operated quietly.

As coal was mined, rock pressed in on the sides and ceilings of the tunnels. This pressure had to be relieved, and in the rigid strata of this region, relief came in sudden, violent bumps. Entire sections could collapse, releasing methane gas and choking ventilation. Mining officials said they could make large bumps a thing of the past by lining up the mine walls of each level, one directly above the other. The workers were uneasy. Many felt this would make the mine less stable.

It was Thursday, October 23, 1958, and the afternoon shift had started as usual at 3:00 p.m. There were 174 men working in the mine. Around 7:00 p.m. they felt a mild bump. There were no injuries, just a release of tension, both in the earth's pressure and in the miners' minds. Suddenly, the coal was easier to extract, and the miners knew that small bumps thwarted larger ones. But in this case, they were very much mistaken.

At 8:05 p.m., a violent bump shook the foundations of the town. Seismographs in Halifax, in Quebec's Seven Falls and in Ottawa recorded earthquake-like activity. In the quiet homes of Springhill, the bump brought a sinking, breathless dread.

Most of Springhill raced out into the night and toward the mine. Dr. Arnold Burden, who'd worked in the mines in his university years, was in the Medical Centre when he felt the building shake. He rushed to the mine to offer help. The local media, equipped with cameras, recorders, and microphones, descended on the anxious throng.

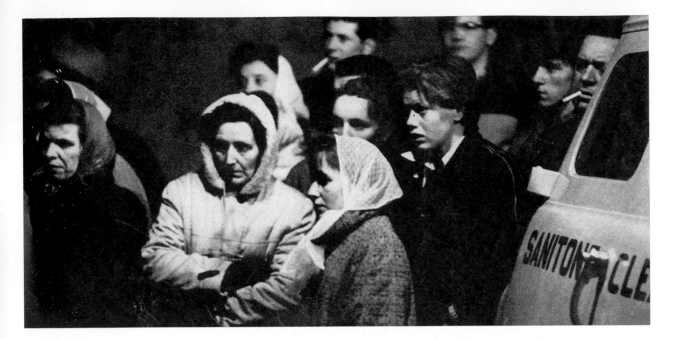

DESOLATE WATCH

Eighteen hours after the "bump," families and friends of men who were still trapped underground waited for them to surface at the pithead.

Manager George Calder was trying to reach the men below by telephone. He finally made contact with overman James McManamon, who informed him that the main slope was intact, but that all contact was severed below 2377 metres (7800 ft.).

The first rescue team rode down to 4084 metres (13 400 ft.) below. They encountered heavy methane gas and, without masks, they could not stay down long. As they headed out, ten draegermen with oxygen masks were on their way down along with a barefaced Dr. Burden. As this second group descended, they encountered a dozen miners who warned that things were bad below. The rescue team continued on.

The enormous convulsion had squeezed tunnels into mere crawl spaces or had completely crushed them. The gas was so potent, it smothered the draegermen's safety lamps. Timber splinters, metal pans, lunch pails were strewn through the rubble. The rescuers used white chalk to mark trickles of blood, still red on the black coal, so that once the blood had dried black and disappeared, they would know where to dig for bodies.

The rescuers located several men with only mild injuries. Some had breathed in the noxious gas and were disoriented. Some had fractures and penetrating wounds. Most had been knocked around by the displaced air. Leon Melanson was found buried in hard-packed coal, just a shoulder and one half of his face showing. He was in agony. Dr. Burden delivered a shot of Demerol in the exposed shoulder, then left the rescuers to chisel the coal away. As they gradually freed Leon's torso, they discovered the leg of a dead miner wedged across Leon's chest. Dr. Burden was summoned to amputate this leg to facilitate Leon's escape. "*Just keep digging,*" he told the rescuers. Something told

Dr. Burden this could be Leon's own leg. He was right. Burden and his colleagues tried unsuccessfully to save the mangled limb in hospital that night. Melanson survived the ordeal.

The exhausting task of finding victims of the bump continued through the night. Draegermen broke into trapped pockets of mine but much of the actual digging had to be done barefaced. The men snaked through the debris, often lying on their stomachs, hacking at the mess with short shovels. By the morning they had managed to free 81 miners.

Now the rescuers began to bring up only dead. The community braced together to comfort families feeling loss. They baked and cooked for one another, or sometimes simply sat together in silence. Two local restaurants offered free meals for those who needed them, while the Boy Scouts volunteered to take on any task: minding children, washing dishes, doing housework.

The Canadian Broadcasting Corporation's Mobile Unit was stationed at the pit mouth, providing, for the first time in Canada, live television coverage of an unfolding drama. But by Saturday October 25, there was nothing further to report. Harold Gordon, General Manager of Dominion Steel and Coal Corporation, somberly faced the press. When asked whether there was any indication that any of the men still below the surface were alive, he replied in a broken voice that there was none. The media retreated. The Mobile Unit drove away. The rescuers went on digging.

On Wednesday October 29, while clearing the coal from around a compressed air pipe, they heard a voice. *It was just a piece of a word,* Earl Wood told the *Chronicle Herald*, *"and very faint but it hit us like an electric shock."* From somewhere far behind the crunched walls, miner Gorely Kempt yelled into the pipe with all his might. He had heard the clink of something hitting the pipe and was shouting, *"We are alive in here. There are twelve of us."* By some miracle, twelve men had lived, trapped in a subterranean dungeon, for six days after the massive bump. Joe McDonald had had his

STRAIN OF RESCUE
Basil Casey, a miner for twenty years, comes up to the pithead for a break before heading back down to continue the rescue efforts for his friends and colleagues. (Below) The long wait.

67

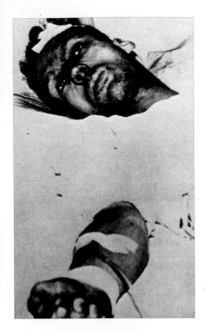

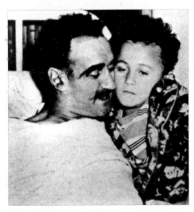

leg crushed by falling rocks, and Theodore Michniak had dislocated his shoulder. The others were largely unhurt.

When the bump hit, it left the men reeling from the heavy doses of methane gas and struggling to focus. Immediately, Kempt suggested that they look for water cans. The stronger of the group then tried to orchestrate their escape. After tunnelling through three walls only to find still more obstruction, the men gave in to waiting. They were entombed for the next six days. The collective four litres (one gallon) of water lasted for only five days. Using the cap of an aspirin bottle, they shared it out, sip by sip.

Three of the twelve, Hugh Guthro, Joe McDonald and Joe Holloway had survived the 1956 Springhill mine explosion. They knew survival was possible. As a group, they bolstered each other's flagging optimism. They pounded on pipes in hopes that they'd be heard. On Friday, the day after the bump, the men heard a scratching noise beneath them; another miner, perhaps, on the level below. And then it stopped, and wasn't heard again.

When the rescuers heard the weak voice at the end of the pipe, they had no idea how much digging lay between the men and their freedom. To find out, they pushed a piece of copper pipe, 30 metres (100 ft.) long, down the air pipe to the miners. They would have to tunnel through a daunting 25 metres (83 ft.) of coal. As the rescuers began to dig, Dr. Burden arranged for water to be sent down the pipe. At 6:00 p.m. the first tankful reached its targets. The doctor was concerned that they would take too much at once. *"I told them to drink one mouthful then count to five hundred,"* he recounts. Why five hundred? *"Because I knew they would count fast."* Next the rescuers sent down hot coffee, and two hours later some hot tomato soup, all the time reassuring the miners that freedom was near.

But the escape tunnel was difficult to build. It was just one metre high by one metre wide (3 ft. by 3 ft.), and filled with stale air. One rescuer would dig, another would pull the coal from between his legs and load it into buckets which were passed out from hand to hand. There was no time to make the tunnel larger or to reinforce it, and as the men worked, the mine continued to experience small bumps. The rescuers would pause while showers of coal dusted their heads. Their efforts attest to courage and compassion so large that exhaustion and fear were of no consequence. It was 2:30 a.m. on October 30 when they finally broke through. *"They cried a bit and we did too,"* Wilfred Hunter told the *Chronicle-Herald*, *"We were all laughing and crying all at once... ."*

Dr. Burden was right behind the rescuers. With a cloth covering his lamp to dim its painful brilliance, he assessed each man in the eerie light, administering pain relief to those in need. The miners were taken by stretcher through the narrow tunnel and up the mine into the light. Their eyes were protected from the glare by blankets, but Wilfred Hunter, weak yet jubilant, raised his cover and waved to the crowd. The people went wild, cheering and applauding.

Springhill had altered since the miners had last seen it. Its anonymity was beginning to dissolve. CBC's Mobile Unit had dashed back to the mine and shared images of the miracle with the rest of the nation. Margie Kempt learned about the trapped miners from her television. The man they were speaking of, alive in the mine, was her husband, Gorely. A cable arrived in Springhill from the Queen, and another from coal miners in Russia, expressing their heartfelt sympathy. And Prince Philip, Duke of Edinburgh, took a detour to Springhill on his way home from Ottawa.

Searchers continued to dig through the rubble for bodies but there was scant hope of finding anyone else alive. Yet, miraculously, on the ninth day after the bump, Byron Martin was pulled from a hole just big enough to contain his folded body. He was alive and behind him, with some digging, his little cave opened into a large one in which there were six more miners.

Among them was Percy Rector, who had also been trapped for four days in 1956. The bump left Percy's elbow caught tight in a wood pack. The others trapped with him could not free the arm without amputating it, an option they were loathe to try. They mustered all available aspirins for him, and checked on him as the days wore on.

Monday October 27 was Garnet Clarke's 29th birthday and the men held a party for him in the dark. They cut a sandwich into seven pieces, one for each man including Percy Rector and Byron Martin, who they'd been unable to dig free. They each drank a capful of water and sang "Happy Birthday" to Garnet.

The following day was more desperate. Percy Rector stopped moaning, and when the others checked on him they found him dead. The water ran out that day, and from then on the men tried anything to moisten their mouths. They gnawed on wood from the props, chewed on pinches of coal,

A QUICK BREAK

Both the Draegermen—named for their German-designed breathing equipment—and "barefaced" rescuers spent long hours in the mine, snaking through cramped and dangerous spaces.

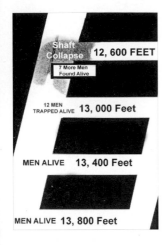

Shaft Collapse	12, 600 FEET
7 More Men Found Alive	
12 MEN TRAPPED ALIVE	13, 000 Feet
MEN ALIVE	13, 400 Feet
MEN ALIVE	13, 800 Feet

SECTION OF
NO. 2 SHAFT

Seven miners were trapped in this area for eight and a half days.

even drank their own urine. Currie Smith tried sipping some oil. They banged on the air pipes until they were too exhausted to carry on. Then suddenly, on Saturday November 1, they heard rescuer John Calder yelling in to them, asking how many there were. "*He sounded just like an angel,*" said Doug Jewkes.

In eight days their quiet town had been catapulted onto the world stage. The media, touched by the town's compassion and caring, spread the names and images of the coal miners and their families from coast to coast and across borders. Gorely Kempt and Caleb Rushton, from the first trapped group, flew to New York City as special guests of the Ed Sullivan Show, accompanied by their doctor, Arnold Burden. Changing planes in Boston they had to battle through mobs of journalists, photographers and television cameramen, and en route to their hotel in New York, they passed a great marquee on West 49th Street and Broadway emblazoned with the words, "*MORE MEN ALIVE.*" Ed Sullivan introduced the Springhillers to his television audience and made an appeal for the disaster fund. Kempt and Rushton, starving in a pitch black hole not three days before, were suddenly celebrities in a brightly-lit window to the continent.

The glory heaped on Springhill, in the bump's aftermath, was almost enough to cloud the stark reality of a death toll of 75. Springhill was awarded the Royal Humane Association Gold Medal in recognition of bravery in life-saving. Five rescuers were awarded Scout Silver Crosses in Ottawa. The Carnegie Hero Fund Commission presented a gold medal and bronze plaque for the rescuers, and the Government of Nova Scotia designated November 2, 1958, a day of public mourning for the mine's victims.

The mine was deemed too dangerous to remain open. And in July 1959, the Springhill mine closed, putting 1000 miners out of work. Springhill emerged from the bump as a scarred war hero, draped in medals, with new economic battles still to face.

PRINCE PHILIP
VISITS HOSPITAL

The mood was grim during the Duke's impromptu visit. But the following day a miraculous rescue brought seven more miners out alive.

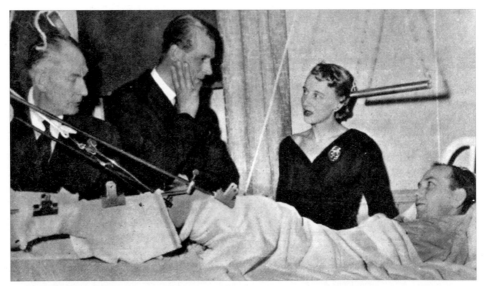

DRUMMOND MINE EXPLOSION

Pictou County, Nova Scotia

MAY 13, 1873

In 1873, the Drummond Mine was considered Canada's leading colliery, a model of a mine, with a manager esteemed by both his men and the community at large. Admittedly, it could be "fiery." Sulphurous fires were not infrequent, but could usually be snuffed out quickly with a miner's jacket, or a pail of water.

Fireman McLeod started a small fire on May 13, with his shot of powder in a high ledge of coal. He battled the flames in the usual manner, but this time couldn't win. After twenty minutes and several buckets, McLeod left to call the manager, and returned to discover a monstrous blaze beyond control. He ran as the first explosion ripped through the tunnels.

Anyone nearby was killed or mortally wounded. The other miners could hear anguished moans coming up through the air shaft. Some offered to descend into the area to perform rescue; others fearfully made their way to the surface.

The second explosion erupted like a volcano. Towers of flame threw rocks, timber and bodies from every opening. Even the old Campbell Workings, connected to the Drummond Mine but closed for some time, reopened with a blast of boulders. All hopes of saving lives were lost as explosion after explosion rumbled from within the earth. Miners and volunteers poured as much water into the burning entrances as they could, then filled all openings with gravel and debris. Seventy men, whether alive or dead, were sealed into the mine.

THE DRUMMOND MINE EXPLODES

An uncontrolled fire caused the coal mine to erupt, shooting timbers, rocks and men high into the air.

71

"In Deepest Misery"

Nanaimo Mine Disaster
Nanaimo, British Columbia
May 3, 1887

There were no charges of criminal negligence. But when the mine blew, the blame fell squarely on the man who had laid the explosives. The Vancouver Coal Mining and Land Company's mine under the city of Nanaimo, British Columbia, extended 1.6 kilometres (1 mile) out beneath the sea. When gas and dust ignited in the mine, the city shook with an ominous tremor. One hundred and sixty men, miners from the British Isles, Nova Scotia and China, were in the mine at the time, and only seven would make it out alive.

THE NANAIMO MINE EXPLODED

Victims were found in groups where they had tried to seal themselves against the gases. Their last messages were scribbled on the walls in chalk.

Dense black smoke billowed from the mine followed by tongues of flame. It was a blaze that would burn for 24 long hours while the city agonized about the miners' fate below. The fire and smoke finally petered out, allowing hesitant rescuers to step inside. One of the first, Samuel Hudson, later died from exposure to the gas.

Despite the twisted and blackened interior, intact bodies were discovered. The first were very near the main shaft, a short run to safety. Several days later, a group of 35 men were found sealed in a protective cave. All had died from lethal carbon monoxide. Rescuers could not interpret the Chinese characters scrawled on the timbers, but scribbled on a shovel, in white chalk was the message: *Thirteen hours after explosion, in deepest misery, John Stevens.*

"NO GAS PRESENT"

Bellevue Mine Explosion
Crowsnest Pass, Alberta

DECEMBER 9, 1910

The December 6 report from District Mines Inspector Elijah Heathcote was succinct: "*I have inspected No. 1 seam and find the timbering and ventilation good, and no gas present.*" Heathcote's report shut down the miners' complaints about unsafe levels of gas. But two days later, a large explosion trapped 47 men underground.

Having no trained personnel or rescue equipment of its own, the company sent an urgent message to the rescue station in nearby Fernie. Mine superintendent Jack Powell couldn't bear the delay. He turned off the fans and then descended underground with a small "advance rescue" party. Soon one of them came stumbling back out, begging for help. The rescue party had been overcome by the gas, and lay in a heap on the main level. Other miners raced in and dragged the rescuers to the surface.

Another 21 men were later found on the main level, victims of carbon monoxide rather than the explosion. Some showed signs of life, yet none of them survived. *Calgary Herald* reporters lamented that on-site rescue equipment might have saved some of these men. Five of their safety lamps were still burning when rescuers found them.

There were heroes that night. Fred Alderson encountered a member of the rescue team who was struggling with a dwindling oxygen supply. He handed the man his own helmet and air supply, and started to the surface to re-equip himself. Within minutes the afterdamp had slain him. Mines inspector Elijah Heathcote, himself, worked until he had to be carried out of the mine. In all, 31 men lost their lives.

MEN AT THE ENTRANCE TO THE BELLEVUE MINE
After the explosion, some of the miners were found unconscious but alive. Unfortunately there was no rescue equipment to revive them.

A TOWN BURIED

A limestone slab—a kilometre (1/2 mile) wide—broke away from Turtle Mountain, crumbling into house-sized boulders and burying a section of Frank and its unsuspecting inhabitants.

THE FRANK SLIDE

Frank, Northwest Territories (now Alberta)

APRIL 29, 1903

The valley beneath Turtle Mountain was sheltered and made green by the cold, clean waters of the Oldman River. The ground sloped gently under poplars and blue lupines. Yet the Kootenay Indians refused to camp here. They regularly used the Crowsnest Pass, west of the valley, but they never lingered near the mountain. For in Kootenay legend, Turtle Mountain was restless and would one day choose to move.

White settlers dismissed the myth, lining the pass with silver tracks for their locomotives and founding the village of Blairmore. And when a seam of jet-black coal was discovered 3.2 kilometres (2 mi.) east on Turtle Mountain's shank, a new settlement sprang up, directly in the shadow of the peak.

The town was named Frank for its founder, mining entrepreneur H.L. Frank of Montana. His business partner in the Canadian-American Coal and Coke Company was prospector Samuel Gebo. With a talent for publicity, the two opened the town with a festival on September 10, 1901. There were speeches, sporting events and tours of the company's mining cottages. Arriving on special Canadian Pacific Railway (CPR) trains from Lethbridge and Cranbrook, spectators enjoyed a lavish dinner, a tour of the already impressive mine, and a tempting view of a future rich with legendary resources.

By 1903, Frank boasted 600 inhabitants. Its homes had electric lights and indoor plumbing. The town centre had amenities like the Union Bank of Canada, four hotels, two doctors, a law office and a dentist.

The mine now penetrated 1520 metres (5000 ft.) into the heart of the mountain. Its wide seams of coal were on an 85-degree slant which made it easy to transport: the coal simply slid down the shafts to the entrance. Little blasting was required to get the coal out of the seam. The mountain practically

mined itself—which cut down on labour costs. By 1903, huge tracts of coal had been torn out of Turtle Mountain.

On the night of April 29, 1903, only the evening maintenance crew of 19 men entered the quiet shafts. William Warrington was in charge of testing and replacing damaged timbers. In the past few months, strange omens had appeared. Timbers, checked thoroughly at night, were found splintered by the day shift. Vertical rooms of removed coal would seal up silently in the night.

As the men worked, the little town slowed its pace and fell into its nightly patterns. The rowdy bars of Dominion Avenue's four hotels quietened as their patrons stumbled home. Across the wooden bridge, at the east end of the avenue, a little row of miners' cottages was in darkness. Just east of the cottages lay the temporary clapboard dwellings of the town's latest arrivals. Behind thin walls, single miners and several families were huddled in their beds, including William Warrington's family.

The coal company's livery stable was quiet, as were the miners' cabins near it, and down by the CPR tracks, workers tottered from the hotels to their construction camp. Some must have noticed the sharp drop in temperature that night, and the strange halo of starlit mist swirling at the summit of Turtle Mountain.

Close to 4:00 a.m. a freight train pulled up to the entrance of the mine. The brakemen, Sid Choquette and Bill Lowes, chatted with a couple of the night shift miners, then leapt aboard as the train headed slowly back down the track towards town. The mine bridge was just in sight, when behind them, a deafening rumble filled the black sky.

Train engineer Murgatroyd thrust the throttle forward and the train lurched across the bridge, with brakemen Choquette and Lowes clinging to its sides. Just behind them, the bridge, the tracks, the earth and the air convulsed, and white dust billowed into the night.

A gigantic slab of limestone—a kilometre (half a mile) or more—had broken from the mountain and hurtled down into the valley. As it fell, it crumbled, into house-sized boulders breaking, bouncing, crushing a path of destruction. The massive avalanche left the valley filled with rocks hundreds of feet deep and stretching part way up the slope of the opposite mountain.

The miners' cottages at the edge of town were in the path of the rock slide. The livery stable, nearby cabins, and construction camp were obliterated, as were the few homesteads in the east of the valley. At the mouth of the mine, men were buried instantly as the huge slide sealed the entrance.

The freight train crew had escaped death by a fragile margin, and as the engine ground to a halt, one thing was certain: they had to warn the Spokane Flyer, the approaching passenger train. It was due into Frank from the east at any moment.

The two brakemen, Choquette and Lowes, each grabbed a lantern and headed towards the main tracks. They were soon climbing over enormous rocks, still hot from the fall. The lanterns were of little use, and the struggle to cross the boulders soon exhausted Lowes. Choquette pushed on without him. Blessed with a keen sense of direction and unflagging resolve, Choquette reached the eastern stretch of tracks just in time to wave his lantern at the oncoming train.

CLARK FAMILY KILLED
Lillian Clark (lower right), out of town at the time of the slide, was the only member of her family to survive. The bodies of many trapped victims were never recovered from the wreckage.

MINERS WORK TO REOPEN THE MINE

Aware that miners may be still alive inside, rescuers struggled with the sheer mass of the rocks.

Spotting the frantic little light directly in his path, the Spokane Flyer's engineer applied the brakes in time.

The centre of town was spared, although the force of the slide hurled people from their beds and threw them against walls. The row of miners' cottages at the edge town did not fare as well. Some were on fire, while others had disappeared completely. A few lucky occupants survived to be pulled from the rocks by townspeople.

Word of the Frank catastrophe sped throughout the country. A cable arrived for Prime Minister Wilfred Laurier telling him, *"Terrible catastrophe here. Eruption Turtle Mountain devastated miles of territory. One hundred killed. Must have Government aid..."*

Speculation ran like water: earthquakes, volcanic activity, mass flooding, reports that the whole town had been buried. The *Calgary Herald* reported that brakeman, Sid Choquette, after saving the Spokane Flyer, had *"gone crazy as a result of the awful tragedy."*

William Pearce, Inspector of Mines for the Dominion Government, arriving on the scene, soon pared down the rumours. The inspector felt that the method of near-vertical mining may have severed the chunk of mountain.

As Pearce began his investigation the day after the slide, a party of men dug through the rubble in search of the mine's entrance. They felt the night shift miners may still be alive.

Seventeen night crewmen were in the tunnels when the mountain broke. Joe Chapman was hurled against a tunnel wall by a blast of hot air. He ran, joining the others, through the terror, all the way to the entrance which had disappeared. Access to the outside world was locked behind at least 91 metres (300 ft.) of stone. Timberman Warrington's leg was severely crushed, and he lay in the main tunnel while his workmates investigated the lower exit. To their horror they encountered water, rising slowly, filling the lower tunnels. Dammed by the slide, the Oldman River was already flooding the mine.

With air shafts choked with rubble, the men raced against mounting noxious gases to chip a new passage to safety. They chose a narrow seam of coal thought to outcrop onto the mountain face. Thirteen hours later, the three who still had energy to work struck through to dazzling sunlight. They crawled out of their trap onto a vista of white destruction. Below them they saw the group of would-be rescuers hacking away at the blocked entrance.

In a strange reversal of most mining disasters, this time it was the freed miners who gathered at the surface for news of their buried families. Carried out of the mine on a plank, William Warrington knew from first glance at the valley that his wife, three children and close friend, hadn't stood a chance.

The rockslide severed road and rail connections across the country. Trains screeched to a halt at the foot of the slide and passengers hauled their own baggage over the rocks before boarding another train and resuming their journey on the other side.

COLLAPSED MOUNTAIN FACE

Still under debate is the exact size of the fall, estimated at somewhere between 70 million and 90 million tonnes (77-99 million tons) of rock.

Calculating the exact number of deaths in the slide proved impossible. A group of men had set up a campsite in the valley. They were all buried by the fall, but nobody knew who or how many they were. The *Calgary Herald*, in its list of the dead, included *"six miners from Lancashire, names unknown, two unknown Welsh miners and nine unknown Russian Poles."* Listed as one of the injured was *"a girl by the name of Nancy"* who had severe contusions. Similarly, the North-West Mounted Police records included the deaths of *"four Finlanders, names unknown."* According to police records, the slide took 69 lives in total, although a commemorative plaque at the site mentions 66, and Harry Matheson, editor of the *Frank Sentinel* at the time, came up with 76 dead. Only twelve bodies were ever recovered.

The exact size of the fall has also been a matter of debate, wavering between 70 million to 90 million tonnes (77-99 million tons) of rock, or "half a mountainside."

In contrast, the cause of the slide could not be clearer. Turtle Mountain was built of steep blocks of sedimentary rock, made all the more unstable by dividing faults and fissures. The days preceding the fall had been abnormally warm, filling the fissures with moisture. The night of the fall was excessively cold, causing that moisture to freeze and expand. What little support the mountain had from its almost perpendicular seams of coal had been removed by the Canadian-American Coal and Coke Company.

In his private correspondence, Mines Inspector William Pearce stated that there was insufficient substance left between the mine walls, and that the reckless habits of the company, in an effort to produce coal at the lowest possible cost, made such a disaster inevitable. Pearce's letters, however, were to remain private until 1979. There was no public investigation, no blame assigned, and mine owners Frank and Gebo survived, their reputations intact.

Government aid to those left homeless, injured and bereaved was not forthcoming, and the Canadian-American Coal and Coke Company rode back into town like heroes. After a quick inspection of the mountain, the company was determined to restart operations, with uncommon attention to safety. They assured the community that the mine would soon be back to its productivity, and its workers would enjoy new housing of exceptional standards.

The town was shifted a little to the north, in accordance with a geological survey, just beyond the reach of any further catastrophes, and the community of Frank enjoyed something of a revival. Sadly, it was short-lived. The mining company's vision of prosperity turned out to be yet another myth. The mountain's resources were already depleted, and before the decade was out, the company was bankrupt. The town was abandoned, then torn down little by little, and of all its myths and legends, only one survived. Restless Turtle Mountain had indeed chosen to move.

TOWN BENEATH BOULDERS
The immense size of the debris hindered rescue efforts.

100 People Buried

The 1889 rockslide laid Cape Diamond bare, killing 47 people. Up to 24 metres (80 ft.) of rock and debris fell onto the residents of Champlain Street.

THE ROCKFALL

Quebec City, Quebec

SEPTEMBER 19, 1889

"*Terrible accident,*" read the telegram to the Ministers of Public Works and the Militia in Ottawa, "*Part of the rock below the Citadel west of Dufferin Terrace fallen. Ten houses destroyed and a great number of persons buried in the ruins.*"

That stormy September evening, a great overhanging crag of slate rock had splintered from Cape Diamond, dropping 91 metres (300 ft.) onto the houses below. It crushed the tenement homes of 28 families, suddenly, stealthily, as if it had fallen from the sky. Now about 100 people lay buried beneath 24 metres (80 ft.) of slate debris.

The police, the military and the fire brigade were on the scene within an hour, mining the buried homes for survivors. Voices cried out from beneath the rocks. Rescuers could hear a woman comforting her crying children, but could not save her in time. Six-year-old Ida Black spoke to rescuers as they dug, begging them not to create so much dust, instructing them to save the piano. She emerged, largely unharmed.

Joseph Kemp lay buried for four days in a coffin-like enclosure, his arms pinned beneath timbers, dust covering his face. Kemp was the last person to be found alive. In total, 47 others were killed.

Tragically, this catastrophe did not come out of the blue. In 1841, a similar accident had killed 32 people, and in 1852, another 7 people died in a rockslide on Champlain Street, the same street now hit. The Dominion Government was well-acquainted with the fissures in Cape Diamond, wedged wider every year by winter ice. After the second rockslide, the land directly under the cliff had been cleared and the largest cracks filled with cement as a structural stop-gap. The houses on the opposite side of Champlain Street, had been considered safe. These were now destroyed by the third, and worst, slide. Their ruins, strewn with rocks, were left to help buttress what remained of the cliff.

SIX SMALL VICTIMS TEMPORARILY HELD AT THE MARINE AND FISHERIES OFFICE

Twenty-eight families lived in the tenement homes that were crushed when an overhang of rock collapsed.

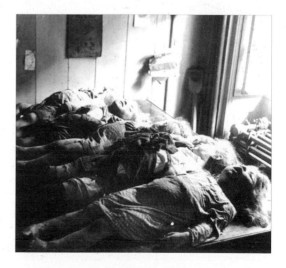

FACES OF HILLCREST MINE

A spark from a gunpowder blast (used to loosen coal) ignited a pocket of gas and exploded. The explosion shot though the shafts setting off a second, and possibly a third, devastating blast trapping nearly two hundred men underground. Hillcrest miners in the photograph are unknown except for the two brothers standing left, John and Charles Ironmonger. Both men were killed in the explosion.

The Hillcrest Mine Disaster

Hillcrest, Alberta

June 19, 1914

In the mine, Friday June 14, was a day like any other. The Hillcrest workings had been checked early in the morning and two hundred and thirty-five men left their modest homes, their wives and children, walking through two holes in the earth into the underworld of tunnels.

The miners laughed and quipped as they descended into the mine's perpetual night. Charles Elick was among them. He'd survived the Frank Slide of 1903, digging himself out from the heart of Turtle Mountain through a narrow seam of coal along with sixteen other men. Tom Corkill, survivor of an explosion at the Kenmore mines, descended happily for what he knew would be his final shift. He had saved enough from years of mining wages to leave it all behind.

By 9:30 a.m., coal production was in full swing. Sam Charlton was 488 metres (1600 ft.) below, loosening coal with gunpowder blasts. Some mine officials discouraged gunpowder blasting, but the miners felt they couldn't do their work without it. And besides, if a mine wasn't safe to blast in, then it wasn't safe to work in.

Charlton set his charges but never had the chance to fire them. Not far from him, and in a split second, a fateful spark leapt into a pocket of gas and dust, ignited, then erupted in a monstrous boom. Propelled through the tunnels, the first explosion set off a second, and possibly a third, devastating blast.

General Manager John Brown knew at once that the worst had happened. He yelled for an electrician to work on the fans at each entrance, to suck gases from the shafts. Already, a toxic-looking brown cloud was accumulating, a forboding signal to the miners' wives and children who ran towards it, fear in their chests. A handful of men arrived at Mine No. 2 but were forced out of the entrance, gasping for air. Three miners who'd been working near the entrance, stumbled from the darkness into view and were helped into the fresh summer air.

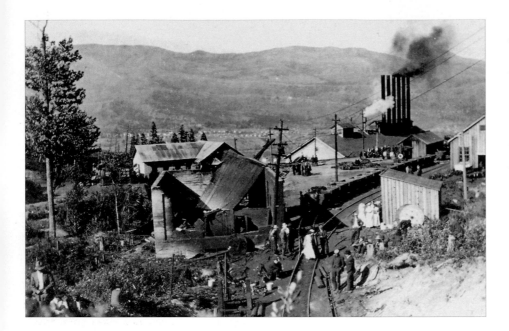

Carbon monoxide clouds in the mine forced a delay in rescue operations. A request for help was sent to Blairmore and a rescue car with oxygen equipment was dispatched. The North-West Mounted Police (NWMP), stationed at nearby Burmis Mines, caught wind of the disaster. Crowds of townspeople surged to the mine.

Twenty tense minutes had passed since the explosion and only now did the mine release further signs of life. A few more men staggered out, in ones and twos. The spectators were frantic. They pushed and squeezed toward the men, desperate to glimpse familiar faces.

Collapsed Mine in Foreground

Clouds of carbon monoxide in the mine delayed rescue operations. Only those close to the surface avoided being overcome by fumes.

David Murray was one of the survivors. Filling his poisoned lungs with clean air, he scanned the faces for his three sons. They must still be in the mine. Murray turned and started back down the shaft. Police Constable Hancock tried to hold him back but Murray was determined and, pushing past the officer, he dissolved into the blackness. Murray would die in the mine, along with his three boys.

Only eighteen men had emerged from their nightmare in the tunnels. As the spectre of catastrophe silenced the crowd, a group of men heaved at the debris that blocked the hoist engine and the tracks. Soon they had both free, and a rescue car ready. It was 10:00 a.m. and the first group was on its way in to save lives. Some who'd only just escaped alive returned with those first rescuers.

They found their first two victims crushed to death beneath timbers and rubble at the main tunnel crossroads in Mine No. 2. They were Rod Wallis and William Neath, two Nova Scotians, due home to their farms on Monday. Nearby, the rescue team located three unconscious miners and rushed them to the surface.

By now, the government rescue car had arrived. With its oxygen masks, the rescue team could descend further. They came across small groups of unconscious, barely-breathing men. In far greater numbers were the dead. Meanwhile, the salvage operations could not have been more difficult. Level 1 South had been blocked off by heaps of rubble, mangled track and buckled mine cars, but the rescuers, using all their might, managed to push through. Their reward: thirty young and healthy miners. All face down in a puddle of water. All dead. The rescuers worked on.

The frantic miners had streamed through the tunnels searching for escape. There were bodies everywhere, very few of them alive. Occasionally, rescuers would find a body with a weak pulse or shallow breath, and whisk them to the makeshift hospital in the mine yard.

On the surface, Joe Atkinson told his story to sympathetic listeners, *"It was just as if I had suddenly gone deaf, or as if two four-inch nails had been driven into my ears."* Atkinson was knocked to the ground by the shock, but he leapt to his feet and began to run as thick, black smoke billowed through the slant. Other workers joined him. *"A short distance ahead we came on Billie Neal, he was lying on the ground overcome. We tried to lift him and carry him along with us but by this time we were too weak with the gases."* They dragged Neal for several yards, over rubble, over a dead horse, until the effort it required was depleted. His body was relinquished to its own fate in the tunnel, while Atkinson and the other miners stumbled on.

Atkinson continued:

> *...then we came to the afterdamp, a solid wall that drove us back and nearly suffocated us and we lay down and rolled back with what strength we had left to a pool of water about 50 or 60 feet back, and here we crawled into the water soaking our shirts and sucking them to keep off the effects of the afterdamp.*

One by one, Atkinson's coworkers began to slip from consciousness. Gus Franz, a German miner, fell face down into the water. Because no one was strong enough to pull him free, he drowned. Atkinson himself fell unconscious, but he was part of a fortunate group that was saved thanks to the undaunted rescuers and to the fans which sucked gases from the shafts.

By noon, there were only bodies left amid the mine's dissipating gases. Two hundred and thirty-five men had entered the shafts that morning. Only 46 came out alive. The battered bodies of the 189 dead accumulated at the surface amid the crowd's swelling despair. Upon arriving on the scene, Inspector Christen Junget of the NWMP took control. Corporals Fred Mead and John Grant, with a group of miners, were assigned the sickening task of washing the dead miners and searching their clothing for identification. Once washed down, many of the dead had to be reassembled, matching up clothing or wounds, before they could be wrapped in white shrouds and placed in wagons. Police Constable Hancock took it upon himself to scour the bloodstained rubble in the mine for missing arms and legs. Bereaved wives and children sobbed at the

AGONY OF WAITING

By noon, there were only bodies left amid the mine's dissipating gases. Two hundred and thirty-five men had entered the shafts that morning. Only 46 came out.

THE MOURNING CROWD

Gradually, 189 bodies were brought up to the surface. Bereaved wives and children sobbed at the washhouse door while a group of miners washed the dead, searching their clothing for identification.

washhouse door. As dusk approached, the crowds of grieving relatives dispersed. This allowed the workers to carry up the more disfigured corpses.

By Sunday morning, June 21, 1914, over 150 bodies had been cleaned, identified and moved out of the washhouse. Pieces of young, strong miners lay in heaps on the washhouse floor and the exhausted police officers slept, awaiting more grisly remnants from below. The complete bodies lay in rough coffins in the Miner's Hall and in the empty yard next to Cruikshank's General Store. They were grouped according to denomination: Roman Catholic, Anglican, Presbyterian, Odd Fellows, Masons and Orangemen.

A reporter from the *Calgary Herald* witnessed one young miner lifting the lid of a coffin, leaning in and kissing the lips of his dead brother before screwing the box shut. He watched widows collapsing and being led away by friends, and young women with babies in their arms standing silently in their oceans of loss. As the burials began, the graves—long and shallow trenches—were still being dug. The crunch of spades in soil filled the tremulous pauses of the Bellevue Band.

In the months to follow there was an inquiry which seemed to foster more arguments than resolutions. Mine workers all testified that gas and coal dust had not been present in inordinate amounts, whereas the District Inspector of Mines said the opposite. The official report stated that the gas explosion was of unknown origin, but that it had triggered one or several coal dust explosions. Harry White, a former fire boss at the mine and one of the first rescuers, suggested that sparks from a rockfall might have supplied the first ignition. His idea was largely ignored until twelve years later, when on September 19, 1926 just such a rockfall set off another tremendous blast. There were only two men in the mine, both of whom were killed.

The Hillcrest explosion left 130 widows reeling from its blast. An estimated four hundred children under the age of ten were fatherless. The wife of Charles Elick (who'd survived the Frank Slide) gave birth to their youngest child the day after the disaster. Survivor of the Kenmore explosion, Tom Corkill, didn't live to enjoy his new homestead.

The Hillcrest Collieries paid each grieving family $1800. There was also more immediate relief from local and regional committees. The Federal Government gave $50 000 to the cause and the Province of Alberta gave $20 000. It was small compensation for those who had lost so much.

The Hillcrest Mine operated until 1949 when it ceased to be lucrative. Money closed the workings and a deliberate explosion of dynamite sealed them shut.

BURYING THE DEAD, 1914
So many men had died that funerals began while graves were still being dug.

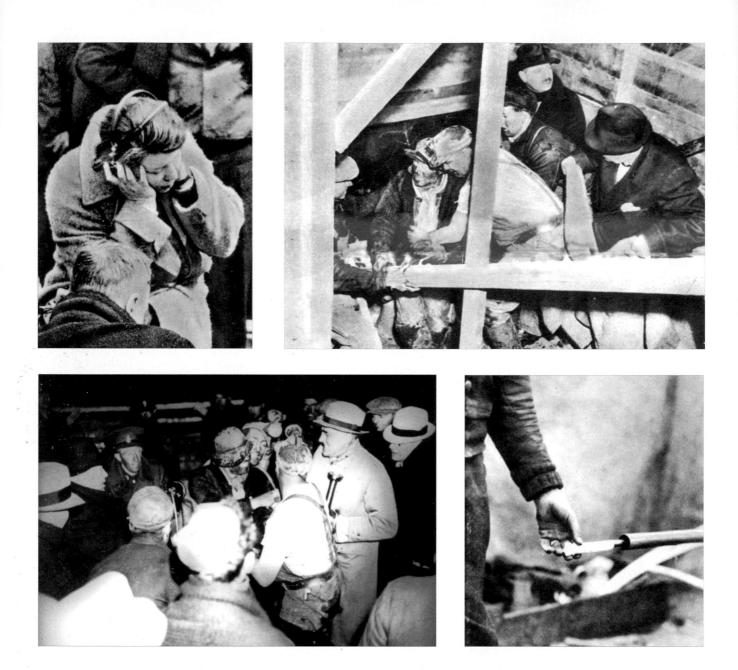

THE DISASTER THAT GRIPPED THE CONTINENT:
THREE ENTOMBED MEN BROUGHT TO THE SURFACE AFTER 242 HOURS UNDERGROUND
(Top left) Mrs. Roberston listens through headphones as rescuers make contact with her husband.
(Top right) After more than 200 hours underground, Dr. Robertson is carried out of the mine.
(Bottom left) Only moments at the surface, Charles Scadding—the 42-year-old time-keeper and
book-keeper—is crowded by joyous miners and reporters. (Bottom right) The 141-foot drill tube
used to send food and a radio transmitter down to the trapped men.

MOOSE RIVER MINE DISASTER

Pictou, Nova Scotia

APRIL 12, 1936

As far as disasters go, it was small in scale. But when the gold mine near Moose River, Nova Scotia, collapsed, trapping three men, the rescue effort and the media response were immense.

The mine's two new owners, Herman Magill and David Robertson, were just leaving the mine with timekeeper Alfred Scadding when the shaft above them came crashing down. The men hurled themselves into a chamber about 43 metres (140 ft.) from the surface where they would remain trapped for the next nine days.

Crouched in the damp, the men were somehow able to build a fire. The smoke filtered through the rocks, appearing on the surface as a sign of life within. Miners tried everything to reach them. They tried to excavate old tunnels, to blast open a new, vertical shaft. They hauled in lumber to reinforce the hole. They brought in a 44-tonne (40-ton) crane and reinforced the muddy mine road. Meanwhile, local and national reporters gathered near the site, literally fighting for the use of the only telephone a quarter mile away. When diamond driller Billy Bell made contact with the men below, Maritime Tel & Tel created a transmitter small enough to fit into a pen and reach the men down the drill hole.

Eight days after the cave-in, Scadding reported to the surface that Magill had died of pneumonia. The mine was flooding, and, though still alive, the two survivors felt their time was running out. They dictated their wills by telephone. Rescuers began to excavate another shaft that was not in use. By now the Canadian Radio Broadcast Corporation's (CRBC) J. Frank Willis had arrived. With his car "patched" directly into a phone line, he was able to report two-minute bulletins every half an hour to radio stations in Canada, and across North America. Millions of people hung on every word of the unfolding story.

The tension mounted as the rescuers inched closer through the tight, risky tunnel. Finally, after nine days of incarceration, the two survivors surfaced to a site strewn with temporary shacks, every imaginable rescue device, clicking cameras and a singing Salvation Army. Across the continent, people wept and cheered as they tuned in to their radios.

J. FRANK WILLIS INTERVIEWS A MINER
The collapse of the Moose River mine was the first disaster to be broadcast live on radio in Canada. The story also gripped American and British audiences. After Moose River, Willis was swamped by offers of employment from American radio stations, but, not wanting to capitalize on the disaster, he refused to leave Canada.

WHEN EARTH GIVES WAY
A dramatic rescue from the doomed housing development at Saint-Jean-Vianney.

LANDSLIDE

Saint-Jean-Vianney, Quebec

MAY 5, 1971

The village of Saint-Jean-Vianney was founded in the 1930s, 10 kilometres (6.2 mi.) west of Chicoutimi. Tranquil and picturesque, the town was built on layers of Laflamme sea clay, souvenir of an ancient flood, which was unstable and apt to slide. The Aluminum Company of Canada (Alcan) established a plant here and built new housing for the young families who moved to the area.

Children and animals sensed it first. On the afternoon of May 4, 1971, some children told confused parents that the ground was shaking and making noises. At around 7:00 p.m. dogs began to bark and whimper nervously, like a thunderstorm was brewing. But the sky was clear, and the night was quiet. Pitre Blackburn tried to take his cows out to their usual pastures, but they refused to stay, following the perplexed farmer straight back to the barn.

Three hours later, Mrs. Lise Laforge of Stanley Street telephoned a neighbour to say she'd felt a slight earthquake. She also mentioned she could see the lights of Chicoutimi from her window, a view usually obscured by a small hill.

Bus driver Jules Girard was picking up night-shift workers for the Alcan plant. As he rounded the bend on Stanley Street, it was five minutes to eleven. He noticed a gully in the gravel and slowed the bus, just as the road dropped away from under the front wheels. The earth was sucking downwards, right before his eyes, and his bus was perched on a rim, its front wheels spinning. Girard ordered his 18 passengers out the rear door of the vehicle, and they ran back down Stanley Street on what felt like an escalator, as the ground fell away from under them. Feeling a firmness beneath his feet, Girard slowed and banged on the door of house number 75 trying to wake the inhabitants. He was on his way to the houses across the street when, suddenly, they dropped downwards, disappearing into the crater. Then the lights went out, and everything plunged into darkness.

More people began to run down Stanley Street, hauling neighbours from their houses, then turning to see the dwellings fall out of sight. *"I could hear people* screaming 'help'," driver Girard told the *Montreal Gazette*, "*then the houses just disappeared into the ground.*" It took just five minutes for the earth to swallow 34 homes, the bus and many cars.

A massive slide of mud sucked and pulled at the surface of the earth, reducing it to liquid. Fifteen million tonnes (16.5 million tons) of heaving, churning slime chewed the edges of Saint-Jean-Vianney.

When they felt their house move, Moncalm and Lise Laforge gathered the three children, all under four, in the kitchen. The refrigerator and stove were sliding over the floor. Stumbling outside, they dropped more than 30 metres (100 ft.), landing on a mound of earth that was floating on some sludge. But their platform did not last. Moncalm watched with horror as the mud pulled Lise and the children to their deaths. He fought his way to solid ground, pulling on roots, rocks, and debris, anything to keep afloat.

Roger Landry was in his basement when his world convulsed. He ran outside, screaming for his wife and five children, but it was too late. Landry spent the night along the edges of the crater in a futile search for his family.

THE EARTH DROPPED 30 METRES

Signs of the impending landslide were seen as curious changes. One woman felt a slight earthquake and mentioned she could see the lights of Chicoutimi from her window, a view usually obscured by a small hill.

Yvon Godin heard his friend, Gilles Bourgeois, crying for help from within the crater. There was nothing Godin could do and, slowly, the wet and eerie rumble of the mud overpowered Bourgeois' voice.

The slide began somewhere on Pitre Blackburn's farm. The grazing field that his cows had resisted was completely washed away that night. As it moved westward, a "dam wall" of trees, roots and rocks formed, blocking the slide's entrance to the Petit Bras Valley. When the pressure grew too great, the dam broke, releasing a mud wave 18 metres (60 ft.) high. Traveling 26 kilometres (16 mi.) per hour, it flowed into the valley of Rivière aux Vases, snapping off a 42-metre (138-ft.) concrete bridge. The bridge is still in the Saguenay River, where the mudwave deposited it.

Sixteen-year-old Denis Ringuette was watching a Stanley Cup playoff game on TV when he saw a wall of mud flow right over the bridge, carrying entire trees with it. The wave pulverized a transformer near the bridge, cutting electrical power to the town. Just two hours later, the Rivière aux Vases, though brown and sluggish, was back to its normal level.

The sinkhole had been quick and lethal. Most of the destruction occurred within five minutes. Thirty-four houses, many cars and an estimated 31 people—most of them children—were whisked into the Saguenay River. Six more houses and several cars toppled gently into the crater in the next twelve hours.

The early morning brought medical personnel, supplies, and a rescue team from the Armed Forces Base at Bagotville, with helicopters and boats, but little could be done for those who had been caught in the abyss. One woman was found balancing on the roof of her car in a sea of mud. She was in shock and shivering but managed to grasp the leather harness lowered from a helicopter, and she was flown to safety.

Daylight broke on devastation. Rescuers in steel-hulled rowboats poked at the debris, finding no survivors. Eleven kilometres (7 mi.) away, at the confluence of the Rivière aux Vases and the Saguenay, furniture and remnants of homes were being fished into boats. Only four bodies were recovered, some washed out into the St. Lawrence River.

The mayor of Saint-Jean-Vianney, Laureat Lavoie, received a telegram from Prime Minister Pierre Trudeau: *"I know what difficulties the rescuers face,"* it said, *"and we await with anxiety the results of their courageous efforts..."* The Prime Minister also forwarded a message from

BROKEN BY THE FORCE
(above) Water and sewer lines were snapped apart, and (below) roads dropped off into the crater. One bus driver noticed a gully in the gravel and slowed his bus, just as the road dropped away from under the front wheels.

Queen Elizabeth, on a tour in B.C. She expressed her *"deepest sympathy to relatives of those who have perished, to those injured and those whose houses have been destroyed."*

Two days after the slide, thirteen mayors from neighbouring communities, lead by Laureat Lavoie, flew over the hole in an Armed Forces helicopter. The view of the wreckage beneath them, with the orderly little town dangling precariously on the lip of the chasm, caught the mayors off guard. Some broke into tears during the flight. *"We must do all we can to help them,"* one told the *Gazette*, *"...that sight was unbelievable."*

The mayors held a meeting with the victims to determine their immediate needs, while clothing, food, and offers of shelter flowed in from communities nearby. Quebec Premier Robert Bourassa arranged for twenty mobile homes and invoked the special measures of the Quebec Police Act to coordinate all available resources.

The housing development was evacuated, with worried families dashing in to retrieve their valuables. Road access was blocked, leaving the area free for the scurrying teams of government and university engineers and geologists. After a two-day study of the site, government engineer Jean-Yves Chagnon was certain that the *"sensitive clay flow slide"* had done its worst. There had been no further rain, and he felt the land around the scar was now stable. Residents of the area refused to believe him, and stayed away.

One engineer, Cameron Kenney of Toronto, suggested that the disaster might have been averted. The clay cliffs of the area were already known to be intensely prone to landslides. According to Kenney, installing drains, and cutting back the cliffs along the Rivière aux Vases would have reduced the danger. Chagnon agreed—that deep, internal drainage would have been useful, but only possible after extensive, costly investigation, and with the benefit of hindsight. Drainage and other stabilizing techniques have since been used for other areas, and all municipalities have been issued maps which indicate potential surface weaknesses.

The village of Saint-Jean-Vianney was moved away, leaving only the foundations. The devastated area now offers relaxation and beauty. There is an aluminum bridge ideal for trout fishing, and secluded trails run through the forest. Those with a mind to explore the cliffs may still find fissures and abrasions deep in the clay, where trees, houses and cars scraped by.

IN FIVE MINUTES 34 HOUSES WERE SWALLOWED BY THE EARTH

A massive slide of mud sucked and pulled at the surface of the earth, reducing it to liquid.

WESTRAY MINE EXPLOSION

Stellarton, Nova Scotia

MAY 9, 1992

When the Westray Mine opened in Nova Scotia's Pictou County, people saw it as a sure-fire business success, and as much-needed relief for high unemployment and a fragile economy. The Provincial and Federal Governments invested heavily in the venture.

The mine tapped into the old Foord coal seam. Four times thicker than other seams in the country, the coal was renowned for its low sulphur and high energy, but also for its explosive methane gas and numerous faults.

Even in Westray's short history, the dangers were obvious: May 1991, a roof collapse; June 1991, electrical arcing in mining equipment; July 1991, coal dust exceeding safe limits; October 1991, another roof collapse. In early April 1992, the Ministry of Labour ordered Westray to come up with a "dust deployment plan." Powdered limestone, known as "stone dust," was commonly used in other mines to control the dust, but in Westray the stone dust sat in bags, unused. Production had failed to reach its targets from the start, and safety issues were pushed to the side.

Two Alberta miners resigned for this very reason. Ken Evans told the *Halifax Chronicle Herald* that when a small fire started from the flames of a cutting torch, no firefighting equipment was available. And Chester Taje, a miner of twenty years experience, quit after his many complaints about safety were ignored. Westray officials later contested these and other criticisms of their mining practices.

The proof, however, came early in the morning of May 9, 1992. Fifteen men were working the coal face, about 350 metres (1100 ft.) down. Another eleven were reinforcing the roof at about the same level. Methane gas had been leaking for days from an abandoned section of mine, and the ventilation system was known to be inadequate. Nevertheless, a variety of equipment was in use that day, including acetylene torches, unprotected diesel engines, and welding equipment. The lethal spark could have come from anywhere. As a pocket of methane ignited, some of the miners had time to grab their emergency breathing kits. Others just ran. The carbon monoxide felled them within seconds. Flames licked along the roof to the main crossroads of the tunnels where the thick dust exploded. None of the 26 men came out alive.

A MINE WITH PROBLEMS

A view down the Westray Mine after the explosion (top) and of the mine entrance that was damaged by the blast that killed 26 men (bottom).

FIRE

This world... ever was, and is, and shall be, ever-living Fire, in measures being kindled and in measures going out.

—Heraclitus
c.540-c.480 B.C.

SAINT JOHN, NEW BRUNSWICK BURNS
JUNE 1877

Fanned by gale-force winds, the fire swept
from the waterfront up through the city centre,
killing eleven people.

THREE MONTREAL FIREMEN ON A SKINNER LADDER
The ladder was pushed down the street while the men fought their way through a sheet of flames.

FIRE

Part Three

Uncontrolled, fire, with its terrifying speed, heat and menace, has always plagued human societies. Roman cities organized fire brigades. And in the ninth century, Alfred the Great of England introduced fire legislation by ordering the *couvre-feu* (origin of today's curfew), the extinguishing of all candles and heating fires for the night.

Canada's earliest fire regulations, in 1692, required home-owners in Quebec City to clean their chimneys regularly. The Sovereign Council of New France was already encouraging the city to import a top-of-the-line Dutch fire engine. The first firefighting organization appeared in Montreal in 1734 after a blaze set by a disgruntled slave destroyed many new buildings. By 1790, both Montreal and Quebec were well-equipped with fire carts.

Englishman John Walker invented the friction match in 1827, replacing the flint and wood drill. At that time, Canadian communities were swaths of wooden buildings thrown up almost overnight. By the end of the century, they were fashionable centres, complete with piped gas, electricity and rosy optimism. And each had already fallen prey to ruinous fires.

The Parliament Buildings first burned in 1849, in a blaze started by Fred Perry, a firefighter! Perry opposed a bill that rewarded traitors while short-changing those, like him, who'd fought for Queen and country. Perry sounded the alarm, and his friends worked valiantly to save the surrounding buildings, leaving the Parliament to light up the sky alone.

Fire was often used as a destructive tool in wartime, but until the middle of the twentieth century, peacetime incidents of arson were rare. The 1972 fire at the Bluebird Cafe in Montreal was particularly vile. Unhappy with the service, arsonists dropped a match on gasoline they'd poured on the stairway leading to the upstairs nightclub. Trapped by the blaze, two hundred people tumbled down the only fire escape. Thirty-seven perished. In 1969, forty seniors fell victim to arson in Notre Dame du Lac, Quebec. In 1979, 47 people were killed in Chapais, Quebec, when a guest at a crowded New Year's Eve dance flicked a lighter at the decorations.

GREAT FIRE OF MONTREAL JULY 8, 1852

Montreal burned throughout one day and into the next, destroying 1100 homes. (Below) Military tents for Montreal's homeless. A shortage of water was blamed for the fire's severity. At that time, a large water tank had been drained while new pipes were being laid throughout the city.

A careless smoker likely caused the death of 77 children in the fire at Montreal's Laurier Palace Theatre, the worst of many fires in Canada to take the lives of children. Fifty-three infants were killed in 1918 in the Grey Nunnery, Montreal, a home devoted to caring for the aged, crippled and orphaned; and about eighty children have been killed in school fires, one in Quebec City in 1927, and the other in St. Hyacinth, Quebec in 1938—promising young lives reduced to statistics.

Outside the cities, the Canadian wilderness and its sunbaked forests ignited regularly. The Miramichi Fire of 1825 shot through the dense

QUEBEC CITY BURNS, 1845

In May and June of 1845, Quebec was decimated by two calamitous fires. Forty people died, about 12,000 homes and 4,000 buildings were razed. The total loss was estimated at over $5 million, of which only $500,000 was insured. The Quebec Relief Fund received money not only from "the mother country and the sister provinces" but also from the colonies and the United States. The fires changed construction materials: brick and stone instead of wood; and tin instead of shingles on roofs.

trees of New Brunswick leaving behind 8000 square kilometres (5000 sq. mi.) of destruction. With fire storms travelling at speeds of 160 kilometres (100 mi.) an hour, at 1093 degrees Celsius, (2000 degrees F) the mining and lumber towns, built entirely of wood, were utterly helpless. In 1908, eighty lives were lost to the Elk River fire in British Columbia which wiped out the towns of Fernie and Michel. Three years later, over a hundred people were killed in the fire that destroyed South Porcupine in northern Ontario.

AFTER THE MATHESON FIRE, MATHESON, ONTARIO, JULY 1916

Two survivors—a man who fled, and a water pump that survived the intense heat—stand in the charred remains of a town.

Contemporary fires have introduced new danger and new spectacle. In 1979, a train carrying tank cars of butane, propane, toluene and liquid chlorine derailed in Mississauga, Ontario. The gases and chemicals leaked and caught fire, exploding tanks like burning rockets into the bedroom community. Mississauga and parts of nearby Oakville were evacuated while the fire was allowed to burn "controlled" until it petered out. No lives were lost. In 1990, 14 million used tires burned to oil in Hagersville, Ontario. Huge clouds of black smoke discharged toxins and carcinogens into the air and soil for 17 days.

While a fire's needs are few—fuel, oxygen and a spark of ignition—its social costs are high in terms of health care services, property damage, post-fire trauma and bereavement. Our approach to fighting fire is changing. More and more, the emphasis is shifting toward prevention and education, away from legislation and fighting the blaze itself. We may yet learn to tame one of our greatest opponents.

OTTAWA HULL FIRE, APRIL 26, 1900

A mangled bridge (above). Ottawa citizens gathered on the escarpment to watch the city of Hull, Quebec, burning on the far side of the Ottawa River (below). Fanned by strong winds, a common chimney fire burned out of control, then skipped across the river on burning debris, destroying parts of Ottawa and threatening Parliament Hill. Seven people died.

AFTERMATH OF THE TORONTO FIRE, 1904
Debris was shovelled by hand, and taken away in horse-drawn carts. The work continued for many months.

THE GREAT TORONTO FIRE

Toronto, Ontario

APRIL 19, 1904

Toronto, in 1904, was a boom town, pushing out and up. The picture of progress, its muddy streets were now gravel and asphalt. Six-storey skyscrapers buzzed with electric light and elevators. And its 200 000 residents had already grown accustomed to the telephone and telegram, to the latest fashions, to convenience and selection.

The threat of fire had not been the first consideration for Toronto architects and builders. In the city core, buildings were covered with wooden towers, dormers, cornices and trim—ideal kindling for any blaze. Generally, roofs were tar with wooden supports. Firebreaks—solid walls between structures—were extremely rare. Great warehouses filled with furs, hats, furnishings and paper goods stood side by side, and only a few with sprinkler systems. Webs of wires for telephone, telegram and electricity were draped over the streets. Unwittingly, the metropolis had built itself the perfect set for an unparalleled spectacle.

It was unseasonably cold the night of April 19, 1904. While flurries fell on the dark city, Fire Chief John Thompson was warm inside the Lombard Street Fire Hall. At 8:04 p.m. his peace was shattered by two alarms, activated simultaneously, close to the station. Two night watchmen had discovered flames at the E.S. Currie building at 58-60 Wellington West, and had raced to activate alarms. Chief Thompson arrived at the scene with three horse-drawn engines, seven hose wagons, an aerial truck, water tower and hook and ladder, only to find the Currie Building beyond salvation. Gusting winds hurled streams of water back into the firefighters' faces, coating them with ice.

The Gillespie-Ansley building, just across the lane to the east, had not yet been affected. Chief Thompson prepared a team to keep the Currie blaze from jumping to the next door roof. He and four men broke into the building, but the

**FIRE CHIEF
JOHN THOMPSON**

A broken leg early in the fire disabled the Chief, leaving firefighters to battle Toronto's worst fire without their leader.

FRONT STREET LOOKING WEST

A photograph from the Customs House on Yonge Street shows the business district in ruins.

FIREFIGHTING EQUIPMENT, 1904

Horse-drawn steam pumps were insufficient to stop the raging fire as it was pushed around the city by erratic winds.

wind sent flames across the lane, and the Gillespie building's upper floors quickly filled with smoke. Disoriented, Thompson and his men staggered to a window and screamed for help. Their colleagues down below propped a ladder up against the wall, but it wasn't tall enough. The trapped firemen dangled a rope out of the smoking window. It was caught by those below, tied to a fire hose and then pulled back up to the window. One by one the men slid down it. When it was his turn, Chief Thompson's left hand slipped and he fell three storeys at great speed, his leg snapping as it jammed into the pavement. The Fire Chief was rushed to hospital, leaving his deputy, John Noble, to lead the team.

Noble and his men watched the wind whip flames south across Wellington, igniting buildings sixty feet away. The fire was also spreading rapidly to the north and east. Deputy Noble sounded the general alarm. It was 8:51 p.m.

Every fireman in the city raced towards the blaze. Every steam engine, hose wagon and ladder truck hurtled through the night streets pulled by horses in wild gallop, bells clanging, engines smoking. The streets began to fill with spectators, anxious to glimpse the action.

When the front wall of a skyscraper crashed eastwards across Bay Street, the *Evening Telegram* building caught light. The building's sprinkler system failed to activate and night-shift employees soon faced burning window frames, exploding glass, and clouds of smoke. Incredibly, they opted to stay and fight the flames. Gasping through wet towels, the *Telegram* workers battled without help for more than two hours, using hand-held hoses and a hydrant on the roof. The *Telegram*'s employees saved their workplace from destruction, and earned themselves a substantial bonus.

The W.R. Block building, a dry goods warehouse on the southwest corner of Wellington and Bay, was also fitted with sprinklers, and these did activate when the building caught, but the flames were so ferocious that the spitting water could not extinguish them. The building steamed and sputtered against the night sky. Firefighters doused the windows until the heat inside became too immense, exploding a section of the building outwards, with showers of glass, white-hot bricks and burning debris.

By the time Mayor Thomas Urquhart arrived, flames engulfed the entire block, rising hundreds of feet above the city. He sent out a call for help and by 11:00 p.m. firefighters from as far away as Hamilton were joining in. Two more engines arrived from Buffalo in the early morning hours. Engines dispatched from Brantford, Niagara Falls, London and Peterborough arrived too late to help.

Thousands of spectators thronged the streets. They came with camping chairs, sandwiches, flasks of coffee. They cheered the thrilling acts of bravery, and sighed as buildings crumbled. And the city put on a show like no other. Firefighters leapt through cascading embers and scrambled from the paths of falling walls. Live wires crashed down into puddles, sparking blue and purple as they flew, and sending shocks into the firefighters' legs. Flailing wires caught on ladders, turning into heavy, frozen sculptures as streams of water hit them.

The noise was deafening. *The News*, in its April 20, 1904 edition, printed:

> *Solid chunks of noise. Pandemonium, mingled with earthquake.*
> *Even the shrill yells and the hoarse shouts of the street crowds were*
> *smothered in that croaking, booming sea of sound.*

IN JUST EIGHT HOURS 5000 WERE LEFT JOBLESS

Many of those left unemployed by the fire found work carting away rubble, and in salvage and construction.

The erratic flames worked westward on a path towards the Queen's Hotel (on the site of today's Royal York). The hotel management whisked the women off to other hotels, along with all the baggage and the hotel silver. Every bath was filled with water and wet blankets draped from every shutter. When the roof of the hotel ignited several times, the employees were able to extinguish it. A scorched roof and blistered paint were the only damage to the Queen's, thanks to an organized plan and well-informed staff.

By now the flames were bridging Bay Street in an impressive red canopy that was raging with a vengeance towards Yonge Street. The prospect of halting the fire's progress to the south and east seemed increasingly doubtful. Mayor Urquhart agreed to destroy some buildings with dynamite in order to create a firebreak. Military engineers rushed to the scene with plans, know-how and enthusiasm, but no dynamite. None could be found. The explosives project was abandoned and the assembled troops were used to control the excited crowds instead.

The four-storey Minerva Manufacturing Co. building, on the north side of Front St. at Yonge, had a solid fire wall on the western side. It was considered a vital stand against the fire's eastern spread. The Minerva staff were soaking the roof in the cold until 3:00 a.m. when it ignited and Deputy Chief Noble's team took over. Down below, the crowd shouted anxiously for them to come down. The men refused to be defeated. They stayed and fought until the fire died.

Across the road, on the south side of Front St., the Customs House would prove to be the fire's nemesis. Stationed inside, firemen lanced water at the blazing next door warehouse until the roof imploded. Injured firemen stumbled from the orange smoke to the crowd's applause. The collapse of the warehouse halted the flames' forward surge. The blaze could spread no further. At 4:30 a.m., the great Toronto fire was at last under control.

BAY STREET LOOKING NORTH FROM FRONT STREET

108

More than 7.7 hectares (19 acres) had been torched, 98 buildings destroyed. The heat had caused complete combustion, an intensity rarely seen in fires, leaving almost nothing to be salvaged.

Miraculously, the fire claimed no lives, although one young man, John Croft, died two weeks later while demolishing the ruins of the W.J. Gage building on Front St. West. A dynamite charge blew up in his face.

The fire scene remained a solemn sight for some time to come. Toronto's new asphalt had buckled into huge blisters that collapsed underfoot. Poles and wires littered streets, and the jagged, ashen ruins of buildings smouldered for weeks. *The Globe* described the scene on April 21:

> *Across Bay Street is a counterpart of ruins. North arises the impenetrable veil of smoke, and through it, here and there, rise the skeletons of walls, looking with their shroud of white smoke, like ghosts of departed prosperity.*

But prosperity had not, in fact, departed. It had merely stepped aside. The progress of the optimistic city had been only slightly checked by the Great Fire. Businesses even offered to assist their rivals who had suffered in the blaze. Soon the 5000 people left jobless by the fire were finding new positions in the city.

PAIL OF FUSED NAILS
The intense heat melted iron and blistered asphalt.

KING STREET
Ruins smouldered for weeks while Torontonians tried to resume their regular lives.

PARLIAMENT BUILDINGS
CENTRE BLOCK BEFORE THE FIRE

PARLIAMENT IN FLAMES

Ottawa, Ontario

FEBRUARY 3, 1916

It was February 1916 and the Great War raged in Europe. Canadian papers were filled with incendiary articles on enemy foul play, torpedoed vessels, arrested aliens and spies. In the gothic buildings of the Parliament——repository of the country's confidential records——Frank Glass, Member for East Middlesex, poured over headlines in the pine-paneled Reading Room. Then, shortly before 9:00 p.m., Glass felt a blast of hot air. Startled, he turned to see a desk on fire. Two policemen on duty in the building ran in with an extinguisher but the fire had grown too large already. In fact, the blaze spread so quickly, that everyone near the Reading Room had to run from the overwhelming smoke. Then at 8:57 p.m. the alarm began to shriek. The fire department was on its way.

Frank Glass burst through the Speaker's door of the House of Commons, interrupting a debate on the marketing of fish in Canada. This was no fire drill, and he told them to evacuate before dashing out himself. Most stared after him, amazed, except for Deputy Speaker Rhodes who, according to the *Ottawa Evening Post*, "*unceremoniously rose and walked quietly out of the Chamber.*" When the members ventured out into the hallways, thick smoke enveloped them and the wild scrambles to escape began. J.D. Hazen, the Minister of Marine and Fisheries, was one of the last to flee. With hands over his face, he dashed through the door near the Speaker's chair, scorching his hands and face, and coughing out black smoke.

Prime Minister Robert Borden was in his office when, shortly after 9:00 p.m., an aide shot in announcing fire in the corridor. Borden escaped down the messenger's stairway, through dense smoke and what he later described as "*long tongues of flame, accompanied by short, sharp sounds like explosions.*" Once outside, Borden, in distress and flustered, was led away from the danger zone, wearing a borrowed coat and hat.

MPs Thomas MacNutt and Dr. Edward Cash found themselves imprisoned in a washroom by the smoke. They fashioned a rope from Parliamentary towels which allowed them to dangle out the window to a reasonable drop above the snow.

M.C. MacCormac of the library staff closed the iron doors of the Parliamentary Library against the smoke. He refused to let anybody out, and consequently saved the building and all of its occupants. The Library was the only structure to survive the flames.

The Speaker of the House of Commons, Albert Sévigny, and his wife had been entertaining two friends, Mme. Florence Bray and Mme. M. Morin. The Sévigny family raced through the smoke to safety, but their two friends returned quickly to grab their fur coats. They were later pulled, lifeless, from a blackened corridor.

A policeman and two government employees were crushed under a falling wall, and the MP for Yarmouth, Mr. Bowman Brown Law perished somewhere near the Reading Room.

René Laplante, Assistant Clerk of the House of Commons, became disoriented in the smoke. A steward, Walter Hill, pulled him into a relatively smoke-free room. Their only way out was through the second storey window. Laplante was too afraid to jump, so Hill escaped alone, hanging from the curtains and dropping into a snow bank. As Hill climbed out of the window, Laplante fell to his knees, praying. *"For God's sake,"* he begged Hill, *"Send someone back for me."* But Hill's fall to the ground knocked him unconscious and he was unable to comply. He awoke much later, in hospital. Laplante's badly burnt body was pulled from the building two days after the fire.

Major-General Sam Hughes was dining at the Château Laurier when he heard news of the fire. Finding an enormous crowd of spectators, almost as unruly as Parliament itself, he called in the local 77th Battalion. The soldiers

contained the crowds and assisted with evacuations, suffering several injuries in the process. The men slipped and fell on treacherous patches of ice. They were cut by shattering windows, bursting in the heat, and had their hands and faces frozen by the firemen's spray.

FIRE DAMAGE

Important papers and documents were burned or damaged by water and ice. Prime Minister Sir Wilfred Laurier's office was completely gutted (left). Firemen and militia at the scene (right).

At 9:30 p.m. the roof of the House of Commons came down with a thunderous crash. The Senate Chamber had yet to be engulfed in flames. Members of the Senate and soldiers tried to rescue some of its valued relics while firemen battled the fire's advance. Working in the virtual dark, they were able to remove many historic paintings by the haunting light of an oak door blazing at the west end of the gallery. Soon the heat became insufferable and advancing flames forced the men's retreat.

The icy wind was no deterrent to the crowds. Ottawa, normally in bed by ten, was up all night. Nearby restaurants did a roaring trade for people ducking in from the cold. The Laurentian Chapter of the Daughters of the Empire set up three field kitchens on Parliament Hill, providing hot soup and coffee to the frostbitten workers.

The cold wind that kept the flames away from the Library also forced them closer towards the Victoria Clock Tower. Despite the steady streams of water, at 11:00 p.m., the structure ignited. The clock had continued to strike throughout the evening, but at midnight, was poignantly silent. At 1:21 a.m., the whole tower shuddered, firemen scrambled from its base, and it fell with an earthshaking thud.

The firemen, soldiers and policemen had the huge blaze under control by 3:00 a.m. Apart from a small outbreak at 10:00 a.m., its defeat was final. The fire's path of destruction had been random. Whole areas were completely

wrecked, with one lucky office in their midst, utterly unscathed. Sir Wilfred Laurier's office was totally gutted, destroyed with all of his notes from his years as Prime Minister. Sir Robert Borden's office was badly damaged, but his hat and coat were untouched and the correspondence on his desk was pristine enough to finish off and send.

One question remained: were the Germans responsible? *The Journal*, in Providence, Rhode Island, had printed an article three weeks before

ICE CASTLE

Doused in water, the buildings transformed into frozen castles. Soldiers, brought in to help manage the chaos, had their hands and faces caked in ice by the firemen's spray.

MAJOR-GENERAL SAM HUGHES MINISTER OF MILITIA AND DEFENSE

Hughes did not share the initial belief that the fire was the result of sabotage.

warning of a German conspiracy to destroy the Canadian Parliament, Rideau Hall and a Canadian munitions factory. The source was an employee of the German Embassy. The Fire Chief himself reported hearing four or five explosions like those caused by shells. Several suspects were arrested. Jules Verlier, a Montreal photographer, was detained and accused of taking pictures of the scene for German agents. He was released an hour later. Also arrested was Charles Strony, a Belgian pianist who had played for guests at the Governor General's house on February 3. His crime was leaving the city in a hurry. He was released the next day after proving that he had rushed off to another engagement. A third suspect by the name of Schuebier, arrested when he departed the Château Laurier without fully settling his account, was interrogated and released.

Major-General Hughes was irritated by the rumours. He maintained from the start that the fire had been accidental. The investigating Royal Commission Inquiry agreed. Although many steps had been taken to guard against espionage, the building's fire safety mechanisms were underdeveloped. In fact, in the previous three years, thirteen accidental fires in the Parliament buildings had been rapidly extinguished. Much of the beautiful, carved paneling was dry, white pine, with heavy varnish. The floors had been shellacked and treated with oil and the Reading Room was fitted with rubber mats, ideal for producing clouds of black smoke. There were no firebreaks or iron doors (apart from those of the Library), no sprinkler system, and there were few fire escapes. No evidence of shells came to light. The explosions could easily have been bursting chandeliers or, more likely, exploding liquor bottles. The Inquiry illuminated the dangers of smoking in the highly-combustible Reading Room and suggested that a final report be submitted later, allowing all possibilities, foreign or accidental, the benefit of time to come to light.

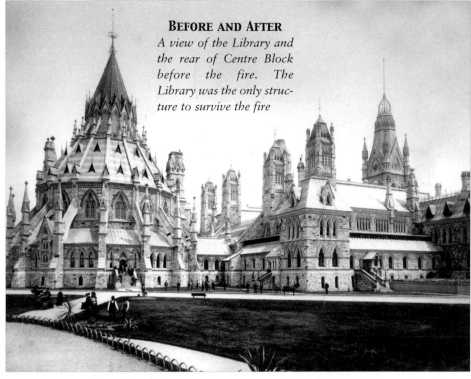

BEFORE AND AFTER
A view of the Library and the rear of Centre Block before the fire. The Library was the only structure to survive the fire

LIBRARY IN RUINS
Thanks to its iron doors. While firefighters soaked the walls from the outside, the Library staff remained inside, shifting books to protect them from the water.

DESOLATION AFTER THE MATHESON FIRE, 1916

THE NORTH IS DEVASTATED

The Matheson Fire, Northern Ontario

JULY 29, 1916

The sun was a copper disc in the dirty sky above the little town of Matheson in northern Ontario. The air was thick with the smell of burning wood, and though it was only just past noon, the sky was darkening as if night approached. Scant rain and a tremendous heatwave had sapped the thick brush of moisture, dried the wooden homesteads and parched the fields of hay.

Fire was a constant threat to settlers in the North. Just five years before, in 1911, almost 1600 square kilometres (1000 sq. mi.) of the area's forest and mining property had been ravaged, leaving three thousand pioneers homeless. Congested towns and all-wooden settlements were not protected by fire regulations and fire was a useful tool for clearing land. In fact, fires were sprouting up everywhere, burning away the brush beside the railway tracks, reducing the piles of scrub to debris on farms, cooking food in the lumber camps. But on this hot day in July of 1916, a demonic wind had caught some small fire, somewhere, and whipped it into a voracious monster. Now an explosive rumble was closing in on Matheson.

Settler William Dowson raced home to the small farm he shared with friends. Its log home, stable and few animals were all surrounded by dry bush. He ran along the railway tracks, and was passing his neighbour's farm just minutes ahead of the main blaze. His memoirs tell us:

> I saw them working to spot out sparks of the fire that were dropping all about their buildings. But the fires started by the rain of sparks were getting ahead of them; everything was too dry and the power of the wind too great. There was no chance.

As Dowson sped on, he could hear the train from Matheson, its whistle just audible above the furnace roar around him. He glanced back to see his neighbours flagging down the train, having given up their fight against the fire.

As the thick black smoke invaded Matheson, many citizens dropped their water buckets, leaping to the safety of the freight train. They stuffed wet cloths into the cracks of the boxcars to keep the smoke out, screaming as the train passed through walls of flame. At one point, two cars ignited in the incredible heat and were disengaged from the train while their occupants scrambled through the sparks to other cars. As the train fought through the flames, it stopped to pick up farming families, exhausted and frightened, with nothing but the sooty clothes on their backs.

Reaching his farm before the devastation, Dowson found his friends working on a plan. The three built a shelter out of some boxes covered with a soaked tarpaulin. They filled a tub with water and placed it near the shelter, ready to re-wet the cover if it ignited. They had no way to gauge the power of the coming force, nor the chances of their survival.

The preliminary fires, the vanguards of heat, were burning all about us. The sun, shining through a lighter smoke, was a blood red ball. When the fire would strike an exceptionally dry and light stretch of timber the flames mounted hundreds of feet into the air driving away for a moment the enveloping smoke.

MATHESON BEFORE THE FIRE

Towns that were built of wood, such as Matheson, Iroquois Falls, and Cochrane, lay in ruins after a fire. The official death toll in the Matheson Fire was 223. Bodies were uncovered throughout the countryside in the following months.

Dry, coniferous branches burned like huge blow torches. Dowson and his friend ran to the pens to release their sow and cows. Frantically, they harnessed horses and led the animals, each with a gunny sack over its head, down into the gully. Once free and with their blinds removed, the horses regained their bearings and headed for Wanzer's Lake, the cow in the lead. The sow chose instead to stick close to the people, trusting in their crude shelter. In their small clearing, it felt as though a tidal wave of heat was bearing down on them, that they were *"at the bottom of a sea of fire thousands of feet high."* Dowson later recalled that the afternoon was as dark as night.

By now, hundreds of thousands of acres burned furiously in all directions, from the town of Matheson up the Black River to Iroquois Falls, to Cochrane in the north, and Timmins in the west. All rural communities in the area were in peril. No lives were lost in Matheson itself, but elsewhere, death and destruction were widespread.

In Nushka, the Reverend Wilfred Gagne tried to shelter 35 of his parishioners in a clay hut by the tracks. As the fire burst in, the Reverend and most of his followers were consumed by the flames. The town would later be renamed Val Gagne for its valiant priest.

Near Matheson, Mr. Frank Monahan had the presence of mind to jam some planks down into a well as a sort of scaffolding. He was able to fit the women and children of three families into the well where he scooped water over them with his hat. When the furnace raged overhead, one twelve-year-old girl's clothing caught on fire. Monahan managed to rip it from her, saving her, but the baby she'd been holding was killed.

In the poverty-stricken area of Iroquois Falls, the light wooden houses burned like paper. Nurse Isabelle Scott dashed in and out of burning shacks, dragging out the occupants and covering them with wet blankets. She was so determined to retrieve much-needed medical supplies from the hospital that she had to be pulled from the burning building before it collapsed around her.

The heat was so intense that it caused the water in the creeks to boil, sending the white bellies of dead fish floating to the surface. In the town of Cochrane, water in the new fire-fighting hoses turned to steam.

Meanwhile, in his shelter, Dowson could no longer bear the heat. Having trouble breathing, he held a shirt over his nose and mouth, but felt the hot air cut his lungs. In a panic, he tried to run from the heat but he was sandwiched between two shafts of flame. There was no escape. His only hope was to get back to the clearing. He turned to face his only horrifying option, to run back through the massive wall of flame.

The great fire wrapped about me for a moment, a solid mass of combustion, like the interior of a furnace, then I was through and in the clearing.

THE TEMPORARY MORGUE
(above) Coffins were stacked up on either side of the road running south from Matheson. Some bodies were so badly burnt that families of three could fit into one casket. The heads of the undertakers can be seen above the coffins to the right.

A TEMPORARY HEARSE
(above left) Caskets were taken by horse and wagon to the graveyard.

As Dowson leaped, only the shirt covering his face caught fire. He staggered into the potato patch, removing his clothing as he went, then collapsed into a patch of clay, which would likely not burn. Drowsy from the smoke, Dowson turned his face to the wind and fought to stay awake in the midst of the flickering, red glare, the driving sparks and the thundering booms of powder magazines as they went off near the town.

On Sunday July 30, the smoke slowly lifted to reveal 200 000 wasted, smouldering hectares (over 500 000 acres). *"North is Devastated"* read the headlines of the *North Bay Nugget*, and for the first time in two years, reports of the war were shifted off the front page. The towns of Matheson, Iroquois Falls, Porquis Junction, Nushka, Kelso, Cochrane and parts of Timmins were in ruins, and the death toll had just begun. Whole families had been caught by the flames, suffocating in their root cellars and wells. Groups of people met their death crouching together in small clearings and gullies. Dowson and his friends survived in their little shelter in the clearing.

On Sunday, the earth hissed and steamed as heavy rains fell, mocking the dry season. The search for bodies began, but was hindered by charred wagons, lack of horses, and burnt bridges. The official death toll came to 223, although the number was probably much higher. The army set up a tent city at Matheson and provided a temporary mortuary. Some bodies were beyond recognition. That autumn, human remains would be uncovered from time to time throughout the countryside.

Just as the railways, particularly the Temiskaming and Northern Ontario (T. & N.O.), provided escape during the blaze, so did they provide relief shortly afterwards. The first train was dispatched from North Bay with a cargo of doctors and nurses, and others followed quickly from around Ontario bringing tents, food, clothing and medical teams. The survivors had already started a relief effort of their own, sharing what little they had left: potatoes baked on the vine, the remains of chickens—partially roasted, and axle grease for burns.

Most survivors remained in the area to begin again. They rebuilt on old sites, drawing faith from the fresh green growth coming up from beneath the charcoal.

BURIAL PARTY

Local volunteers, friends and neighbours dig graves in the cemetery on the hill. In the centre is St. Andrew's supply minister, Reverend James Conn, performing the burial services. After the fire, the dog (at right) "adopted" him, following him everywhere. The charred jack pine trees in the background were bent by the fire.

SAINT JOHN, NEW BRUNSWICK BURNS

JUNE 20-21, 1877

While the exact cause of the fire that destroyed a large part of Saint John, New Brunswick was never determined, its origin was narrowed down to a building on the south of York Point slip. The blaze raged along the waterfront, consuming building after building, even before firefighters arrived at the scene. A gale-like wind buffeted flames in all directions, sealing the fate of the city. Most wharf-side structures were beyond repair, including all the schooners docked in the market slip. Once the flames reached the city's core, down came the banks, churches, missions, schools and hotels. Eleven lives were lost.

Although nine newspaper offices were destroyed, the *Canadian Illustrated News* thoroughly covered the event, complete with grave editorials. On July 30, 1877, the paper called for radical municipal reform and prevention, declaring:

These frequent and disastrous fires, this repeated destruction of our cities and towns strike at the very root of our national prosperity.

SAINT JOHN ON FIRE

Starting at the waterfront (below right), the fire quickly spread to the venerable city centre of Saint John (below).

St. John's, Newfoundland Burns

July 8, 1892

The days leading up to July 8, 1892, were the hottest on record in southern Newfoundland. There had been weeks of drought, numerous forest fires, and continuous, gale-force winds. So when fire broke out in Timothy Brine's barn on Long's Hill, St. John's, it spread in no time at all. The normally abundant water supply had been cut off that morning to facilitate pipe repairs, and the emergency water reservoir, for some reason, was practically empty. The wind hurled burning shingles far and wide as the fire swept, unimpeded, down the hill towards the city.

The people put their trust in the few stone buildings, frantically stashing their valuables in churches before fleeing from the fire's path. They lost everything. Twelve thousand people were left homeless, and many of them penniless as more than two thirds of the city fell to ashes. Luckily, all but two citizens escaped the flames.

It would take a month of investigating the smoking ruins before Justice D. W. Prowse would submit his shocking report on circumstances surrounding the fire. Regarding its origins, Prowse suggested arson. A man named Fitzpatrick, subsequently arrested for cutting the tongues of Timothy Brine's horses, was thought to have tossed a burning match into the farmer's barn. The nearby reservoir had been allowed to go empty through gross neglect by the Fire Department. The fire engine was unprepared, and every other firefighting tool found to be inadequate. *"The whole costly apparatus on which we relied for protection against fire, failed,"* reported Prowse, *"...And if this department is ever left again in the same hands, all I can say is that we deserve to be burnt."*

THE ASHES OF ST. JOHN'S, 1892
Even buildings high on Signal Hill (left background) were destroyed by the blaze.

STEAM FIRE ENGINE
With ill-prepared, ill-func-tioning equipment, Victoria's firefighters struggled to contain the blaze of 1907.

THE SECOND FIRE
The Five Sisters Block is destroyed along with adjoining businesses in Victoria's second devastating fire in 1910.

Island City Ablaze

Victoria, British Columbia

1907 and 1910

Victoria's first "Great Fire" destroyed patches of the city on July 23, 1907. It started somewhere on the west side of town. The flames literally leapt over some homes, sparing them, then devoured adjoining neighbourhoods. The Fire Department hurtled to the scene, only to be paralyzed by a lack of water pressure. Even their Deluge fire engine failed to raise enough steam power during most of the crisis.

A row of small frame, shack-like homes between Herald and Chatham Streets lit up like tinder, as did the red light district. Blazing for four hours, the fire left 250 people homeless, five city blocks and more than 100 homes in ruins. The Fire Department was admonished for inadequate, ill-functioning equipment.

Just three years later, with the city's wounds almost healed, a fire started in a department store in the business section. The next-door tobacconist sounded the alarm. This time the firefighters were ready. As they arrived, however, flames were already shooting up the store's elevator shaft to the roof, and were spreading quickly from building to building along the rooftops.

The streets filled with spectators, many straight from the theatre and in evening dress. They tried to help with the hoses, but it would take 150 servicemen from nearby barracks to bring the fire under control. The damage was extensive, and almost as costly as the fire of 1907. But once again, Victoria bounced back quickly.

The Driard Hotel Escapes

Though damaged, Victoria's finest hotel was left standing after the 1910 fire. Hotel guests ran out into the smoke-filled streets with their suitcases.

125

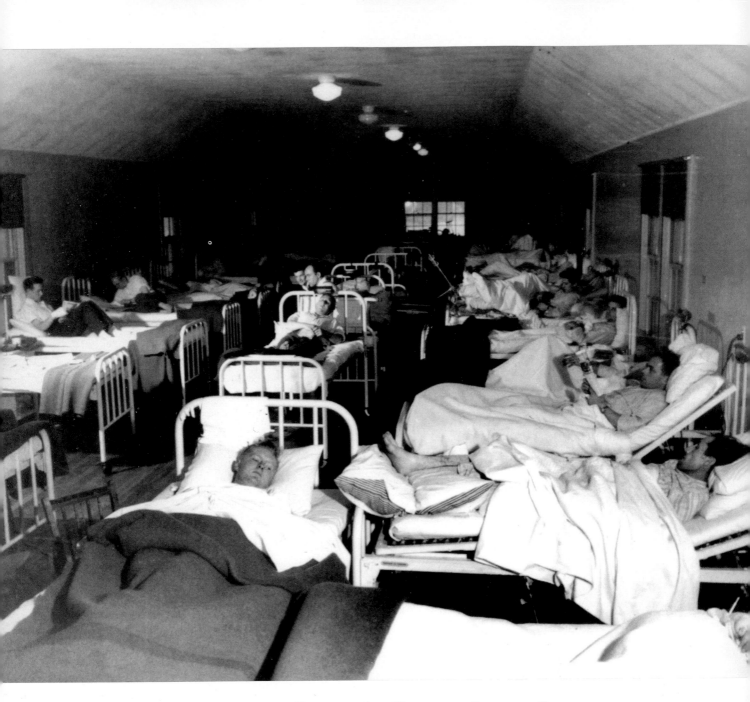

HOSPITALIZED VICTIMS OF THE KNIGHTS OF COLUMBUS FIRE

The 107 people injured in the Knights of Columbus fire were rushed to hospitals around St. John's. Burn experts were flown in for advice. Not all of the 99 victims died of burns. Many had succumbed to carbon monoxide poisoning. Survivors spoke of people lying on the floor of the burning building, incoherent, but seemingly uninjured.

KNIGHTS OF COLUMBUS FIRE

St. John's, Newfoundland

DECEMBER 12, 1942

The Knights of Columbus Hall in St. John's, Newfoundland, was a well-appointed building. To the many servicemen staying in its dormitories, it offered a restaurant, recreation room, and a quiet reading lounge. On the night of December 12, 1942, its large auditorium was crowded with over 350 military personnel, civilians and children, who formed the live audience for the weekly radio broadcast of "Uncle Tim's Barn Dance." The windows were covered in plywood in accordance with wartime blackout regulations.

It was a Newfoundland soldier who first discovered smoke seeping from a storeroom above the auditorium. He left the door to the storeroom open, running to raise the alarm. The fire flashed out into the hallway, flames licking up the wall and to the ceiling.

The radio show's M.C., Joe Murphy, was suddenly aware of a crackling static through his headphones. At home, Mrs. Murphy was listening to the show on the radio. "The Moonlight Trail," sung to solo guitar, was suddenly interrupted by a loud bang, screams of "*FIRE*!" then silence.

Within minutes the fire had spread explosively throughout the Knights of Columbus building. It burst through the ceiling of the auditorium, spewing molten asphalt and blazing Christmas decorations onto the fleeing audience. Flames shot like blowtorches through walls and out windows. An orderly exit was impossible. Hysterical people scrambled over each other. Some were literally blown out of the exits, while others smashed windows and tore at the blackout shutters.

KNIGHTS OF COLUMBUS BUILDING, ST. JOHN'S
The night of the fire, the building on Military Road was buzzing with activity.

127

SPECTACLE

The Knights of Columbus Hall in flames. The fire spread so fast that many suspected it was sabotage.

"Uncle Tim" (Bill Duggan) leapt from a backstage window, then tried to break the fall of each member of his dance troupe. Joe Murphy followed the same route before the stage imploded, sending a flaming piano crashing down to the basement.

To witnesses outside, the quiet, shuttered building had become a fireworks display, with flames and people flying from every opening. In his book, *Newfoundland Disasters*, writer Jack Fitzgerald records an interview with eye-witness Margaret Ryan:

> *The whole Knights of Columbus building from end to end was one golden mushroom of flame. I saw men diving from the 20 foot high [6m] upstairs window, their pyjamas burning as though they were human torches. Over and above the roar of the flame I could hear the pounding of the poor trapped souls.*

In seven terrifying minutes, 99 people died. Firefighters were barely in position when the building was given up for lost. They turned their attention to saving nearby structures.

Through the early hours of that devastating Sunday morning, armed forces personnel pushed into charred sections of the smouldering building to remove the bodies. And all day, in a fierce snowstorm, they salvaged anything they could, and hauled away the mess. They were so efficient, in fact, that they seriously hampered the investigation into the fire's cause. Electrical panels, switch boxes and radiators were already at the dump, and had to be retrieved for examination.

Several indicators pointed to sabotage by the enemy: the explosive nature of the fire; the predominance of military personnel in the audience; and the location of St. John's on the enemy-infested Atlantic. However, Sir Brian Dunfield's inquiry, while admitting the possibility of sabotage, concluded it was more likely the work of a single pyromaniac. No evidence of gas leaks or electrical trouble came to light, but the building itself, constructed of local timbers, had been highly flammable.

Two funerals were held on Tuesday, December 15. A sombre procession accompanied the bodies to the cemeteries. They were buried in two mass graves—the Protestants at the General Protestant Cemetery and the Catholics at Mount Carmel—each with a gun salute and the tragic call of the bugle's "Last Post."

FUNERAL, DECEMBER 15, 1942

Coffins for Navy personnel were draped with the Navy's White Ensign, while those for Army personnel lay beneath the Union Jack. Bulldozers worked through a heavy snowstorm to dig the mass graves.

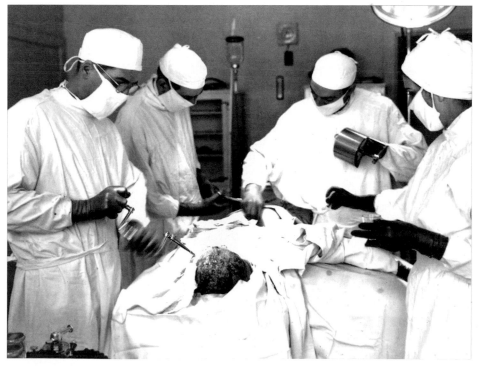

SURGERY ON FIRE VICTIM

Part of a series of photographs showing the medical response to the fire.

NEW WESTMINSTER FIRE

New Westminster, British Columbia

SEPTEMBER 10, 1898

FRONT STREET FROM LYTTON SQUARE

The fire consumed all major hotels, the city hall, the courthouse, the public library, two banks, the post office, many businesses and both fire halls.

New Westminster's fire brigade, founded in 1861, prided itself on its speed in reaching the scene of a fire. But when a large, hay-filled warehouse ignited, throwing flames to spread in every direction, the fire department was unprepared. Six city blocks and three steamers at the piers were soon on fire while firefighters scrambled to find horses to pull their equipment to the scene. The city reservoir had been allowed to drop to a low level, so when firefighters tried the hydrants, there was little water left to dribble out. And the fireboat in the harbour simply wasn't ready for action.

Residents fought to save their own families, businesses and possessions amidst showers of sparks and whirlwinds of ash. Prisoners were released from the city jail to work on saving that building. It would be the only structure of substance in the city to survive the fire.

New Westminster had suffered a serious setback, but fortunately, there was no great loss of life. Only one man died of a heart attack during the fire.

VANCOUVER CONSUMED

Vancouver, British Columbia

JUNE 13, 1886

Still in its youth in 1886, the city of Vancouver already displayed a distinct, vibrant spirit. The port's lumber mills welcomed customers from South America and the Far East while the building of the railway brought a constant flow of workers into town. New structures popped up along Burrard Inlet's southern shore. They were built using timber from the balding hills behind the city, where great piles of brush now lay drying in the sun.

It was early on a lazy Sunday afternoon when someone noticed that a wall of flame was advancing down a hillside towards the inlet. Shouts of "*FIRE*" rang out, but the blaze was so formidable that fighting it, or saving any property, was impossible. The only option was to flee. "*The city did not burn*," said one survivor, "*It was consumed by flame. The buildings simply melted before the fiery blast*."

Racing to the water, people leapt into boats and onto rafts. Others hurled themselves onto anything that would float. Some climbed into wells and were strangled by the smoke. Flames reached out across the inlet burning those who lagged behind. The 30-40 people who failed to react immediately, burned to death. On that black Sunday, this lively, hopeful city was reduced to ashes.

POST FIRE CITY HALL
Only seven buildings remained after the great blaze of June 13, forcing Vancouver—a tent city in its early days—to erect temporary shelters. The city, so young and optimistic, had neither coroner nor cemetery. The dead had to be taken to New Westminster in wagons.

AFTER THE FIRE AT THE LAURIER PALACE THEATRE, MONTREAL
Approximately 800 children were in the theatre when it caught fire.

PICTURE HOUSE PANIC

Montreal, Quebec

JANUARY 9, 1927

The Laurier Palace Theatre was packed full for the Sunday matinee. About 800 children filled the seats, jammed the aisles, and milled about. The younger ones, between the ages of four and thirteen, were crammed into the balcony. Eleven-year-old Edward Murphy and his older brother Michael slipped in late. Michael fought his way into a balcony seat, but Edward had to stand in the aisle. Near them, thirteen-year-old Roger Frappier and his two half brothers watched the screen with rapt attention.

Projectionist Emile Masicotte removed the Mary Pickford reel and began the comedy the children had been waiting for. Amid shouts of delight and roaring laughter, somewhere in the balcony glowed a single cigarette.

Shortly after 2:00 p.m., smoke began to sting the laughing eyes. A man yelled "*FIRE!*" The children scrambled from their seats as flames licked along the floor of the balcony. The five hundred teens who had been sitting in the orchestra, ran into the lobby and out into the street. But the smaller children in the balcony had a bigger challenge. Two dark stairways lead down to the ground, but they were narrow, with sharp turns and no handrails, and one of them was locked.

Panic gripped the children in the darkened theatre. They crushed into the single exit. Amid pushing, crying and fighting, some stumbled out to safety. Then one child fell, tripping others, and a squirming mass piled on top.

By now, the upholstered seating, plaster walls and wooden structures of the balcony were all on fire. The air was choked with smoke, the escape route with bodies. The chaos peaked in two short minutes. A passerby ran across the street to Fire Station No. 13 and firefighters raced to the scene. But by then the little bodies— piled eight deep already—were so tightly packed together, prying them apart was almost hopeless. Firefighters doused the human blockage with water, then fought the balcony fire from within.

Roger Frappier lost sight of his half brothers. He catapulted over the railing of the balcony, landing in an empty aisle below. His brother Paul Leduc, eleven, met him outside, bruised and trampled, with little recollection of crawling through the staircase mob. Thirteen-year-old Roland Leduc did not come out alive.

By the time Edward Murphy reached the staircase, there was no way through the crush. Panicked, he ran to the back of the theatre. A man grabbed him and pulled him through a small window into the projection booth. From here, Edward escaped onto the theatre marquee. There was no sign of his brother Michael.

Emile Masicotte, the 27-year-old projectionist, was the one who had rescued Edward. And he saved many more children, hanging through the projection booth window to grab them, and shouting to direct them through the smoke. *"It was the most terrible thing ever anyone saw,"* Masicotte told the press later. *"The children were crazed with fear and screamed for their mothers."* As he caught them and pulled them up, they fought like animals,

MONTREAL IN SHOCK

Headlines in The Gazette *tell the story (right). The theatre in ruins (below). A dropped cigarette was thought to be the cause.*

134

WEATHER FORECAST
Fresh to strong northerly winds; partly cloudy and colder, with light local snowfalls.
For complete weather report see page seven.

The Gazette.

TEMPERATURE YESTERDAY
Max., 13; Min., 4
SAME DAY LAST YEAR
Max., 28; Min., 8

VOL. CLVI. No. 8   LATE EDITION   MONTREAL, MONDAY, JANUARY 10, 1927.—TWENTY-TWO PAGES   PRICE FIVE CENTS

SEVENTY-SIX CHILDREN KILLED IN PANIC ON STAIRWAY AT FIRE IN EAST ST. CATHERINE STREET MOVIE THEATRE SUNDAY AFTERNOON

I.M. OCCURRED | TWO FAMILIES | FOUR MEN HELD | LANE ATTACKS BRIDGE | CLARITY OVER

desperate to make it to the stairs. Masicotte hauled about thirty children to freedom before he began to suffocate on the smoke himself. Outside the theatre, the frantic children swarmed over the marquee before being helped down a ladder to the ground.

The fire was extinguished quickly, and the firemen turned their attention to the crushed children, cutting the stairs away to reach them. Some had been just steps from safety. Police and firemen began to lay the little bodies out onto the icy pavement.

Constable Albert Boisseau ran to a telephone and called his wife. Had their three children been in the picture house that afternoon? Mrs. Boisseau was confident that they had not. The policeman returned to help remove the dead and injured. He then discovered his thirteen-year-old daughter, Germaine, lying among the bodies. He tried to go on helping, but broke down. Roland, eleven, and Yvette, eight, had not yet been located. Boisseau would find them later at the city morgue.

In total, 78 children died, most asphyxiated by smoke. About 25 children were crushed to death. Only a handful died directly in the flames. Montreal was aghast at the tragic loss. The press spewed accusations: the theatre had been operating without a license; it had not conformed to fire codes; the children's attendance was illegal. The archbishop of the city lamented that so many children had been in the picture house on the Sabbath. Theatres all over Montreal closed pending fire inspections, and the four workers at the Laurier Palace Theatre, all Syrian and doubly suspicious for their foreignness, were arrested.

But the accusations were unfounded, and the four suspects were absolved. Embers from a cigarette may have caused the fire, although no one could be sure. At the time, Quebec law prohibited movie theatres from admitting children under the age of 16 without parental or adult accompaniment. However, a 1919 amendment to the act permitted youths to go alone to films that were specifically for children. In the grieving aftermath of the fire, this amendment was repealed. For the next forty years in Quebec cinemas, anyone under 16 had to be escorted by an adult, no matter what the subject matter. Montreal's cramped and spirited matinees became a thing of the past.

S.S. *NORONIC* AT DETROIT

*The largest passenger ship on the Great Lakes, the Noronic was 110 metres long (362 ft.)
and weighed almost 6400 tonnes (7000 tons).*

THE NORONIC FIRE

Toronto, Ontario

SEPTEMBER 17, 1949

FIRE: This steamer is equipped with modern fire prevention apparatus, in addition to which the steamer is patrolled day and night by experienced watchmen for the protection of the passengers.
—from the card posted in
each *Noronic* state room

The largest passenger ship on the Great Lakes, the *Noronic*, slid into Toronto Harbour, her upper decks tinted gold by the sun. She was 110 metres long (362 ft.) and weighed almost 6400 tonnes (7000 tons). Gliding through the sheltered area of smaller vessels, her gravelly whistle scraped the fall air. On its last voyage of the season, the *Noronic* had set out from Detroit and was stopping over in Toronto for the night. Most of her 525 passengers streamed off at Pier Nine to sample the city's nightlife. Captain William Taylor disembarked to dine with friends. He'd granted the night off to all but fifteen of the 171 crewmembers aboard the ship.

By 2:15 a.m. on September 17, most of the revellers had returned to their berths, leaving just a few lingering on the promenade deck or sipping night caps in the *Noronic*'s lounge.

The skeleton crew was scattered through the five dark decks. On watch until midnight, First Officer Gerald Wood retired to his cabin on the "A" deck. Taking over, Second Officer Bowles made his way down to the gangway, chatting to Pepper and Donaldson, the two wheelsmen left on duty. At least one of these men should have been in the wheelhouse at all times, ready to sound the alarm in case of fire. But tonight, the wheelhouse stood empty for long stretches.

Deep within the ship, seven engineers maintained vital services—hot water

NORONIC'S ELEGANT SUNROOM
The ship was known for its parties and romantic atmosphere. After the tragedy, officials had difficulty identifying some bodies; desiring a romantic tryst, some couples had travelled under pseudonyms.

and electricity. A smattering of bellboys emptied ashtrays, scrubbed hallways and cleaned the observation lounge after the evening's dance. Two "Special Officers" were assigned to fire patrols, but by some quirk of scheduling, neither was on duty after midnight. The wheelsmen, Pepper and Donaldson, had assumed their fire duties, but rushed through the procedures. No one seriously considered the possibility of real fire while they were docked. There had been no drills, no clear course of action outlined for such an emergency.

Long off duty, the maids had stowed equipment and locked the linen cupboards. It was in one of those cupboards on the port side of "C" deck that a smouldering ember sparked at the contents.

2:30 a.m. A wisp of smoke seeped from the cupboard into the corridor, wafting to the starboard side. It was just enough to dim the ambient air and sting the nostrils of Don Church, a fire insurance specialist from Ohio, who was strolling to his cabin. Church followed his nose to the smoking cupboard. Hearing the faint rustling of someone caught inside it, he strained to open it. This was the first of many critical delays.

Church ran for help and found young bellboy, Ernest O'Neill. O'Neill had a key for the cupboard and he and Church returned to open it. The dark, smoke-filled interior showed the beginnings of a blaze. Confident that he could put out the puny flames, O'Neill went to find a fire extinguisher. While he was gone, the open door fed the little fire with oxygen. Church tried to smother it, but the blaze began to overwhelm him, and by the time O'Neill returned there was little he could do. Church and O'Neill raced away again to grab a hose. Church opened the hydrant valve while O'Neill unravelled the hose, aiming the nozzle at the spreading flames. Nothing happened. The hose was flaccid, as the

LISTING AND IN FLAMES

Firefighters continue the battle, hours after the fire broke out.

138

fire savagely consumed the corridor. Church fled to wake his family, O'Neill to sound an alarm.

The commotion in the hallway awakened a few passengers. Mr. Gibson, in a cabin opposite the fire, roused his wife and the two hurried out. And Josephine Kerr, a personal friend of the captain, peeked into the fiery hall. She then retreated to her cabin to haul her two young nieces out of bed and off the ship.

Ernest O'Neill broke the glass of a fire alarm box in the social hall on "C" deck. Now the whole ship had to be alerted. He ran to the "E" deck gangway to report the fire to Donaldson, the first wheelsman he could find. Donaldson raced up the main staircase to the officers' quarters, pounding at the cabin door of First Officer Wood. Wood ran to the deserted wheelhouse, sounding the klaxon horns. Some passengers were scrambling for the gangplanks already. Wood tried to blast a series of warnings on the whistle, but it jammed on the first pull of the cord, spearing the smoky air with a throaty and unbroken howl.

At some point in his mad dash around the ship, wheelsman Donaldson had passed Captain Taylor. The captain was standing at his cabin door, fumbling to find the right key for the lock. Later he'd explain how his keys were all in random order because his key ring had come apart the night before.

After alerting the wheelsman, O'Neill returned to get clothes from his quarters before leaving the ship. He woke some crewmates, warning them of the danger, but it didn't occur to him to evacuate passengers. Several crewmembers had been assigned fire extinguishers but, unable to reach their stations in the smoke, they found the quickest way to shore.

RESCUE
(above left) A woman is lowered to the pier on the ship's lines. Others had no choice but to jump.

SPECTATORS
(above) Hundreds turned out to watch the aftermath of Toronto's deadliest disaster.

2:44 a.m. In just under fifteen minutes, a sleepy, starlit ship had become a thunderous inferno—a blaze so advanced that the Toronto fire chief, arriving at the docks, was surprised that anyone on board was still alive. Passengers, in all states of undress, struggled through the smoke-filled hallways, pushed and stumbled down overcrowded gangplanks. A woman fell and was trampled under fleeing feet.

Those on the starboard side had a terrifying choice: stay and be burned alive; or leap from dizzying heights into the black water. They began to leap. On the port side, firemen directed ladders through the smoke up to the desperate people, saving many. Firemen themselves climbed into the fire and back out again, rescuing children and burned passengers. Those who could not reach a ladder were forced to jump onto the concrete and wooden docks. Many were badly, sometimes fatally, wounded.

Josephine Kerr, the captain's friend, hammered at her brother's cabin door. There was no response. She gathered her two nieces, Barbara and Kathleen, and ran. The smoke left them no choice but to climb up to "C" deck. Headed for the bow, they dodged screaming people and bursts of fire until they reached an impasse. The water was sixty feet below. Eleven-year-old Kathleen scrambled over the side and onto a thick steel cable that reached to the dock. As she squirmed down slowly, burning her hands and feet, a woman slipped down the cable, knocking Kathleen thirty feet into the water. The girl swam to shore. A stranger took hold of six-year-old Barbara, and carried her down the cable on his back. Josephine, the flames mounting behind her, launched herself into the air, bruising and scraping herself on the anchor cable as she fell. The girls' parents and eight-year-old brother, Philip, never made it off the burning ship.

Ross Leitch had been sitting in his water taxi with two friends, George English and Cecil Mackie, when they saw the *Noronic* light up the sky. They manoeuvred the little boat around the people, hauling them aboard and taking them to safety, dodging falling bodies as they worked. Donald Williamson, a 27-year-old passer-by, had just finished a shift at Goodyear Tire. He found a raft near the ship's stern, pushed it amidst the injured people, and dragged them from the water. In two hours he helped at least twenty victims to shore.

Detective Cyril Cole and Constable Robert Anderson of Number 1 Division saved the remainder of the swimmers. As soon as they arrived at the scene, the two policemen shed their outer garments and leapt into the water. On that long September night they dove for survivors until they were on the verge of collapse. Later when the whistle finally drowned in the lake, and the charred ship settled in the mud beneath its slip, divers plunged into the ash-littered water. Braced to encounter many bodies, they would only find a single victim on the harbour floor, thanks to the heroes of the night.

The next morning, firefighters started to carry human remains from the smouldering ship. Of the *Noronic*'s 525 passengers, 119 perished in the blaze. All were American but one. The entire crew escaped alive.

A subsequent inquiry blamed the ship's owners and Captain Taylor for the fire and the staggering loss of life, alleging the captain's drunkenness and his lack of leadership. Would a more rigorous fire patrol have made the difference? An evacuation plan? Some firefighting training for the crew? Presiding Justice Kellock held the captain to account for his sleeping passengers. Canada Steamship Lines, the *Noronic*'s owners, were required to cover the cost of the inquiry, and to pay more than $2 million to the families of the dead. Captain William Taylor was suspended for a year, but never returned to the profession, choosing to slip quietly from public view.

Some weeks after the fire, air was pumped into the holds of the *Noronic* until, with a blackened belch, she lurched to the surface. Her last voyage was a tedious limp, towed by two tugs along the shore of Lake Ontario to Hamilton. Altogether scrapped, the *Noronic*'s only artifact is her whistle which now lies silent in a nautical collection at Toronto's Harbourfront.

REMOVING THE BODIES

Firemen wrap charred remains in tarpaulins. The Royal York Hotel (left background) sheltered many survivors.

THE *NORONIC'S* DINING ROOM
The dining room seated nearly 300 people (top). Pictured above are its molten remains.

TIRE FIRE

Hagersville, Ontario

FEBRUARY 12, 1990

Straza's Tyre King was a storage depot for used tires, and by February, 1990, fourteen million bald and wounded treads sat in hillocks of black rubber on the depot's two hectares (4.6 acres). The fire that spread from pile to pile on February 12 was deliberately set—a malicious act with disastrous environmental consequences. Composed of synthetic and natural rubbers, oil, Carbon Black, fibres and chemicals, the fire's fuel was highly energetic and combustible.

The Ministry of Natural Resources went to war against the blaze. Three Canadian CL-215 water bombers skimmed Lake Erie for water before swooping over the dense smoke in an aerial attack, while a team of forty firefighters scattered the tires and smothered them with water and foam. The blaze was stubborn, the battle against it long and tough.

A plume of black smoke emitted carbon monoxide and sulphur dioxide into the air along with toxic heavy metal oxides. Several hundred people from within a five-kilometre (3-mi.) radius were evacuated from their homes to escape polluted air. Meanwhile, so much oil drained from the melting tires, that it was syphoned from surrounding ditches and recycled. Seeping into the soil, the oil posed an ugly threat of contamination to surrounding groundwater.

MILLIONS OF BURNING TIRES IN HAGERSVILLE
Tyre King owner, Edward Straza, had been ordered by Ontario's Ministry of the Environment to protect the site and build a water reservoir for potential fires. He delayed compliance by launching several appeals. (above) Straza's home enveloped in a toxic inferno.

WIND, WATER, ICE

Poor naked wretches, whereso'er you are,
That bide the pelting of this pitiless storm,
How shall your houses, heads and unfed sides,
Your looped and windowed raggedness defend you
From seasons such as these?

—William Shakespeare
King Lear, 1605-06

TORNADO IN ALBERTA

Up to seventy tornados hit Canada's populated areas each year. Though many are too weak to cause significant damage, the most severe can be up to 400 metres (1300 ft.) wide, and generate wind speeds of 360 kilometres (224 mi.) per hour.

WIND, WATER, ICE
Disaster's Trinity

Part Four

An earthquake, a landslip, an avalanche overtake a man incidentally, as it were—without passion. A furious gale attacks him like a personal enemy, tries to grasp his limbs, fastens upon his mind, seeks to rout the very spirit out of him.

Joseph Conrad, *Typhoon*

WIND

The furious gale is simply wind—air in motion. Above us, the ocean of gases is constantly stirred by rivers of air: the cold air diving towards the equator, and the hot wafting upwards to the poles, intercepted by serpentine jet streams circling the globe. Wind distributes energy, information, warmth and moisture. Without it, the planet would dry up, freeze and suffocate.

But in the wake of the blessings come the curses of violent storms, from gales to hurricanes. Tornadoes—dark, spinning funnels dipping down from

BARRIE TORNADO
On May 31, 1985, several tornados, in parallel series, hurtled east-northeast across Ontario. The city of Barrie was worst hit. A funnel of black dust pummelled a seven-block area, damaging 857 buildings, and killing eight people.

towering clouds—are the most violent wind storms. The pressure inside is so low that it produces a vacuum effect, stripping people naked, shearing sheep and pulling bark from trees. Though short-lived, the intense tornado core can devastate—precisely and impressively—as it did in 1987 in Edmonton, Alberta. Edmonton's tornado killed 27 people.

The cyclone and its larger brother, the hurricane, are storms that spiral around an atmospheric depression, sucking moist air up from the tropics and dropping a deluge of rain. But far more frequent, and just as terrifying, are the storms of medium strength that fill the skies for days. 1775 was known as "The Year of the Great Storm" in Newfoundland. According to Governor Duff, the island received *"a very severe stroke from the violence of a Storm of Wind"* in which an incredible 2000-4000 perished. The Great American Gale of 1851 descended on a large fleet of American schooners fishing off Prince Edward Island. For weeks afterwards, ships filled with bodies haunted islanders by drifting onto their shores.

Even when the wind is calm, it is capable of mischief. In 1862, the Variola virus crept around in the stagnant air of the outskirts of Victoria, British Columbia, spreading a smallpox epidemic to thousands of Indians. Though several hundred Native people received the new vaccination, the population was by and large ignored, and then banished by the whites, and left to spread the disease to the north. The death toll, up to 20 000, devastated an entire way of life.

WATER

As much as life on earth depends upon the wind, so does it require water to survive. Ocean currents, giving off their vapour to the air, help keep the planet's surface temperature within its narrow, liveable limits. Water also forms a part of almost everything on Earth. Even the driest flakes of dust, blown through the prairie droughts, contain some small amount of water. The cells of every plant are filled with water. Trees and plants release vapour into the air—one hectare (2.5 acres) of corn produces more moisture than a lake of similar size. Drawing water from the earth, root systems weave a stabilizing carpet for the soil which, if removed by overgrazing or unwise farming, creates conditions vulnerable to drought. Ironically, in the 1930s, the desert-like farms of

RED RIVER, MANITOBA
Life in the flood basin of the Red River, Manitoba was an ongoing struggle against the river's temperament. (Below) The flooded streets of St. Boniface, 1916.

the Dust Bowl, so desperate for rain, were damaged even further by rare, pounding thunder showers.

The conditions necessary for water to appear on the planet were so unique as to be highly improbable: oxygen and hydrogen had to stay in the atmosphere and meet; Earth had to be the right size and distance from the sun. When the first fluid fell from the sky, miraculously, it was water. On Venus, clouds rain concentrated sulphuric acid, one of the most corrosive fluids in the universe.

Aside from the droughts of the 1930s, Canadians have historically taken their vast freshwater resources for granted. It has, for a long time, been plentiful, easily accessible and clean, which is why the gross contamination of the water supply in Walkerton, Ontario, in the spring of 2000, had such an impact on the country. A deadly strain of E-coli bacteria washed into the water supply, killing between five and eleven people.

The Earth's water can have frightening power; enough to wash away lives and solid structures, and to alter landscapes. Over years, the liquid can erode any surface. Leonardo Da Vinci once said, *"In time, and with water, everything changes."*

ICE

Drop the temperature slightly and water freezes. Snowflakes—filigrees of frozen fluid—drift from the sky, so light they land unnoticed on eyelashes. But en masse, snow can become a sodden blanket that has been known to slip down mountains, smothering communities below. In 1965, a slide engulfed half the Granduc Mine camp, north of Stewart, British Columbia. Twenty-seven men were killed. One man stayed alive for over three days beneath two and a half metres (8 ft.) of snow while rescue helicopters landed right on top of him, compacting his tomb. When a bulldozer finally exposed the man, he was still conscious. He lost a hand and foot to

WHEN FOG FELL ON HIGHWAY 401, SOUTHWESTERN ONTARIO, SEPTEMBER 3, 1999

Fog descending upon Highway 401 resulted in a calamitous series of accidents. Five separate crashes snared 63 vehicles, 45 people went to hospital and eight died.

ICE PUSH ON THE VICTORIA JUBILEE BRIDGE, MONTREAL

During Spring breakup, ice can accumulate on rivers, exerting phenomenal pressure. Using shovels, men try to break up the mound of ice threatening the bridge.

frostbite, but the air-rich snow had allowed him space to breathe, and insulated him from hypothermia. In 1999, in the little town of Kangiqsualujjuaq, northern Quebec, a New Year's gun salute may have triggered an avalanche that crashed down on a party in a school, killing nine people.

In warmer weather, moisture that is carried high into the clouds can freeze around dust particles, forming hail. The ice falls, gathers more moisture, is carried higher still by warm updraughts, and freezes into ever bigger balls. Eventually, their weight brings the ice flying to earth. Calgary, Alberta is regularly hit by hail, with costly consequences. In 1991, Calgary residents shovelled hail from $400 million worth of damaged property. The following year, another hail storm was even larger.

Frozen water has the strength of steel, enough to push up bridges, tear down transmission towers, and to coat the world in crystal armour. Aside from convulsions in the planet's crust, it is simple ice that has, more than any other factor, changed the face of the earth.

THE FORGOTTEN ICE STORM
HAMILTON, ONTARIO, DECEMBER 6, 1898

(Below) December 5 and 6, 1898, southern Ontario felt the pressure of 41 centimetres (16 in.) of snow. Frigid, windy conditions turned the snow to ice, destroying orchards, freezing railway lines, and damaging houses. One hundred years later, in 1998, Ontario was hit by another ice storm. This time, miles of transmission towers crumpled, leaving us surprised at the vulnerability of our modern world and its conveniences.

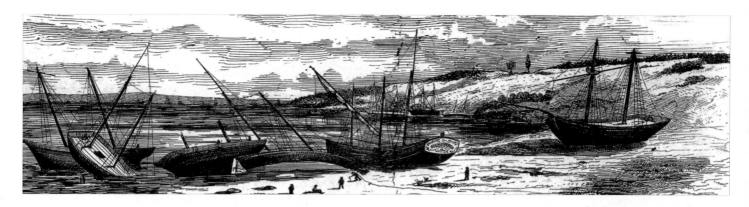

500 LIVES LOST, 12,000 VESSELS FOUNDERED, 900 BUILDINGS DESTROYED
GREAT NOVA SCOTIA CYCLONE, AUGUST 24-25, 1873

(Above) Long remembered by Nova Scotians as The Great Cyclone, the storm of 1873 lashed the shores of Cape Breton Island with extraordinary severity. A recent expansion in the Dominion's coal trade brought seasonal fleets to the area, seeking freight for transport. Over a thousand of these vessels, anchored in the island's harbours on the night of the storm, were driven onto the rocks. The gale also destroyed an untold number of bridges and wharves, and swept away homes and churches. Over five hundred people died.

An interruption in telegraph service between Toronto and Halifax had prevented storm warnings from getting through, and this was felt to have contributed to the high losses. After the cyclone, officials were convinced, more than ever before, of the need for an improved Canadian storm-warning system.

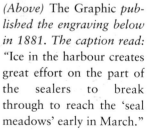

INTO THE ICE FLOES
(Above) The Graphic *published the engraving below in 1881. The caption read:* "Ice in the harbour creates great effort on the part of the sealers to break through to reach the 'seal meadows' early in March."

ARMADA DRIVEN AGROUND
(Left) Quebec City had been expecting an attack from the English for a month. And by August 22, 1711, a spectacular armada—including 9 warships and 60 troop carriers—under command of Admiral Hovenden Walker was sailing up the St. Lawrence River towards the city. The English plan of attack was thwarted when a violent storm seized the fleet, sending eight ships crashing onto the rocks of Ile aux Oeufs. Nine hundred lives were lost.

SMITH STREET, REGINA

A deadly funnel cloud created by colliding storms tore through the centre of Regina on June 30, 1912. Twelve city blocks were left in ruins.

MURDEROUS CYCLONE

Regina, Saskatchewan

JUNE 30, 1912

There had been so many days of debilitating heat that most people in Regina were relieved to see the skies darkening on Sunday afternoon, June 30, 1912. Out for a walk, Judge Hannon noticed clouds converging somewhere over Wascana Lake, where they shed an unearthly hue through the sky.

The judge ran home through sheets of pelting rain, forked lightning snapping through the clouds. The racing wind pushed him up his front steps.

Hannon's verandah curtains had been shredded into ribbons, and his heavy, steamer chair slid from one end of the verandah to the other. He slammed the front door and the wind shrieked through it in a wild, weird moan. Suddenly, his parlour and dining room windows blew out and all of his furniture began a crazy dance.

The judge hustled his family down to the cellar, then struggled to secure the back door, which refused to close. Looking out, he noticed that his neighbour's small frame house was completely gone.

The colliding storms had convulsed into a towering funnel that tore across the lake. It took only six minutes for the funnel to cut a swath through the heart of Regina. It ripped northwards up Lorne and Smith Streets. It rampaged through the railway yards. It spread out and flattened the northern outskirts of the city. Then, it was gone. In the half hour that followed, more than an inch of rain doused the devastated city.

The people called it a cyclone. But within this cyclone, the funnel was tight and tense, with the violent, predatory nature of a tornado. Debris was picked up and transformed into bullets and spears by the wind's fury.

Flying gravel left holes in walls, and shards of glass were driven into brick. And in the core of the sweeping spiral, the pressure was so low that a powerful vacuum effect was created. At once, volumes of trapped air expanded outwards. Tightly-sealed houses, their occupants quivering in the cellars, literally exploded, the windows blown out into the vacuum. The damage was bizarre, severe and concentrated, while the rest of the city was left unscathed.

As it crossed the lake, the funnel swept up a massive waterspout that demolished the Boat Clubhouse. It catapulted canoes into surrounding buildings. One crashed through a fourth-storey window more than half a mile away.

HOMES HAD EXPLODED

Volumes of trapped air expanded outwards, literally causing houses to explode. Windows and household items were sucked out into the vacuum.

The Beelby family of Smith Street sought safety in their attic which was subsequently torn from the house and hurled into a neighbour's yard. The family climbed out of a window, stunned but unhurt. The Telephone Exchange Building, at Lorne Street and Eleventh Avenue, lost its roof and a wall. Its heavy switchboard fell through two floors and into the basement, carrying four people with it.

As the funnel careened past the new Legislative Buildings, with one great inhalation it sucked out all the examination papers of Saskatchewan grade schools.

A livery stable housing fifty horses was reported lifted from the ground and dropped onto the railway tracks. The horses did not sustain serious injuries. C.P.R. freight cars and their loads were tossed and juggled and a substantial grain elevator simply vanished.

"In the upper story of the YWCA," said Judge Hannon, *"was visible something looking like a ladder driven through the wall from the inside and standing straight out some six feet."*

The path of damage was three blocks wide by twelve blocks long. Thirty people were killed, two hundred injured and more than two thousand left homeless. Upwards of 500 buildings were damaged or destroyed, and estimated loss of property was a staggering $4 million. The Dominion Day celebrations of the following day were cancelled. Drenched flags drooped at half mast. Businesses were closed and papers reported: *"Dominion Day. For Regina the day of the dominion of death."*

For five years, the city had been cradled in the arms of prosperity. As the province's chief distribution centre, it was expanding, planning, and radiating wealth. So despite the catastrophic storm, the people were galvanized by western optimism. They took up tools and, within eighteen hours, had already begun to repair and rebuild. Mayor Peter McAra Jr. organized his city with admirable efficiency. All men were requested to volunteer to help clear the wreckage, Boy Scouts were designated messengers, private homes were opened to storm victims, and the nightly anti-looting patrols were scarcely necessary. While the bereaved people invested their energy in hope and regrowth, the city's banks and firms invested their money in building loans. By the end of 1912, Regina was rising, *"Phoenix-like from its ruins,"* just as the *Morning Leader* had predicted, only three days after the disaster.

DOWNTOWN REGINA
Before the tornado struck, the young city had been enjoying an economic boom. Afterwards, relief supplies for stricken families poured in from across the country.

FLIPPED TRAIN
Grain elevators, warehouses and railway cars were tossed around like toys as the funnel cloud swept through the rail yards.

BODIES FROM THE *WEXFORD*

Members of the steamer's 16-man crew washed ashore near Goderich, Ontario.

GREAT LAKES GALES OF 1913

Lakes Superior, Michigan, Huron, Erie, and Ontario

NOVEMBER 7-12, 1913

Superior, Michigan, Huron, Erie, Ontario: together these lakes are the world's eighth sea. Saltwater seamen have scoffed at the danger of mere lakes, but there is no denying the lethal power of these tempestuous waters.

November is the most malevolent month, when the cold polar air moves in, sucking the lakes' summer-soaked heat in large gulps and letting loose wild, frigid gales. The waves churned up are stocky and fast. Snow and freezing spray grip the railings, choke the ventilation ports, and seal the lifeboat davits, while just beneath the foaming surface lie thousands of threatening reefs. These lakes have taken more than 4000 vessels.

Early November 1913 had been placid and abnormally warm, but two intense low pressure systems drifted on a collision course over the Prairies and the plains states. When they struck, they flung a cruel storm onto the end of the shipping season. If the shipping captains missed the omens of destruction, the animals did not. Throughout Friday November 7, Sudbury loggers and hunters noticed deer, moose and bears deserting trees and gathering in swamps and hollows.

By Friday's end, weather alerts were issued, and gale-warning flags were hoisted in ports along the shores. The storm began over Lake Superior where ships out on the water felt the first jabs of the onslaught.

The *Huronic*, a passenger liner of the Northern Navigation Company, was on her last run of the season across Lake Superior. She was struck by the gale that Friday evening. Tossed and beaten by the waves, the windows on the bridge were smashed in, and the crew and passengers terrified, until the ship straggled into Whitefish Bay and was beached on a sandbar. Her Captain, Malcom Cameron, was nearly frozen, her crew exhausted.

After several hours in the storm, the steamer, *Turret Chief*, was utterly lost. Superior's violent seas battered the ship, tore apart her steam lines, and drove her a 160 kilometres (100 mi.) off course. When the ship was finally thrown onto a reef early Saturday morning, the 22-man crew scrambled down a line onto the rocks, making it to shore. They huddled beneath an improvised shelter, waiting out the blizzard. After three excruciating days and nights watching their ship become a giant iceberg, the men set off in search of help. They soon discovered that they were on the Keweenaw Peninsula, with the town of Copper Harbor only six miles from their ship.

That same night, the large freighter, *L. C. Waldo*, filled with iron ore and bound for Cleveland, was impaled on Gull Rock on Superior's southern shore. Nine-metre (30-ft.) waves thrashed at the ship, lifting her up only to break her on the rocks again. Her crew of twenty crowded in the bow, burning anything in the captain's bathtub just to keep warm, and choking on the smoke. It was days before the U.S. Coast Guard reached them.

Captain of the freighter *William Nottingham*, Louis Farwell, wrestled with Superior for more than two days, by which time his coal supply ran out. Farwell knew that without power, his ship and crew would be at the mercy of the reefs. In desperation, he ordered his men to open up the hatches and shovel grain down the coal chutes and in the bunkers. Furiously burning wheat, they just made it into Whitefish Bay when they were forced onto a reef off Sandy Island. Three of the crew were sent for help, but the wind bashed their lifeboat into the ship, hurling the men into the icy waves. The remaining fourteen men and a female cook awaited rescue on the ship.

The freighter, *Leafield*, vanished on Lake Superior with her eighteen crew. Last seen by the captain of the *Huronic*, dangerously close to the rocks off Angus Island, she disappeared from view in the dense snow. The *Leafield* has never been located.

The large American freighter, *Henry B. Smith*, and her crew of 25, were consumed by the storm. Her captain, Jimmy Owen, desperate to deliver one more load of ore before winter, ordered his ship cast off from the Duluth docks. Owen stubbornly set a course across open Lake Superior, into the teeth of the storm. Three days later, scraps of the ship were found on a beach near Marquette, Michigan.

By Saturday November 8, a second storm, blown up from the Caribbean, and bursting with moisture, collided with the low-pressure system over the Great Lakes. It began by wreaking havoc on Lake Huron's Georgian Bay before hitting each of the other huge bodies of water.

American sister freighters *Isaac M. Scott*, and *Charles S. Price*, both heading north on Lake Huron loaded with coal, were taken by the waves on November 11. Their crews of 28 men each were drowned. American sister ships the *Hydrus* and the *Argus* shared the same fate, both overwhelmed by Lake Huron on November 11 and 12. None from their 28 and 25-man crews survived.

THE PORT HURON TIMES-HERALD.

EXTRA

PORT HURON, MICHIGAN, SATURDAY, NOVEMBER 15, 1913 — 12 PAGES TODAY — PRICE TWO CENTS

BOAT IS PRICE
DIVER IS BAKER
SECRET KNOWN

**MYSTERY OF THE
CHARLES S. PRICE**

*(Above) Composite photo
of S.S. Charles S. Price in
1912 and her overturned
hull after the November
1913 storm. (above right)
Headlines six days after
the mystery hull was dis-
covered. A diver had identified the ship as the* Price.

The *James C. Carruthers*, was only five months old and one of the largest freighters on the lakes. She managed to survive the tremendous blow on Lake Superior but was taken by Lake Huron. All hands were lost. And the *Regina*, a small freighter delivering supplies up Lake Huron's eastern shores, was sucked to the bottom with a broken hull. A few days later, the bodies of three crewmembers washed ashore in a lifeboat—dead from exposure.

Without wirelesses on board, there was no communication from the foundering ships. But some of the victims made poignant efforts to reach out. A week after the storm, a message in a bottle washed up on the eastern shore of Lake Michigan, dispatched by Chris Keenan of the barge *Plymouth*. Towed by a rickety old tug, the *Plymouth* had set out across Lake Michigan two hours before the storm warnings began. Progress soon became impossible. The tug steamed on alone to better shelter, leaving seven men aboard the vulnerable *Plymouth*. When the tug returned two days later, the *Plymouth* had disappeared. The note in the bottle read:

> *Dear wife and children. We were left up here in Lake Michigan by McKinnon, captain [of the]* James H. Martin, *tug at anchor. He went away and never said goodbye or anything to us. Lost one man yesterday. We have been out in the storm forty hours. Goodbye dear ones, I might see you in Heaven.*
>
> *Pray for me. Chris K.*

Ten days after the storm, a wooden board from the steamer *Wexford* washed up on a shore near Goderich. Scrawled across it were the words: *"I am with the boat, lashed to the wheel. —B."* The *Wexford* had disappeared on Lake Huron with Captain Bruce Cameron and his 16-man crew.

Captain Hugh Williams of the *U.S. Lightship #82* also scribbled one last message on a door, before his 24-metre (80-ft.) vessel lost her battle to stay afloat in Lake Erie. To his wife he wrote: *"Good-bye, Nellie, the ship is breaking up fast. Williams."* His body was washed onto the rocks a few days later. His crew of five had also drowned.

When the waters of the Great Lakes had regained their slate-grey composure, bodies began to drift ashore. Some arrived alone, others in small groups tied to lifeboats, caked with ice. Search parties and local residents located 56 victims.

The body of Emily Walker, the cook aboard the *Argus*, washed up wearing evidence of two last acts of gallantry: her captain's life preserver and the chief engineer's coat. The body of Chief Engineer John Groundwater of the *Charles S. Price* was found snagged on the rocks wearing a lifebelt from the *Regina,* sparking theories that the two ships met up in the storm. But when the wreck of the *Regina* was finally found in 1985, it lay 32 kilometres (20 mi.) from the *Price*.

Thomas Thompson of Hamilton, Ontario identified a body as his son, John, a firefighter aboard the *Carruthers*. The body had several identifiable features: some teeth missing, the initials J.T. tattooed on the left forearm, a burn mark on one shin. The paler hair colour was likely due to prolonged immersion in cold water. The family discovered they had the wrong man only after the burial, when the real John Thompson walked in on the wake.

HULL OF THE
CHARLES S. PRICE
Decades later, the Price *sits in depths between 12 and 18 metres (40 and 60 ft.).*

LIFEBELTS
Lifebelts from foundered ships such as the Wexford, *and* James C. Carruthers *were collected from the shoreline after the storm passed.*

The 1913 gales destroyed eleven large, steel freighters, two barges and a lightship. After six days of terror, up to 300 victims were lost in the depths of the world's eighth sea.

Canadian ships lost:	Length		Number of crew
James C. Carruthers	550 ft	(168m)	25
Regina	269 ft	(82m)	20
Wexford	250 ft	(76m)	17
Leafield	248 ft	(75m)	18
American ships lost:			
Henry B. Smith	565 ft	(172m)	25
Charles S. Price	524 ft	(160m)	28
Isaac M. Scott	504 ft	(154m)	28
John A. McGean	452 ft	(138m)	28
Argus	436 ft	(133m)	25
Hydrus	436 ft	(133m)	28
Plymouth	213 ft	(65m)	7
Halstead	171 ft	(52m)	6
Lightship # 82	80 ft	(24m)	6

Length of ships and crew sizes from David D. Swayze's Shipwreck, *courtesy of Harbor House Publishers, Inc., 1992.*

HENRY B. SMITH
Pressured to meet their quotas, captains often took risks. Such was the case when the Smith *sailed into the storm of 1913. The ship and twenty crewmembers were lost.*

The Great "Yankee Gale"

Prince Edward Island
October 4-6, 1851

The "Yankee Gale"—Prince Edward Island's two-day storm of 1851—owes its name to the hundreds of American schooners it tormented. Their sails were clearly visible that October 3 white against a darkening sky. They had flocked here for the superb mackerel fishing off the north shore of the island.

The storm blew in overnight with unimaginable fury. The wind swung from south to east to north. Most ships were caught between heading for the open and riding out the gale at anchor. A veil of rain and spray obscured the ships from view until the morning of October 7, when the winds finally died and the islanders could finally see the damage.

Schooners, driven aground, littered the Cavendish dunes. On one ship, caught on rocks, thirteen exhausted sailors hung from the rigging, awaiting rescue. Islanders boarded another waterlogged vessel to find ten drowned crewmen hidden in her cabin. The *Shipjack* from Liverpool, Nova Scotia, went aground on Robinson's Island. She yielded thirty barrels of mackerel and ten dead fishermen. The casualties of men and ships cannot be calculated, but between East Point and North Cape on the northern shore of P.E.I. there were at least eighty ships wrecked and 150 men drowned.

The Americans later acknowledged the Prince Edward Islanders, who did their utmost—attempting rescues even while the storm raged, providing food and shelter, cleansing and burying the dead. The schooner *Seth Hall*, captained by Seth Hall of Maine, was salvaged after the storm and offered as transport for the dead back to New England. Many had already been buried, so they were exhumed and loaded on the ship. After sailing past East Point, the *Seth Hall* struck another storm. All hands, and the dead, were lost.

Oil Painting of The Yankee Gale by George Thresher

(Below left) Off the northern shore of Prince Edward Island, the 1851 storm whipped the waters into a maelstrom. Over 150 fishermen lost their lives.

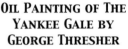

Ravages of a Gale

(Below) An engraving of a victim of the gale, reproduced in Roland H. Sherwood's The Wind That Made Them Widows.

NEWSPAPER CARRIERS FOR THE *WINNIPEG FREE PRESS* TAKE PRECAUTION

Homemade gauze or cheesecloth masks were worn in most cities for protection. Though advised to wear the masks for only two hours at a time, and to boil them before re-use, most people wore them the entire day. The porous material would have offered no protection from the virus.

164

"THE DISEASE OF THE WIND"

Spanish Influenza Epidemic

1918

The Spanish Influenza did not originate in Spain. The first victims of the virus were in China, in February 1918. Then Chinese workers brought it unwittingly to France. It was passed around in the cramped trenches of Europe, and carried by WWI troops as they traversed the globe. In March of 1918, the flu appeared in North America, infecting 107 American servicemen at their camp in Kansas in a single day. The disease next appeared in Britain, finally reaching Spain by May.

Spain, being neutral in the war, did not censor its media as other countries did. Spanish newspapers were the first to announce and name the epidemic, although it was called many things throughout the world. The Swiss called it The Coquette because it gave so freely of its favours. In Hungary it was The Black Whip; in Japan, Wrestler's Fever; in Britain, Flanders' Grippe. The Persians called it The Disease of the Wind.

The Germans knew it as Blitz Katarrh, or Lightning Cold. As the flu bombarded German cities, their supply lines to the front faltered and battles had to be postponed. The disease may have even helped to shorten the war. U.S. President, Woodrow Wilson, contracted the flu during peace negotiations in Versailles. Many suspected he had been poisoned when he became so ill so quickly. Some even attribute the flawed and vulnerable peace treaty directly to Wilson's sickly state.

By early June 1918, Canadian troops brought the flu back home with them. Soldiers were acutely ill with the disease aboard the hospital ship *Araguaya*, sailing from England to Canada on June 26. Almost every ship to arrive on Canadian shores carried illness. Symptoms started with a cold-like stuffy nose and coughing, progressing rapidly to severe muscle and joint aches,

FILTERED AIR MACHINE
Inventions to avoid Flu-cont- aminated air did little to check the epidemic that killed up to 50,000 Canadians, and up to 25 million people worldwide.

fever and overwhelming lethargy. Many developed pneumonia and were too weak to fight off death. Strangely, the virus mainly targeted the young adult population, twenty to forty years old. The feverish young soldiers boarded trains bound for their home towns and fanned out across the country.

Throughout the summer, the infection rate in Canada was low, but it escalated in the autumn. When cities across the nation began to report dramatic numbers, there was no federal health office to respond. Municipal and provincial authorities had to invent their own courses of action. And as quickly as the flu spread, Canadian health officials recoiled into denial, soft-pedaling its dangers.

WWI—PERFECT CONDITIONS FOR THE SPREAD OF INFLUENZA

(Top) In crowded and dirty trenches like this one at Vimy Ridge, the disease was transmitted at an alarming rate. (Bottom) The virus was carried on home-bound ships and on trains transporting troops across the country.

Canada's first civilian outbreak was in Victoriaville College, Quebec. In early September, most students and teachers had fallen ill and were bussed home all over the province. Over 500 soldiers were already fighting fevers in a St. Jean military camp. But an army spokesperson informed the public that the epidemic was under control, that it was *only a matter of days, now.* It was to be only a matter of days before the whole province was affected. In Montreal, the demand for hearses led the city to devote a trolley car for transporting coffins. In the province of Quebec alone, more than 500 000 people were infected and over 13 000 died.

On September 30, in St. John's, Newfoundland, three ailing sailors were carried down their ship's gangplank into the city. On October 3, three more arrived in Burin. The lightning-fast transmission started. The mail boat, *Sagona*, left for the coast of Labrador stopping at every port to deliver letters, lumber, clothing, oil, groceries—and the virus. The little settlements would face immense suffering during the winter. With most falling ill in the autumn, there was not enough wood chopped to heat their homes for the cold season, and when many succumbed to pneumonia, surviving relatives lacked the strength to open the frozen ground for burial. In Okak, an isolated family died, leaving one eight-year-old girl to fend for five weeks by herself.

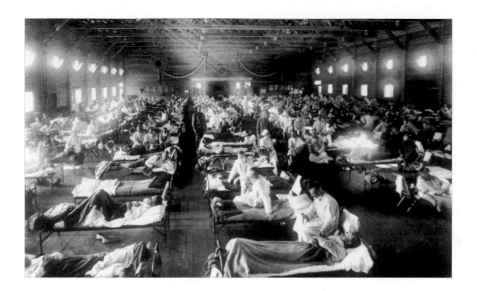

Huskies ate her parents' bodies right before her eyes. The girl survived through weeks of temperatures thirty below zero, burning every candle to melt drinking water.

The native people of Okak had expected disaster to befall them: the northern lights showed bright red that year, turning the snow pink. But how could they have known the tragedy would be so crushing, leaving so many young orphans? Of 266 Okaks, only 59 survived the epidemic. And in Hebron, only 70 of 220 managed to pull through. The dead were weighted with stones and dropped through holes in the ice. Small funeral services were held in Labrador's raging blizzards.

In late November, the Hudson's Bay Company sent a plea for government assistance on behalf of the people. A curt letter came back refusing aid due to a lack of coal for the journey. However someone did dispatch a doctor, some medicine, a carpenter and some lumber for coffins—in June of the following year! By then, more than a third of Labrador's population had perished.

Halifax, Nova Scotia, was still reverberating from the great explosion of 1917. Churches and schools just reopened, were forced to close again. Large placards hanging on the doors of infected households read "Spanish Influenza."

When, in early October, fevers broke out all over Ontario, health officers considered closing the schools, but were advised against "irritating the public" for "no useful purpose" by Ontario's Board of Health. In Brantford, Ontario, the chairman of the Board of Health, T.J. Minnes, denied outright the existence of the disease in his city, even though there were 800 cases of the "grippe" reported at the time.

From the Department of Militia and Defence in Ottawa came a message for the director of medical services in Toronto:

VICTORY PARADE

Armistice celebrations are tempered by the spectre of disease, their jubilance muffled by cheesecloth masks.

HOW TO MAKE A MASK

(opposite page, top) Instructional poster showing how to construct a face mask. Believed to be a barrier from the disease, the warm, damp cloth actually provided a breeding ground for bacteria.

The disease, although extremely contagious, is not a serious one and every effort must be made to control alarm, not only among the troops but among the public and in the Press.

Seven days later, the Military Base Hospital in Toronto was begging civilian nurses for help with the soaring numbers who were dying from pneumonia.

The virus travelled by locomotive to the prairies and the first two deaths were reported in Saskatoon on October 3. By the middle of the month, residents were wearing masks and were being fined $50 for spitting in the street. Dr. Arthur Wilson, Saskatoon's medical health officer, told the *Saskatoon Daily Star* on October 21 that the epidemic was nothing but the old form of grippe, festooned with more publicity. These were hardly words of comfort to families like Alan McLeod's of Stonewall, Manitoba. An eighteen-year-old war hero, the wounded Alan had shot down three enemy planes before his own caught fire. Climbing out onto the wing, he had guided his burning craft to a crash landing in No Man's Land. Six months later, safely home in Manitoba, the young hero caught influenza and died.

The flu grabbed a foothold in Alberta and British Columbia travelling on trains coming from the East, and then on ships arriving in Pacific ports. Vancouver's Medical Health Officer, Dr. Frederick T. Underhill, told the city that if proper precautions were taken, Vancouver should come through without a serious epidemic. By October 16, Vancouver's General Hospital was bursting at the seams. The university's auditorium and several classrooms were converted for the sick. Vancouver would have one of the highest flu-related mortality rates.

Northern communities were mercilessly cut down by the disease. Beaver Indian Reserve in the Peace River Area of Alberta lost 85 percent of its population. Those who should have been strong enough to combat the illness were weakened by lack of food. Hunters simply dropped in the wilderness and never returned, while survivors were too weak to lift the dead out of the dogs' reach. In the North, the influenza continued to crest as late as 1922.

The world had not yet seen the deadly virus. Still alive today in various mutations, the virus is so small that 20 to 30 million can fit on the head of a pin. Only the finest filters are able to strain them from the air. In 1918, some scientists suspected a bacteria, Bacillus Influenzae, was responsible. The organism had been discovered in Germany in 1892 and was used to produce a vaccine. Provincial health boards and private laboratories sprang into action, producing the vaccine and shipping it throughout the country. But it was powerless against the virus.

Homemade masks of gauze or cheesecloth were felt to offer protection and were worn in most cities. Health officers advocated wearing them for only two hours at a time, and then boiling them before reuse, but few followed this advice.

Household cures included hot poultices of onions, mustard, salt and flour, wrapped in muslin and pressed to the chest. Some used hot bran, or lard with camphor, chloroform or turpentine. Many warded off the evil with bags of menthol or camphor worn around their necks, by soaking their masks in formaldehyde, or by ingesting oil of cinnamon, castor oil or violet-leaf tea. Some tried to smoke the culprit out by carrying hot coals sprinkled with sulfur through their homes.

Smoke, in any form, was latched onto as a safeguard. People took up chain smoking, or puffing on cigars, while *Popular Science* magazine illustrated how to smoke while wearing a mask, by cutting a small hole in the material and plugging it when not in use.

But it was alcohol that proved the most controversial medicine. The Prohibition Act of 1917 forbade the use of valuable foodstuffs for the distillation of liquor, but sale of intoxicants was permitted by prescription through government vendors. Doctors could charge $2 per prescription and lineups were enormous outside liquor dispensaries.

Across the nation, the virus also crippled business. Shops and hotels were empty; theatres, restaurants and dance halls were ordered closed; and every industry was desperately short-staffed. Medical facilities could not keep up and provincial budgets shuffled funds to try to keep them going. Clearly, health care resources needed coordination, and by March 1919, a bill was finally passed establishing a federal department of health.

The Spanish Influenza killed between 30 and 50 thousand Canadians, and 20 to 25 million people worldwide. As destructive as it was, it also fuelled important research. As the crisis waned, scientists searched for the cause, shifting their focus from bacteria to viruses. The breakthrough came in 1933 when Drs. P. Laidlaw and C. Andrews not only discovered the offending virus but also how it travelled in air.

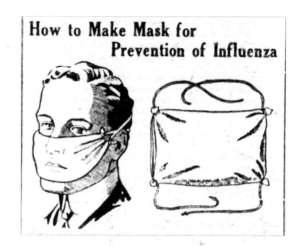

How to Make Mask for Prevention of Influenza

OPERATORS AT HIGH RIVER, ALBERTA
(Below) Despite long hours and staff shortages, these operators are still smiling beneath their masks. With thousands taking sick leave across Canada, every industry felt the blow of the Spanish Influenza.

TORNADO STRIKES EDMONTON

Robert den Hartigh's photograph of the tornado taken from an office building. A local newspaper printed a story about den Hartigh who was selling his photo to raise money for disaster relief. Three weeks later he donated $10,000 to the Canadian Red Cross, matching the largest corporate donation made to Edmonton's Tornado Relief Fund.

TWISTER

Edmonton, Alberta

JULY 31, 1987

It had been another hot, wet day in Lois Theroux's mobile home. Looking out the window, she could see a funnel of black cloud reaching down to touch the ground. In a flash, she was racing from the trailer park, her two children with her in the car. Before she could get away, the engine stalled, and the car's front end was lifted off the road.

"*It was unreal,*" Theroux told Marylin Moysa of *The Edmonton Journal,* "*Water was coming through the doors. Big balls of hail were hitting the car all over. I couldn't see anything.*" Somehow she got the engine started and, with wheels spinning, hail pounding and her children's cries lost in the screaming wind, she drove to safety.

The tornado absolutely shattered the Evergreen Mobile Home Park. Its 700 trailer homes were tossed into heaps. The industrial park nearby fared no better. Cars and trucks were thrown around, roofs torn away, and workers hurled into walls or hit by flying debris. Twelve freight cars flew off the railway tracks. Those who lived through it later told the papers that they had felt the world was coming to an end. The furious wind, blasting like a supersonic engine, hurt their ears.

The erratic funnel had taken a forty-kilometre (25-mi.) path. At 3 p.m. it touched down south of Edmonton, tearing north-wards, east of 34th Street and between the Whitemud and Sherwood Park Freeways. Minutes later, stunned and severely injured people staggered through the carnage while the rest of the city battled flooding, hail and power cuts. Caught in the tornado's path, 27 people had been killed and 215 injured.

HOMES SHREDDED
Wreckage is checked for survivors after the Evergreen Mobile Home Park is flattened.

RED RIVER FLOOD, 1950

Flood waters engulf Winnipeg's Riverview district, including three hospitals (at right).

WAR ON THE RED

Red River Floods, Manitoba

1826, 1950, & 1997

The river wends its way northwards from west-central Minnesota toward Manitoba, reddened by silt particles suspended in its waters. It twists through Winnipeg, the largest city on its banks, and, joining with the Assiniboine River, it meanders into Lake Winnipeg. The basin of the Red and Assiniboine Rivers is the exact geographical centre of North America, once the site of the large, glacial Lake Agassiz. In Native myth, southern Manitoba was originally a vast sea from which a muskrat lifted a chunk of mud. From this mud the land was created. Periodic floods of the Red River have nurtured the land, making it rich. But every so often, the river strives to recreate the sea.

DEFEAT: 1826

Dispossessed of their lands in Scotland, Scottish crofters were lured to settle along the Red River in the Earl of Selkirk's wilderness colony. For fourteen years they fought with nature, set upon by wolves, blizzards, droughts and plagues. A few hopeful years encouraged them to stay, and a fair-sized village began to grow around the Hudson's Bay post, Fort Garry.

January of 1826 was gripped by an intense freeze. Native hunters on the Prairies were starving, their horses killed and the buffalo driven from their reach by the cold. The Hudson's Bay Company sent dogsleds of provisions and clothing to the snow-bound families. The cold stretched on. The land drained poorly. The preceding autumn, it had been soaked with heavy rainfall, and then as the cold set in, the soil was coated with heavy snow. By spring, ice more than 1.5 metres (5 ft.) thick had formed a solid shell over the angry river. The river rose to the level of its banks.

On Friday, May 5, the ice gave way with an explosive crack. Surging violently over its banks, the river rushed toward the colony, pushing along great and jagged ice floes. At once, 47 houses were swept away. Residents climbed to their roofs or into the trees. Many fled. Young Francis Heron, a Hudson's Bay Company clerk, wrote in his journal:

May 6th Saturday. The waters continued to increase during the last night and this day. The ice during the same time ran past without inter-mission in immense masses, mingled with the wrecks of houses, fences, trees, etc.

FLOODING VIEWS
(above) Residential areas inundated, 1950. (opposite page) Two nuns canoe through St. Mary's, 1950.

In Fort Garry, the clerk had been moving the store's provisions to higher shelves for two days, preparing for the inevitable. But now his company mustered all the boats for rooftop evacuations. According to resident Alexander Ross, Hudson's Bay Company employees, *"exerted themselves to the utmost and did good service with their boats."* Sixty families and 200 cattle, trapped on the last dry spot, were helped to higher land by company workers.

The area looked like a lake, with fleets of abandoned houses, barns, carriages—flotsam for Lake Winnipeg. As the water kept on climbing, settlers moved to higher land, drove their cattle into the hills, and endured a miserable two weeks of unrelenting rain, sleet, thunderstorms and high winds. On May 14, the Hudson's Bay Company gave up hope for their fort and evacuated their property from the garret windows. Only the largest boats could cope on the stormy water.

Encamped with the refugees on the banks of the Assiniboine, Heron noted that company sales were good. All food had been distributed free of charge, but ammunition and tobacco sales were brisk. Other entrepreneurs also fared well: two men sold sturgeon caught in the rapids, while a group of De Meurons (Swiss merceneries), who were known only rarely to possess cattle of their own, made a suspicious business of cheap beef sales.

One De Meuron man drowned when he ventured out from his camp at night. Another man and three children drowned when their canoe capsized.

The water crested on Monday May 22—two and a half weeks after the flood began—and started to recede gradually on Tuesday. For many settlers, the flood had been the final adversity. They prepared to leave Canada forever, trading their last cash, furs and valuables for travelling supplies from the Hudson's Bay stores. Just when everything of value had been traded and the desperate mob was eyeing the Company loot, the water went down enough to allow the Company workers to escape with the goods.

On June 15, they shifted the Company's belongings back by boat to what remained of Fort Garry. Not a single home in the colony had survived the flood. Settlers who returned to rebuild their lives had to start from scratch, with only a modest contribution from the Hudson's Bay Company as relief. Grub worm destroyed their first, post-flood crops.

George Simpson, manager of the colony, considered the flood, *"an extinguisher to the hope of Red River ever retaining the name of a Settlement."*

A WORTHY BATTLE: 1950

The settlement without a hope had actually become the thriving metropolis of Winnipeg, its suburbs stretching along the banks of the Red and Assiniboine Rivers. Though struggling to maintain financial dominance in western Canada, the city enjoyed a guarded, post-war prosperity. There had been years of flooding, but in the last one hundred years, Winnipeg had managed nicely. The Americans were spending millions on flood protection, and Winnipeg talked about such schemes, but none were put into place. Weather forecasting was still in its adolescence, while disaster response and relief plans were still unheard of. Essentially, Winnipeg, in fact the whole region, was defenseless.

Nature lined up her weapons of assault: heavy rain all autumn, a long winter with copious amounts of snow, a cold spring with nothing thawing, and loads of thick ice on the river. Fearing heavy flooding, Manitoba threw a plan together, signing on the Army and the Red Cross. By the end of April, the town of Emerson had been evacuated, Fort Garry was hurling sandbags onto a small dike, and most other communities south of Winnipeg were battling the onslaught.

From May 1-5 the water rose higher every hour, pushing into the streets and homes of Winnipeg. Under the coordination of the Red Cross, the relief initiative was staffed entirely by volunteers. Some town councils were demanding federal assistance, but Manitoba's Premier Douglas Campbell was declining offers of aid from other provinces. His province, he felt, was coping very well. Mass evacuations were taking place throughout the rural south, with farmers shooting cattle they could feed no longer. Winnipeg's hospital patients and elderly were being carried from the danger zone.

When the dike at Fort Garry broke, the water swept 26-year-old Scotty Org into the basement of a house he was guarding. A diver later retrieved his body from the rafters.

On Saturday, May 6, the chief flood-fighters met with the Premier, urging him to centralize resources and ask for federal support. Campbell approached Ottawa and finally declared a state of emergency. But it was too late to save Campbell from his critics. Duff Roblin, a freshman member of the Manitoba Legislative Assembly, spoke out against Campbell's administration, calling it *"bungling, dallying and procrastinating."*

Brigadier R.E.A. Morton took on the fight against the water. Recent war veterans were called back into uniform

A CITY UNDER SIEGE

(Above) Cars sit as though in rush hour traffic. (Below) A CBC reporter slogs through water.

at their prior ranks and rates of pay. Conditions were deteriorating beyond any expectations or experience. The threat of typhoid spreading prompted the donation of a chlorinator by the city of Ottawa and the typhoid vaccine by the University of Montreal. Meanwhile, Brigadier Morton discretely planned "Operation Blackboy": the evacuation of all of Winnipeg.

But Winnipeg held her ground. Sandbaggers of all ages worked on dikes in every community. *"We called it the sandbox, and we filled bags with the stuff for eight to ten hours a day for many, many days,"* recalled Allyne Brown of Portage la Prairie. *"...Our hands were shredded and bleeding. Our feet, unaccustomed to rubber boots, were blistered. Our backs ached and it rained. But we toughened up."* Even the Grey Nuns of St. Boniface pinned up their robes and shovelled sand into bags.

Though "Operation Blackboy" was shelved, more than 80 000 women and children were removed to rural towns and summer homes, relieving pressure on food resources and reducing the potential for epidemic. "Flood bachelors," men cut off from their homes and families, relied on soup kitchens for survival until well after the water crested on May 15.

As the water level slowly dropped, a Flood Relief Fund rose. Eventually it would reach $10 million. Donations poured in from across Canada, Britain and the United States. The greatest portion came from Manitobans. A "Flood the Fund" rally and variety show at Toronto's Maple Leaf Gardens that was broadcast by CBC raised $230 000. Celebrities included Hollywood comedian Jack Carson, ukulele player George Formby, the Toronto Symphony, Sir Ernest MacMillan, and Fred Waring with his Pennsylvanians.

Residents were cautiously returning to their fetid homes, while federal engineers began to study future flood control. They introduced three new solutions: first, a 40-kilometre (25-mi.) dike south of Greater Winnipeg to form a detention basin; second, a channel to divert the Assiniboine around Portage la Prairie to Lake Manitoba; and third, a floodway, a 42-kilometre (26-mi.) ditch to divert flood water at St. Norbert back into the Red River near St. Andrew's dam. The report sat on Premier Campbell's desk for years, as its costs and benefits were picked through, until the premier was defeated at the polls by Duff Roblin.

VICTORY: 1997

"Duff's Ditch," or the Red River Floodway, was completed in 1969. The engineering masterpiece shifted more earth than the Panama Canal project. Huge steel diversion gates, eleven metres (35 ft.) high, sat beneath the Red River at St. Norbert, to be hydraulically raised when necessary. Other defenses were also in place. Dikes were improved all over the province, the Portage diversion channel had been dug, and the Shellmouth Dam had been built at the upper end of the Assiniboine River.

Several years of high water not only tested the new measures in flood control, but also the effectiveness of the Emergency Measures Organization, which was formed in the 1960s. Not surprisingly, there was much to iron out. Flood culture had been mutated by promises of protection, so that people living within the floodway had become complacent, while those outside it had grown angry. There was a sense that governments should control and compensate disastrous "acts of God." In 1997, the winter conditions warned of severe flooding on a par with 1950. Then, in April, a blizzard buried the valley in snow. This promised to be the flood of the century.

In late April, Manitobans watched television footage of Grand Forks, south of the border, utterly devastated by the height of the water—the highest they'd ever seen. The dikes at Grand Forks had been useless, and fires rampaged through the downtown core. The Canadian Forces had already moved into Manitoba, prepared to build dikes and rescue

WINNIPEG, 1997
Most of the city was protected by a dike system. For the remainder, sandbag walls had to be built.

people and livestock, when the province declared a state of emergency on April 22. The Forces mounted "Operation Assistance." With 7000 troops, it was the largest military action since Korea.

While Southern Manitobans evacuated, Winnipeggers looked nervously at their floodway. Hydrology engineer, Ron Richardson, had noticed a gap in the flood protection which would allow a deluge of the size they were anticipating to flood into the La Salle watershed. The homes of 100 000 people were in danger.

SUBMERGED FARMLAND

Wayne Jorgenson heads out in a boat to check on his family farm near Morris, Manitoba.

ALAIN ROLLIN OF THE 22ND INFANTRY CHECKS A DIKE

(opposite page, top) 10 000 human and some mechanical "sandbaggers" filled the 6.5 million bags of sand to stave off the rising Red River.

THE TROOPS ROLL IN

(opposite page, bottom, right and left) Winnipegers braved the rain to cheer on troops from Quebec who helped during the flood. It was the largest troop deployment since Korea.

Hearing Richardson's prediction, authorities hurried to the scene. The floodway's existing dike system would have to be extended, but there was not much time. The Morris River to the south was already flowing backwards, pushed by the Red's floodwaters. A conventional elevation survey mapping out the best dike route over the highest ground would have taken weeks. A private company, Pollock & Wright, offered to do it in a day. They covered the area by truck, a satellite dish mounted on its roof, taking elevation readings from a geostationary satellite. They chose a zigzag route and by the next morning, work had begun.

Incredibly, the Brunkild Z-dike, 24 kilometres (15 mi.) long, was built in under a week. Heavy equipment bulldozed farmers' fields, hauled limestone, and dropped monstrous sandbags into place. A breakwater was built of old school buses.

Winnipeg was bracing for the worst. Most of the city was protected by about 120 kilometres (75 mi.) of "primary dike." The rest would require sandbags. In January, Winnipeg Mayor Susan Thompson had ordered a million sandbags. In April, she ordered a million more. The sand pit was north of the city, near Birds Hill, where 10 000 volunteers, many of them students, filled the bags. The city also owned two Sandbaggers, twelve-armed machines invented by Manitoban Guy Bergeron. With a crew of fifty people, a Sandbagger could fill, tie and load 7000 bags an hour. In the end, Winnipeg would use 6.5 million bags of sand.

Prime Minister Jean Chrétien showed up to throw a ceremonial sandbag on the Scotia Street dike, before returning to Ottawa and calling a general election. In the midst of crisis, Manitobans were outraged. Campaigning and voting were last on their lists of priorities. Leader of the Reform Party, Preston Manning, satirically suggested the government provide inflatable polling booths.

The water crested on May 1, well below the capacities of the primary diking system. A frenzy of media reports, focusing on breached dikes, rumours, and personal accounts of trauma, blurred the larger picture: Winnipeg was sheltered by its defences. Towns up the valley were safe behind their ring dikes. Only 28 000 people had been moved from their homes, and most as a precautionary measure. In short, Manitoba was victorious.

The media attention did, however, kindle generosity across the country. As the main relief agency, the Red Cross received $10 million in corporate donations, while the Salvation Army received $4 million. Contributions also flowed in from individuals, with the victims of the 1996 Saguenay Floods in Quebec proving particularly generous. Peter Gzowski, in his last season with CBC Radio's Morningside show, staged a national benefit concert raising $1.5 million. Winnipeg-born actor, Tom Jackson, organized the Red River Relief concert, involving the talents of Burton Cummings, Randy Bachman, and many others, to raise $2 million for flood relief.

Manitoba has recovered from its battle with the flood of the century. Now the province has to decide if the benefits of more extensive measures of protection—extending the floodway south to the American border, for example—outweigh their construction costs. Flooding is a cyclical phenomenon, and 1997's water heights may not be seen again for another hundred years. Anything lower than these levels may now seem manageable. But should the Red rise higher, to the level of the first-recorded floods or beyond, Manitoba's fight to stay the sea may yet be lost.

Montreal's Chaboillez Square, 1887

High River, Alberta, 1942

SWOLLEN RIVERS

Scrapbook of Flooded Cities and Towns

BOW RIVER FLOODS, CALGARY, ALBERTA

LETHBRIDGE, ALBERTA, 1902

TORONTO, ONTARIO'S DON RIVER
SPLIT THE CITY, 1918

NORTH SASKATCHEWAN RIVER,
EDMONTON, ALBERTA, 1915

SAGUENAY FLOOD, JULY 1996

Chicoutimi, Quebec, one of several towns besieged by the 1996 floods. A cyclonic depression stalled over the Saguenay-Lac-Saint-Jean area, dumping torrential rain onto already saturated soil. Over 28 centimetres (11 in.) of rain fell within hours, bursting dikes and overpowering dams.

SAGUENAY DELUGE

Saguenay-Lac-Saint-Jean Region, Quebec

JULY 20, 1996

It was only rain. But there was a lot of it. A large low-pressure system had sucked up waters of the Caribbean, and was dumping them into the waterways that feed into Quebec's Saguenay River and Lac Saint Jean. In fifty hours, as much rain fell as was normal in the whole month of July. The area's silty, clay-like soil—legacy of the ancient Laflamme Sea—was already saturated by two weeks of wet weather. From the runoff, ditches were forged, then ravines that turned from streams to torrents. Reservoirs filled to capacity, dikes eroded into mud slides, and throughout the region, swollen rivers began to tear at cliffsides, bridges and homes.

As water levels rose, people fled, some just barely getting out in time. Though no one drowned in the raging waters, ten people died in the clay slides created by the torrents. Living a kilometre (0.6 mi.) from the Ha! Ha! River in La Baie, the Paquet-Garceau family lost two children to a deluge of mud in their basement. Their home, like many of those destroyed by the floods, had been built on unstable land. City planners had known for decades that the land was not safe but they had caved in to developers. By July 22, 488 homes had been destroyed, 1230 damaged, and 16 000 people evacuated from the area.

An inquiry into the flood found that the region's web of dams and dikes, set up to harness the maximum energy from the water's flow, was poorly maintained. Recommendations were made to update floodgates, lower reservoir levels and ensure the integrity of dams and dikes. The commission also suggested halting all construction in zones likely to be flooded within twenty years. But with our altered climate and more erratic weather patterns, some scientists doubt that any of the recommendations will be enough to avert future catastrophes.

THE POWER OF FLOODWATERS
A road through Chicoutimi is under repair.

BURIN PENINSULA

Residents of the Burin Peninsula felt the earthquake. Once their initial fears had eased, most people returned to everyday affairs, unaware that a "tidal wave" was on its way.

THE TSUNAMI

Burin Peninsula, Newfoundland

NOVEMBER 18, 1929

At 5:15 p.m. on November 18, 1929, a violent tremble shook the southern shores of Newfoundland. It startled those who lived in the hardy settlements clinging to the cliffs of the Burin Peninsula. Merchant George Bartlett and all his assistants rushed out of his Burin shop, deafened by a roar, the shop's contents tumbling about their shoulders as they ran. And then it was over, leaving no damage. *"People gathered in little knots,"* Bartlett said, *"And discussed the occurrence, and went home to their tea. That night the moon rose with its silvery light and it died out calm, not a ripple on the water."*

The tremor baffled everyone. Nineteen-year-old Pat Antle of Fox Cove thought it was an aeroplane, until the noise became too terrifying. Some, remembering Halifax, believed a munitions ship had blown up along the coast. This seemed the best explanation.

It was the first earthquake that the Burin Peninsula residents had ever felt. It measured 7.2 on the Richter scale and its epicentre was 560 kilometres (350 mi.) south of St. John's in the Atlantic Ocean.

Once the initial fear had eased, most people put the tremor out of their minds, returning to the details of their evening meals and closing shop. The evening was still. But in the ocean to the south, the shifting earth had cast an enormous tsunami shoreward, its energy invincible. It would slow a little on approaching the coast, only to build dramatically in the shallows.

Shortly after 7:00 p.m., two hours after the tremor, people in the village of St. Lawrence observed the water in their harbour, normally ten

GREAT BURIN, BEFORE THE TSUNAMI
Wooden homes and structures stood no chance against the massive wave.

metres (33 ft.) deep, draining out towards the sea until the harbour floor was visible. Many panicked, and raced to higher ground.

When the wave hit shore, it crushed with a stealthy, grasping power from below. It tore apart the sea bed, ripped boats from their moorings, destroyed wharves and stages, and lifted houses from foundations. In St. Lawrence alone, 31 buildings were dragged away. The water rose to thirty metres (99 ft.).

George Bartlett, playing cards aboard the steamer *Daisy* in Burin's harbour, was alerted by a sailor who yelled that the town was sinking. Rushing onto deck, Bartlett saw entire buildings swallowed by the sea. The *Daisy* was floating up over the wharf, the dark waters around her an unbelievable soup of bobbing houses and wreckage. After several minutes, the ship was dumped onto the wharf, and the men climbed down. Bartlett waded ashore to find that his shop, in a building at least nine metres (30 ft.) high, had vanished. He found it eventually, far inland, resting in a meadow. Its well-stocked winter provisions were unharmed.

Five-year-old Pearl Brushett was already in bed when the wave came to the beach in Kelly's Cove. By the time her mother woke Pearl and her sister, their house was grounded on the other side of the harbour. The water was barely visible for all of the debris. A second wave thundered in and washed the house, water lapping at the kitchen window, back to the beach at Kelly's Cove. Pearl's mother smashed the parlour window so she could pull her five children from the house to higher ground.

Marion Kelly, aged thirteen, of Kelly's Cove, was working on her English homework when she heard the water's roar. It was a mountain slowly moving towards her. With a burst of adrenaline, Marion grabbed her three-year-old brother and jumped the fence behind the house. She turned to see her mother make it to the yard, only to be washed away with the house, and everything else near it. Her mother, younger sister and home were never seen again. *"It took everything when it came,"* she said. Marion's father had been out in the woods, gathering the winter's wood supply. He knew nothing of his loss until he returned one week later to a vacant lot.

Pat Antle tells the story of one man who was overtaken by the wave and dragged inland, nearly drowning. Clinging to a floating chicken coop, he was pulled back out to the harbour. As he was carried out to sea, the man saw a house on the water with its second storey windows just above the waves. He swam to it, smashed the window with his fist, and climbed in. A frightened cat leapt to his shoulders. It was his own cat. He was standing in his own bedroom.

PEARL BRUSHETT

Five-year-old Pearl Brushett (bottom right) slept through the tsunami, waking to find her house had floated to the far side of Kelly's Cove.

HOMES WERE TOWED BACK TO SHORE

Swept out to sea, one man swam toward a house, its upper windows bobbing just above the waves. Breaking through a window, he climbed inside, only to discover he was in his own home.

**PORT AU BRAS AFTER
THE 1929 TSUNAMI**

*The water rose to thirty
metres (the height of a ten-
storey building), tearing out
entire sections of villages.
Port Au Bras was one of the
most severely afflicted, losing
ten homes, all wharves and
most of the winter provisions.
Papers reported: "There are
not 5 barrels of flour in the
place and no coal."*

The tsunami reached the communities of Fortune and Grand Bank, but sheltered by Fortune Bay, they were only mildly disturbed. The wave also struck
Cape Breton, Nova Scotia, drowning one person, and it frightened French residents on the islands of St. Pierre and Miquelon without wreaking too much
havoc. But to Newfoundland's Burin Peninsula, the effects were crushing. Along
the 113 kilometres (70 mi.) of coastline, the sea took 28 lives, over 100 fishing
boats and 26 schooners, and destroyed about 500 buildings. In total, the tsunami
would affect ten thousand people in 40 settlements.
The earthquake had, as *The Globe and Mail* reported:

> *threshed the bed of the Atlantic with sufficient force to sever ten of
> the twenty-one cables connecting the Eastern and Western
> Hemispheres.*

In Burin's greatest need, all communication with the outside world had been
cut, and at a time when no road linked it to the rest of the province. The people
could send no S.O.S. When the wave receded, dumbfounded survivors had to
improvise their own rescue teams, striking out in remaining skiffs and dories to
search for relatives and neighbours. As they scoured the debris, a fierce storm
blew in, pummelling the little vessels with gale-force winds, dropping temperatures, and lashing the bereft villages with sleet and snow.

There was an occasional miracle. Rescuers came across a house, still intact
and bobbing in the harbour. A kerosene lamp was still alight in its second-storey
window. Inside they found an unharmed sleeping baby. On the first floor, the
baby's mother and three siblings had drowned.

The people of the peninsula, isolated and storm-battered, reached out to
neighbours, providing food and comfort. Dorothy Cherry, an English nurse who

ran the dispensary in Lamaline, was determined to reach all the victims of the peninsula. Beginning in her home village, she worked her way along the shore, braving the storm, to Burin. When her horse could no longer carry her, she continued on foot, at times wading through freezing streams where bridges had been swept away. "*Our Florence Nightingale*," they called her.

It was Thursday morning, two days after the tsunami, when the coastal steamer, *Portia*, made a scheduled stop at Burin's altered port. The waterfront was piled high with wreckage, and a flood of stories finally found an outside ear. A wireless message to St. John's brought help from the SS *Meigle*, loaded with doctors, nurses, blankets and food. Nurse Dorothy Cherry was one of the first to be picked up, numb with cold and near collapse.

Pearl Brushett remembers her ten-year-old brother Fred weathering the two-day storm in girls' dresses retrieved from wreckage on the beach. It would be months before their cuts from the broken parlour window healed, and years before little Pearl's nightmares would cease. Mrs. Brushett lived the rest of her life with the noise of the sea roaring in her head. The family watched as their house was towed back to Kelly's Cove where it would be used as a fish store. Most of the other buildings taken by the wave were gone for good. Many families in the forty villages were left destitute, having lost their season's catch, food, coal, fishing gear, boats and, in some cases, homes and families.

In St. John's, the South Coast Disaster Committee raised $250 000 for a survival fund. The aid proved indispensable, for the lacerated ocean floor yielded meagre crops in the Depression years to come.

TRUCKS OF THE SOUTH COAST DISASTER COMMITTEE
Funds raised by the St. John's committee proved indispensable. Not only had the towns along the Burin Peninsula been damaged, but their fishing grounds were also ravaged.

DESTRUCTIVE EFFECTS OF WIND EROSION

Clearing the land of vegetation coupled with years of drought and snowless winters left rich topsoil at the mercy of the winds.

BREAD BASKET TO DUST BOWL

Alberta, Manitoba, Saskatchewan

THE 1930s DROUGHT

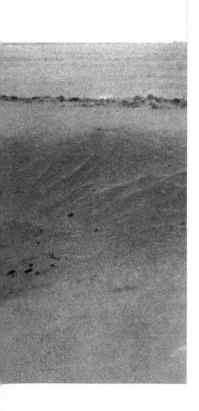

It would never be viable as farm land. Explorer John Palliser covered the vast, central tract of Canada in 1857—its dust, scorching wind and sparse brush—and prepared his report. Palliser's Triangle, from today's Lethbridge, Alberta, across to Melita, Manitoba and to an apex north of Saskatoon, Saskatchewan, should not be farmed, he advised. But the Dominion's founding dreamers saw things in a different light. This land was a bridge from one half of the nation to the other, and it needed to be settled.

At the end of the nineteenth century, millions of homesteading acres in the Triangle were handed out to settlers from America, Ontario and Eastern Europe. Used to farming well-watered soil, they were unfamiliar with this new land. With luck and timely rains, there were good years mixed with bad, and the settlers kept flowing in until the rains stopped in 1930. Palliser was right. The land dried out completely and the driest, foulest weather was only just beginning.

The catastrophe was not just environmental. The New York Stock Exchange had plunged in October, 1929, destabilizing the entire continent. Then a shattering collapse in world commodity prices made a mockery of world trade and capital. Butter prices fell to 10 cents a pound and chickens to 23 cents each. In the mid-1920s, more than 70 percent of Prairie wheat was exported to international markets, bringing in over $1 a bushel. By 1932, it had dropped to 35 cents. After paying transportation costs, those who managed to coax a crop from the parched earth were left with nothing.

The nation was focusing on other things: grasshopper plagues in the plains states; floods in China killing thousands; the Japanese invasion of Manchuria; and every city in North America sagging under lay-offs, pay cuts and relief rolls. Then suddenly, on August 1, 1931, a Red Cross appeal dominated headlines: "*125 000 destitute families need food and clothing on the prairies.*" Canada shifted its focus to its own central provinces.

191

DUNES COVER A FORMER FARM

The dust was so pervasive that people turned their car headlights on during the day to penetrate the brown haze. (Below) Gravel roads were layered with sand.

Not only had the wheat crops failed, but also the fodder crops for live-stock. Most of the farmers in Saskatchewan were on some form of relief. Canadians sent hundreds of tons of clothing, bolts of flannelette, coats, boots and children's clothing, both new and used. Hundreds of hand-knitted socks arrived from Ontario and the Maritimes. One church in Brussels, Ontario sent 57 000 pounds of fruits and vegetables. A great quantity of salted cod arrived from the East Coast, although most Prairie families had no idea how to prepare it. All through the 1930s, any extra food or supplies were sent to the Palliser Triangle. It would be needed desperately, for the worst was still germinating.

In order to sow seed, farmers had pulled up the fibrous roots of natural prairie plants and burned off the stubble. The earth simply blew away, drifting into dunes. In the snowless winters of those years, strong westerly winds whipped the soil into black blizzards. In the spring, gusting sand cut through growing grain, slicing it off at the ground. The soil eventually became the texture of fine flour, and any rare, harsh rain further exposed it to erosion. The dust was all pervasive. The people ate it, drank it, wore it and slept in it. They turned their car headlights on during the day to penetrate the brown haze. Some days they couldn't see across the road. The soil blew from bad field to good, suffocating any struggling, viable crops. Unable to fight after three successive crop failures, depressed and dusty families walked off their farms, drifting into urban centres and unemployment.

The abandoned land became the incubating grounds for the decade's most destructive pest: the grasshopper. Swarming up on the winds from the south,

the sun blood-red behind their wings, the grasshoppers bred in fantastic numbers. They would land, devour everything in sight, and move on. They returned year after year to chew through clothes on wash lines, shirts on farmers' backs, pitchfork handles, brooms, and even the roots of plants deep in the soil. When, by some miracle, grasshopper damage was light and crops had enough moisture to grow, the wheat would be destroyed by something else: wheat stem rust, sawflies, wireworms, or abusive hail.

Hardship stacked up against the people. D.B. McRea of the Regina *Leader Post*, and R.M. Scott of the *Winnipeg Free Press*, trailed across southern Saskatchewan in 1934, reporting on farming. In many households, lard pails had replaced worn out kettles, cardboard replaced broken windows, clothes were patched, then patches patched, and children had no shoes. Decrepit farm machinery was wired together, and many farmers used the Bennett Buggy—a car pulled by a team of horses—for transportation.

The frigid winters kept families living in their kitchens, crowded around their stoves. With no money to pay teachers, schools were closed. Only the need to search out food or fuel could make a farmer leave his kitchen. In spite of pitiful conditions, McRae and Scott spoke of a buoyant faith that good rain would return. Fields were prepared for the following year, livestock and machinery carefully attended to, and optimism endured.

Poverty also fanned invention. Dependent on their radios to connect them with the outside world, some farmers designed wind-powered chargers for their batteries. Many wells had gone dry and families hauled water from the lakes. They conserved every drop. Bath water was kept for washing vegetables and clothes before it was poured onto straggling gardens. James Gray, a reporter for the *Winnipeg Free Press*, met two little boys on a farm whose most thrilling memory was taking a bath in a rain barrel. One boy told him:

> *We'd jump in and get wet and come out and put soap on and jump in! Boy! My dad says if it rains again this summer, we can do it again. We sure hope it rains, don't we Bobby?*

The boys' mother was proud to serve her guests real coffee instead of "coffee" made from roasted barley seeds which most farmers used. Otherwise, her kitchen offered the standard Prairie diet. Gopher stew was a staple for most families. Since the scrawny rodents were both plentiful and a threat to crops,

GRASSHOPPER PLAGUES

Grasshoppers often flew in clouds so thick they obscured the sun. They devoured fields, biting the wheat shaft in the juiciest part, just below the head. When food became scarce they could be seen chewing paint off wood.

DESTITUTE FAMILY

Many families abandoned their farms and moved to cities in search of work. One paper reported that 125 000 Prairie families were destitute and needed food and clothing. Saskatchewan's total provincial income plummeted 90 percent in only two years.

they were also smoked, pickled, breaded and fried, and baked in pies. Some spoke of year-long, unbroken diets of potatoes, eggs and milk, spiced up now and then, with leafy weeds, the only greenery around. Nothing was wasted. Butter and beef-tallow doubled as axle grease, while buffalo dung and stinkweed seeds made stove fuel.

With almost nothing to farm and mass unemployment in the cities, it was another challenge to find amusement and occupy the long days. Horseshoe tournaments, baseball tournaments and picnics were frequently arranged and well attended. On weekend nights, each tiny, deserted schoolhouse was emptied of its desks, its windows rattling to dancing feet and a local fiddler. During this period, people read books more than before. The Wheat Pool library lent every book on its shelves, including political pamphlets and publications. Political meetings, filled with locals desperate for distraction, became rousing, lengthy, shouting matches. Politicians were assailed by pointed questions from patched, dusty and thoroughly-informed farmers.

So extreme was 1936, so filled with horrors and trials, that further hardship could scarcely have been contemplated. The relentless winter was the coldest on record. Howling blizzards immobilized the countryside, battering the threadbare farms. The cattle had nothing left to eat. Many suffered from "hardware disease"—they'd been eating doorknobs and gate hinges. Cattle carcasses littered the ranches in the spring. The record-breaking summer heat that followed brought squadrons of army and cut worms. Dozens of people died of heat prostration. The soil drifts were ten feet high. While the horses died of sleeping sickness, polio threatened humans.

1937 was no better. A black winter, devoid of any flakes of moisture, led into spring dust storms and near hurricanes in summer, the worst in thirty years. The government stepped in, shipping starving cattle to northern Alberta and Manitoba where there was feed available. In Minton, Saskatchewan, even the chickens ate relief feed. There was nothing for them to scratch from the earth. Lake Johnston, south of Moose Jaw, dried up and white alkali dust from the lake bed coated the plains with a sickly pallor. The furnace-like winds sucked every drop of water out of Fife Lake, near Rockglen, and The Lake of the Rivers evaporated, exposing a cemetery of buffalo bones several feet deep. Local farmers ground it up as fertilizer, their only good cash crop of the decade.

July 5, 1937 brought farmers to the precipice. It was the hottest day ever recorded—43-45 degrees Celsius (109-113 degrees Farenheit) all over the Triangle. How much more could these people take?

Then, on July 16, 1937, the drought ended. Heavy clouds split open over southern Saskatchewan and it rained and rained, filling ditches, drowning roads and drenching the earth's cracked wounds. A billion Russian thistle seeds sprang to life, sprouting carpets of green across the countryside. The Dirty Thirties delivered a few last blows to the Palliser Triangle—a vicious winter storm, an infestation of wheat stem rust and the worst known grasshopper plague in 1938—but these were the final convulsions of a dying phenomenon. In 1939, a respectable crop of wheat was produced.

It had been a decade of the greatest misery and widespread privation, and yet it nurtured a bumper crop of human triumphs. The Dominion Experimental Farms system, set up in the 1880s, performed its finest work in the 1930s. Striving to find the best farming methods for the area, trying any farmer's ideas or inventions, the Experimental Farms catalogued and dispensed all useful findings throughout the region.

C.S. Noble, a farmer north of Lethbridge, with the help of the Experimental Farms, invented the Noble Blade. This simple, shallow blade could cut weeds off at the root, just beneath the soil, without disturbing their structure above ground, which held the soil in place. Summer-fallowing, the practice of using two years' precipitation to grow one crop, was perfected for dry-land farming. The Swift Current Experimental Farm, under Gordon

LINING UP FOR RELIEF
(Above) A line of horse-drawn wagons stretches to the horizon as farmers wait for relief trains from the East. (Below) Farmers moving off the land in portable homes.

"ON TO OTTAWA TREK"

Frustrated by six years of hardship, unemployed strikers from western Canada boarded trains for Ottawa to confront Prime Minister R.B. Bennett. The trek was halted in Regina where 2000 men clashed with police, sparking the Regina Riot.

Taggart and his team of scientists, was the first to exchange steel tractor tires, which pulverized topsoil, with the fat, gentle airplane tires used today. And at Swift Current, a new reaper and thresher—the combine harvester—was put to the test.

BREAD FROM ONTARIO

Most Saskatchewan farmers were on some form of relief.

Entomologists also made their mark. Normon Criddle, who grew up on a farm near Brandon, Manitoba, worked out how to bait and poison grasshoppers, and the Criddle Mixture became a world-wide pestilence solution.

It was a struggle, but Canada's link from East to West was established. Cross-fenced community pastures, dams, irrigation schemes and new farming methods have changed the complexion of the Prairies. Never again will drought conditions be so catastrophic for Prairie populations. The dust bowl inhabitants of the 1930s were scarred by their experience, but through their remarkable endurance and ingenuity, their hope was transformed into technology that is still used to combat the encroaching deserts of the planet.

DEMONSTRATING AGAINST THE POLICIES OF THE R.B. BENNETT GOVERNMENT

Unemployed workers protest against Prime Minister R.B. Bennett. His inaction failed to bring relief to out-of-work Canadians during the Great Depression. The man wearing the top hat is dressed like Bennett, mocking him for his lack of rapport with the common people.

THE HOLLAND MARSH FLOODED BY HURRICANE HAZEL

*The Holland Marsh, a farming community about thirty miles north of
Toronto, was completely flooded. A marooned family is shown circled.*

HURRICANE HAZEL

Southern Ontario

OCTOBER 15, 1954

The official weather forecast was mildly interesting. Issued Friday evening, October 15, 1954, the forecast warned that Hurricane Hazel was heading north from the Carolina Coast towards Lake Ontario, but so depleted, she could no longer be classified as a true hurricane.

This weakening storm will continue northward, said the Dominion Public Weather Office, passing just east of Toronto before midnight. The main rainfall associated with it should end shortly thereafter, with occasional light rain occurring throughout the night.

After days of rain, what was one more night? The people of southern Ontario continued with their regular Friday night routine. Kenneth Gibbs kept up his deliveries in the west end of Toronto despite being lifted off the ground by the gusting wind. His last client's driveway had been completely washed away by the rain. Gibbs watched as cars floated around a nearby parking lot. That night, passengers on buses opened their umbrellas to keep the rain, driving through closed windows, from soaking them. One bus had to open its doors to let the water out after driving through a gully. On some Toronto streets, the storm covers had given way to 1.2-metre (4-ft.) geysers. This was no ordinary rainstorm.

To Ontarians, a hurricane was a southern storm, with palm trees bending to the ground and angry seas lashing tropical shores. And that's just how Hazel began, taking 500 lives as she swept across Haiti and the eastern coast of the United States. As it pushed inland, the storm's fury diminished, but it still carried a punch, its screaming 88-kilometre-per-hour (55-mph) winds, gusting to 116 kilometres per hour (72 mph). To make things worse, Hazel's warm air collided with a cold front, dumping billions of gallons of rain on land that was

199

HUMBER RIVER

Torrential waters carved away the river bank leaving houses clinging to the shoreline.

already saturated. The little creeks and streams of the Humber watershed soon became raging torrents. No one mentioned battening down hatches, or filling bath tubs with emergency water. People were out with their children, as usual.

Driving home, Gerald Elliot was crossing a bridge over the Humber River when both banks suddenly washed away. Firefighters found him stranded on the precarious structure and threw him a hose. Gerald tied it around his waist, but it broke as they pulled him through the violent current, and Gerald was swept away. He reached out and grabbed a slender willow tree, clinging there for the next four hours until the brave and skillful Max Hurley rescued him in a small boat.

In their home on the Holland Marsh, the de Peuter family's flood preparation included buying extra candles and stacking furniture on tables. Mr. de Peuter nailed the back door shut, and as the water level rose outside, the whole house was afloat. The lights stayed on until the hydro wires snapped, freeing the house to sail all over the Marsh, bumping into barns and poles, and spinning in the currents. One young son became seasick. At dawn the winds were lighter and the house became tangled in, of all things, a floating field of carrots. The family was evacuated by canoe. On the Holland Marsh alone, 465 families lost everything that night.

Individual police and fire departments around the region raced out into the night to help, aided by armed forces and volunteers. But, at the time, no civil body existed to coordinate crisis response at the local level. On their own initiative, and to their credit, rescuers searched out people in need.

In dramatic rescues, Toronto firefighters extended their aerial ladders almost horizontally. *The Globe and Mail* described some incidents: "*With Captain (Fred) Rose perched far out on the tip, the aerial lifted two small children through a second floor bedroom window, pulled a hysterical woman from a tree when she was up to her neck in water, grabbed a motorist just as his car was sucked out from under him.*"

While trying to rescue three youths trapped in the Humber River on their car, a fire truck was pulled down into the water, four firefighters clinging to its sides. A fifth, Frank Mercer, clung to a sapling in the raging current. Policemen arriving at the scene formed a human chain out into the water. Detective Greer was within arm's distance of Mercer when a large wave dragged the firefighter out of reach and into darkness. Inching towards the fire truck, which was lodged downstream, the policemen hurled a rope to the firefighters. It fell short. As the human chain struggled closer, the fire truck was turned over in the waves. Its four occupants, weakened and weighed down by their heavy suits, were drowned.

From their Island Road home in Long Branch, the Thorpe family handed four-month-old Nancy to a fireman who ferried her to a safer home. Returning for the family, the fireman found the house was gone, carried off by a raging Etobicoke Creek. The baby was handed from one person to another, balanced on rooftops, until she reached the arms of 16-year-old Sylvia Jones, who kept her warm for several hours. Nancy Thorpe was eventually taken to St. Joseph's Hospital, where she lay unidentified for some time before being found by her grandparents.

Farmer Jackson Glassford and his son spent hours trying to reach four people who were clinging to their floating car near Beeton. When Glassford finally sent a small boat close enough to rescue them, it capsized beneath their weight and the four drowned in the currents.

HIGHWAY 400 WASHOUT

The highway vanished into the Holland Marsh, cutting traffic off along this major thoroughfare.

CAR SWEPT MILES
This Chevrolet was torn from its garage, and found nearly 5 kilometres (3 mi.) away wrapped around a tree.

One family in Woodbridge spent the entire night waiting for help, standing on their verandah railing. Another Woodbridge man spent the night snatching up drowning pets as they spun past his front porch. He rescued 27 cats and 14 dogs.

Later, a Transport Canada study revealed that since 1900, 25 such tropical storms had passed over or near Ontario. None were as memorable as Hurricane Hazel. Almost 23 centimetres (9 in.) of rain had fallen on the Humber Valley over 48 hours. The Highland Creek, Don River, Humber River, Etobicoke Creek, Credit River and Sixteen Mile Creek all burst their banks. Over twenty bridges were destroyed. The Humber River washed away 17 homes on Raymore Drive killing 36 people. A Woodbridge trailer camp was left in chaos, with twenty people dead. The official death toll was 81.

The storm's forces had been concentrated yet random. While many fled their homes and fought for their lives, others slept soundly, completely oblivious to the nearby destruction. They awoke to fantastical reports of devastation in next-door neighbourhoods. People shovelled rivers of mud from their houses. Others found bodies in the trees, or half-buried in mud on the river banks. Some people were still huddled on the roofs of their homes, drenched and exhausted.

GRIM SEARCH
Volunteers search for bodies. The hurricane's devastation was selective. Those badly hit shovelled rivers of mud from their houses. Others found bodies in the trees, or half-buried in mud along the riverbanks. Eighty-one people died.

Once the water had receded, Frank and Mary Wakeman of Weston returned to their new home. In her book, *Hurricane Hazel*, Betty Kennedy relates their story: *"There was a telephone pole through our front window, golf clubs on the table inside, and various pieces of silver and china scattered throughout the house—* none of which were ours. On our front lawn was a two-storey house broken in half."* They were touched by the overwhelming generosity of neighbours and strangers, and stunned when looters took everything remotely salvageable, including plants from their garden.

The Salvation Army and Red Cross brought aid and assistance, joined by the Molson's Brewery Limited Mobile Emergency Unit from Montreal. Equipped with a first-aid station and operating room, kitchen, and radio room, the Mobile Unit stationed itself between Toronto and Bradford, giving Typhoid inoculations to hundreds of residents.

Major General Frank Worthington, long-time advocate for civil defence, toured the stricken area in the following days. He had nothing but praise for the Red Cross, Salvation Army and for the ingenuity and courage shown by individuals and organizations who helped out in the crisis. Worthington lamented the shameful waste of life and property, made significantly worse by the absence of an emergency response team.

It was not until 1974 that the Government of Canada created Emergency Preparedness Canada, a civilian branch of the Department of National Defense. Its mission: to safeguard lives and reduce damage to property by fostering better preparedness for emergencies in Canada.

LIFE OVERTURNED

Hazel destroyed homes and left a swath of destruction and mayhem.

LABOUR-INTENSIVE CLEAN UP

Hundreds of produce crates had to be gathered from lake-like farmland.

DIGGING FOR VICTIMS, MARCH 4, 1910

Rescuers burrow into the mountain of snow to save 62 railway workers buried by the Rogers Pass avalanche. Six hundred men worked to excavate the site. Many were volunteers from mining and logging camps, some walking three miles through the snowstorm to help.

AVALANCHE

Rogers Pass, British Columbia

MARCH 4, 1910

It had been a brutal season. Slide after slide had battered Rogers Pass. Nine days of thick snow and rain had left a heavy snowpack barely clinging to the sheer peaks. Then a March 4 storm pounded the slopes of Cheops Mountain, until, with a rumble, the snow lost its grip, hurtling down into Rogers Pass. The avalanche uprooted trees, grabbing boulders as it flew. It narrowly missed a passenger train inching through the stormy pass, dumping seven metres (23 ft.) of snow and debris right behind it.

A crew quickly arrived to clear the railway tracks. With Conductor R.J. Buckley in charge, the huge blades of the rotary plough churned an indent in the snow. When branches and roots blocked its progress, a shovel gang went in with saws and picks.

The men forged along the tracks, walls of hard-packed snow rising to six and half metres (21 ft.) on either side. The storm still raged above their heads, but the men were sheltered in the cut. They knew that the slide had cleared Cheops Mountain of danger, and that the opposite slope was too heavily timbered to launch an avalanche. They were making good time.

Foreman Johnny Anderson left the men hard at work and trudged for a mile or so in the storm to find a phone. He called Revelstoke to say the railway tracks would be clear within two hours. As Anderson came back along the tracks towards his crew, he became disoriented. The lantern lights were gone. The beam of the plough had disappeared. Running forward, Anderson saw no cut, no people, no plough or engine, only snow. Hearing weak cries, he stumbled towards them. On a parallel track, in the broken timbers of a snowshed, he found fireman William Lachance, cold and battered.

Somehow, the rush of air that preceded the avalanche hurled Lachance upwards, and despite internal injuries, a broken leg and lacerations, he was

BIRD'S—EYE VIEW OF ROGERS PASS

(Above) Rogers Pass and Hermit Range from the summit of Mount Abbott, Glacier, B.C. (Top right) Men struggle to dig out the rotary plow and its driver in the 1910 avalanche.

able to pull himself out of a deep burial. Foreman Anderson wrapped Lachance in his coat. There was no sign of the other 62 men. Anderson began the long walk back to the telephone for help.

At midnight, Revelstoke's fire bell clanged out an urgent call. Two hundred of the town's inhabitants responded—doctors, nurses and other volunteers—and they were soon aboard a relief train, climbing through the storm toward the pass. They arrived as dawn was filtering through the falling snow. Nothing of the railway could be seen.

As rescuers burrowed into the mountain of snow, more volunteers arrived from nearby mining and logging camps. A trainload of men from the town of Golden had to walk the last five kilometres (3 mi.) through the storm. By mid-day, the avalanche site was crawling with 600 digging and shovelling men.

What they found astonished them: the shovel gang was deep in the hard-packed snow of the original cut; all were dead, and most were upright, frozen in action. One worker was bent over a shovel. Others still held picks raised above their heads. One was rolling a cigarette. Three foremen were found standing together, as if still chatting, one with his pipe in his hand. In a flash, the avalanche had simply packed them all in ice.

The engine, weighing 150 tonnes (165 tons), had been overturned and wrecked. And the 100-tonne (110-ton) plough had been lifted out of the cut and thrown to the nearby snowshed. Some of the men had been swept into Bear Creek chasm along with 457 metres (1500 ft.) of snow. Four bodies were discovered there two months later.

The fireman, William Lachance, was bundled up and hauled on a toboggan 5 kilometres (3 mi.) to Glacier Station, where he was put on a train for Revelstoke. A telegraph message was sent ahead, warning that Lachance, the only survivor, was not expected to survive the journey. At each section house en route, people gathered to wish him well. Lachance pulled through.

Along with the lives of 62 men, all confidence in the pass' safety was swept away in the avalanche of 1910. Work began on Connaught Tunnel which, by 1916, bored eight kilometres (5 mi.) through Mount MacDonald, its double tracks safe within the solid rock.

ROTARY PLOUGH

When the rotary plough seized up, caught on trees and roots, the shovel gang moved in to clear the first avalanche. As they worked, a second avalanche buried them.

WINTER SCENE NIAGARA FALLS

Mound of ice at the base of the Falls. Conditions in 1938 produced enough ice to destroy the Falls View Bridge.

BRIDGE IN RUINS

The famous Falls View Bridge over the Niagara Gorge ("Honeymoon Bridge"), felled by the 1938 ice jam.

"Honeymoon Bridge" Victim Of Ice

Niagara Falls, Ontario

January 27, 1938

The famous "Honeymoon Bridge" spanning the narrow Niagara Gorge was in trouble. Chunks of ice had been crashing over Niagara Falls forming a giant ice pyramid which, by January 27, 1938, was pressing up on the bridge's underpinnings. The ice jam, about 45 metres (150 ft.) high, was also being forced down to the river's floor, creating an effective dam wall. Water was building up on the Falls side, adding to the pressure on the bridge, and had risen high enough to flood an Ontario Power Company plant and to cake it in ice.

As more floes thundered through the gorge, fusing with the mountain of ice, a handful of men on the U.S. side hacked away at the ice on the bridge with picks and shovels. Tied to the shore in case a sudden shift should sweep them down river, they chipped out fragments of ice, making barely a dent in the mound. Thousands of spectators watched, spellbound, from either side of the river. The ice did not budge and, by the end of the day, the workers were removed from the site.

Rivets were beginning to snap when Douglas and Wesley Styles, aged twelve and thirteen, crept past the guards with a box camera to get a good shot of the spectacle. Suddenly the bridge shuddered. A policeman yelled at the boys who ran to safety just as the structure cracked, and then crumbled, its giant steel bones littering the ice.

By the time the ice pyramid had cleared, freeing up the dammed river several days later, plans were already underway to build a new "honeymoon bridge" for the newlywed traffic into Niagara Falls.

FALLS VIEW BRIDGE, BEFORE ITS COLLAPSE
The bridge, popular with sightseers, linked the twin cities of Niagara Falls.

209

FROZEN WONDERLAND, JANUARY 1998

An unusual combination of weather systems stalled over parts of Quebec, Ontario and the Maritimes, coating the area in ice. With every branch and twig of every tree covered, the air was filled with an intense tinkling sound.

THE ICE STORM

Ontario, Quebec & the Maritimes

JANUARY 5-10, 1998

El Niño reigned, pushing vast volumes of warm water eastward across the Pacific. Warm air hit the land and continued east in low, wet clouds, pelting rain onto the southern United States. A high-pressure mass, stalled over the Atlantic Ocean, forced the warm flow up towards Canada, where it sprawled on top of frigid, Arctic air in the Ottawa and St. Lawrence valleys. When the torrents fell, they shot through the cold so quickly, they had no time to turn to snow. The water droplets held their liquid form, became "supercooled," and hit the earth's cold surfaces, spreading into an impenetrable glaze. It was January 5, 1998, and the Ice Storm had begun.

The weather systems were held in place by the Atlantic's high-pressure wall, and for the next five days, the freezing rain blanketed a patch of the continent in 7-11 centimetres (3-4 in.) of ice. Trees—every branch and twig clattering in the wind like chimes of quartz—split under the oppressive weight, their branches shattering onto the glaze below. Wrist-thick ice coated hydro wires that sagged then snapped, hissing and crackling with electric fury. First utility poles cracked and then transmission towers crumpled, taking out the heat and light. Canadians tucked inside their homes, cut off from the great umbilical cord of power, were forced to accept the fragility of their industrial world.

It was to be the country's most expensive natural disaster. Over 1000 power transmission towers and 30 000 utility poles were destroyed. 1.4 million people in Quebec and 230 000 in Ontario were plunged into darkness for up to 32 days by 3000 kilometres (1865 mi.) of damaged power line. One hundred thousand people sought refuge in shelters. The military deployed 11 000 troops to dispense food and stabilize the chaos.

With roads and sidewalks fit for ice skates, transportation was crippled. Air traffic was delayed or cancelled as de-icing each aircraft took an hour and a

half. Iced switches and debris that was frozen to the tracks interrupted rail service.

In all affected cities, the hospital conditions were alarming. Back-up power was guarded closely to ensure that only necessary equipment was used. Transportation problems eroded staffing, and blood was in very short supply. Emergency departments had to deal with a surge of chest pain complaints caused by emotional stress, and by the strain of trying to clear the wretched ice.

For two million Montrealers, water, light and heat trickled through the last remaining ice-encrusted cable, stretching from James Bay. Officials watched the line all night while the island city teetered on the brink of blackout. Massive evacuation plans were on the table. Workers had instructions to bulldoze buildings in order to contain fires. When some of the broken cables were successfully repaired, the city sighed with relief.

Those without power found themselves in an eerie world of peculiar contradictions. The beauty of the ice, its white, crystal uniformity, belied its menace. It was treacherous to walk on, and lethal when it fell. At least one person was killed by falling ice. People used hammers and shovels to break through the coating on their cars. And yet, just a slight vibration—a human shout or laugh—would be enough to bring great iced branches crashing to the ground. To those without generators, the noises of urban industry were replaced by a softer soundscape. Intense tinkling filled the air until, with the violence of gunshot, a branch would break and crash, shattering fragmented sound across the rink beneath. The nights were almost luminous, brighter than usual, but without electrical definition of towns, cities and roads, those travelling at night felt disoriented and lost.

TOPPLED TOWERS
(Above) Over a thousand power transmission towers crumpled under the weight of the ice. (Top right) Bent tower, St. Constant, Quebec

Electrical appliances sat useless in their freezing kitchens, so Ice Storm victims reverted to old, and invented new methods of survival and of comfort. Families dragged their beds close to the wood stove or fireplace, closing off the rest of their homes. They toasted food on open flames. Mr. Larocque of Limoges, Ontario, used his blowtorch to make coffee. Geoffrey Sharpe fashioned his own barbeque with a President's Choice cookie tin and an old grill, fuelling it with old election signs.

Without telephones, TV, and fuel, the people of eastern Ontario and western Quebec were disconnected from their world. Yet what developed was a new, surprisingly vibrant, human connection. Families, crowded in a single room, had no choice but to interact. Neighbours checked on strangers around them, sharing generators and sump pumps. When Dave Brown, of Chaffeys Locks, installed an oil-fired water heater, he offered his shower to the neighbourhood. Rose Graham offered the wood stoves in her bakery to everyone in Kemptville. Taxi drivers in Kenata volunteered to drive seniors to the shelters. Hotels with power offered greatly reduced rates, and even free rooms to those who were most in need. Generosity welled up and over. Gifts of food flooded in for the armed forces and hydro linemen, toiling for long shifts in the cold. Locals wearing hockey and bicycle helmets slipped over the ice to feed them coffee and homemade muffins.

Opportunists slipped through the cracks, charging extra for essentials like rock salt, wood, and gasoline, and looting stores while alarm systems were disabled. But they were few, and overshadowed by the spirit of cooperation.

DEAD CATTLE AT ST. ALBERT, ONTARIO
Reliant on power for ventilation and heat, many farms suffered heavy losses in the storm.

The Ice Storm was a trial, a disruption and a worry, but to the farmers it was far more than that. Dairy herds required large amounts of water, careful ventilation, and regular milking—all impossible without power. Other provinces donated generators, but with transportation hitches and milk processing plants shut down, more than ten million litres (10.6 million quarts) of milk had to be dumped. One Ontario farmer found 13 of his cows electrocuted by a broken live wire. A farmer in Quebec lost 2200 pigs when

DOWNTOWN MONTREAL IN CHAOS

Clearing the ice from the roads was an impossibility. Motorists faced the dual dangers of slippery surfaces underneath and crashing branches overhead.

both of his generators malfunctioned. 12 000 chickens froze in a hatchery that had no power.

Politicians scrambled to do—and say—the right thing. Prime Minister Jean Chrétien, Quebec Premier Lucien Bouchard and Ontario Premier Mike Harris postponed their trade mission to Latin America, staying in the afflicted areas. In a January 13 radio broadcast, Chrétien announced, *"We know the terrific personal toll this crisis is exacting. We know that individuals and families are being put to extreme tests.... We also know that communities are pulling together as never before. And that this darkness is being lighted by thousands of individual acts of kindness... You are not alone, and you will not be alone as long as you are in need."*

Despite the shelters and support, many people chose to tough out the storm in their own, cold homes. About 25 died in the attempt. Some were overwhelmed by carbon monoxide fumes from poorly-ventilated generators, others by fire when electricity surged into their homes. Some suffered heart attacks while trying to shovel the heavy ice.

As the ice was conquered, and life returned to normal in Quebec, a seed of doubt began to germinate. Premier Bouchard faced a barrage of questions about Hydro-Québec. Why had transmission towers collapsed in such numbers? With better preparation on the part of the utility, could the storm's blows have been softened?

It has been suggested that layoffs at Hydro-Québec, said to have been approximately 5000 over a period of five years, had resulted in inadequate maintenance of the transmission network, and also that high-voltage transmission lines had been raised without supervision by engineers, contrary to accepted industry practice.

A private investigation resulted in a report to one newspaper that the structure of some towers had deteriorated, prompting them to buckle and fall before they had attained the maximum ice load for which they had been designed.

Premier Bouchard established a commission, led by engineer Roger Nicolet, to enquire into relevant details of the power grid, and of emergency preparedness. It is said that the commission lacked jurisdiction to compel testimony or to offer immunity from prosecution to those who testified. It was suggested that the lack of such powers and jurisdiction discouraged testimony from persons who could have assisted the commission. The focus of the commission tended to lean to issues such as emergency communications during the storm, and the social and economic impact of the weather. Those appointed to the commission tended to be from the ranks of former employees of Hydro-Québec and from persons in the employ of the ministry of the provincial government that had responsibility for that utility. Given the size of Hydro-Québec one can understand the difficulty in finding persons experienced in the field, with no connection to the utility, past or present. The report of the commission was brought in at a cost of some $7 million, which was added to the direct cost of the Ice Storm, estimated to be as much as $2 billion.

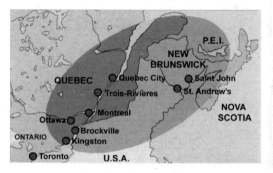

DE-ICING METHODS
(Top) Falling from a warm weather mass through a cold one, the water droplets remained liquid rather than turning to snow. The ice they formed on landing was virtually impenetrable.

STRICKEN AREA
The highlighted oval on the above map shows the area affected by the 1998 storm.

While considered rare, the freakish weather patterns that caused the ice storm havoc could certainly recur. Hydro researchers have been exploring response options for the future. Most of the trauma was caused by the weight of accumulated ice on hydro lines. In Newfoundland, a component snaps the wires free when they are too weighed down, leaving the transmission pole or tower standing. Manitoba warms its lines and melts the ice with extra power. Other options for melting ice include infrared light and lasers. There is also talk of spreading out the sources of supply and creating back-up links. Patching, repairing, improving: all are necessary for our electrically-tenuous lives. For those who believe that our consumerist society dangerously warms the globe with every passing day, increasing the probability of wild and unpredictable weather, different answers must be found. These answers are surely embedded in education, self-accountability, and in finding more sustainable ways to live.

TECHNOLOGY AND HUMAN ERROR

Man errs as long as he strives

Johann Wolfgang von Goethe
"Prologue in Heaven"
from *Faust*, 1808-32

COLLAPSE OF SECOND NARROWS BRIDGE,
VANCOUVER, BRITISH COLUMBIA
JUNE 15, 1958

TRAGIC COLLISION, MEDICINE HAT, ALBERTA, 1908
Three kilometres (2 mi.) east of Medicine Hat an outbound engine hit an incoming passenger train on the Canadian Pacific line killing eleven people.

TECHNOLOGY AND HUMAN ERROR

Part Five

The ruggedness and sheer vastness of Canada's terrain was a challenge to those engineers and labourers who strove to extract its resources, link its territories by rail, and span its many rivers. Railways and bridges were designed and built... and disasters followed. Human error had a role to play—however small—in each of them.

In the 19th and early 20th century, travelling by rail was considered the safest means of transport, moving thousands of people from one end of the country to the other without the fatal mishaps seen in shipping. When a rail disaster hit, human error was usually behind it.

The earliest train wreck occurred in Ontario in 1854, when a passenger express plowed head-first into a locomotive, shunting a load of gravel. The express was seven hours late, and the gravel train, backing along the track, failed to warn oncoming trains of its position.

Safety improved gradually through the years. Communication progressed with the introduction of the telegraph, the telephone and, finally, the radio aboard each train. The air brake, developed in the 1860s, though not infallible, was an excellent addition. And the "block" system, using signals to limit blocks of single track to one train at a time, further reduced the frequency of wrecks. Today, computerized systems track all trains and signals.

Bridges were growing in strength and size and were elegant testaments to engineering artistry, but they were still prone to rot, stress, weather and human miscalculation of their capacities. Canada's worst train-bridge disaster, in which an engine hurtled off an open, swing bridge into the Richelieu River, was compounded by a lack of communication.

An almost comical miscommunication in the Narrows of Halifax's harbour led to the explosion of 1917. Although both a marine and fire disaster, the Halifax explosion was primarily caused by human error. One of the colliding ships carried fuel for our most dangerous technology—instruments of war. The accident happened so easily. And with such tragic consequences.

There were other explosions. Boilers on ships. Gases in mines. In June of 1930, thirty people died in a river-boat blast in Brockville, Ontario. In one particularly deadly incident, an Air Canada DC-8 exploded in the air three times at Toronto Airport in July, 1970. Wing spoilers deployed too early caused the plane to bounce on the runway, lose an engine, and catch fire as it was catapulted back into the air. All 109 on board were killed.

Most aircraft catastrophes have been caused by combinations of human error and failure of technology. But the DC-4 that plunged to the ground

QUEBEC BRIDGE, 1906
The elegant, cantilevered arm of the bridge stretching out from the south shore shortly before it crumpled, trapping 77 men in steel.

site for a day until crash investigators arrived, but they failed to stop hordes of souvenir hunters from carting off bits of plane and personal possessions.

Crash investigations escalated in November 1963, when an Air Canada DC-8F crashed at Ste. Thérèse, Quebec. A salvage team of 1500 people worked around the clock to excavate the crater, recovering most of the shattered plane. In the end, the aircraft's instruments were blamed.

Aircraft disaster investigations reached new and costly heights with the Swissair tragedy off Peggy's Cove in 1998. The Transportation Safety Board was charged with determining the cause. The Board had been created by Ottawa after the botched investigations in December 1985 of the Gander disaster, the worst air disaster on Canadian soil.

While horrifying statistics from lethal flights grab the headlines, everyday road transportation is possibly more sinister, insidiously taking lives

near Issoudun, Quebec, in August of 1957, was cursed with an unstable pilot. Three years previously, pilot Norman Ramsay had been discharged from a different airline company for deliberately diving a plane into the ground. Still deemed unfit to fly, he secured a position piloting the Maritime Central Charter DC-4 from Heathrow to Toronto. The plane was overloaded, the crew was overtired, and Ramsay failed to refuel when he had the chance. With empty fuel tanks, when he met a storm west of Quebec, Ramsay had no choice but to fly straight into the hostile weather. Of 78 passengers and crew, only one infant survived. Local authorities were asked to protect the

GLASS AND DEBRIS LITTERS CLASSROOM FLOOR AFTER AN EXPLOSION IN THE HALIFAX HARBOUR
The explosion blasted out classroom windows at Dalhousie University, four kilometres (2.5 mi.) away, where students were injured by glass shrapnel. At the time of the blast, many of the students were away at war.

a few at a time. Canada's worst single vehicle accident occurred north of Quebec City in October, 1997. The driver of a bus carrying senior citizens lost control of the vehicle, killing 43 people. This disaster was closely matched near Eastman, Quebec in August, 1978, when the brakes of a chartered bus failed killing 41 passengers as it careened into Lac d'Argent. In Canada, on average 3400 people are killed in road accidents each year. Growing congestion on streets and highways has even produced its own sickness—road rage.

In our increasingly computerized society, a single maliciously-invented virus, released to attack a world of linked computer hard drives, is capable of frightening damage. The threat of the great Millennium Bug gave cause to reflect on the utter chaos that might ensue should our computers, so much in control of our lives, break down, en masse.

PLANE CRASH AT GANDER, NFLD. 1985

(above) The recovered wreckage showed signs of an explosion and fire before the crash. Some of the wreckage was moved into piles by bulldozers before it could be investigated thoroughly.

DIVERS SALVAGING SWISSAIR AIRPLANE DISASTER, 1998

The divers survived depths of 55 metres (180 ft.) tethered to the world above by a thick "umbilical" cord, containing sources of light and gas, communication cables, a depth gauge, and heated water to warm their diving suits. Though the divers were well-trained, the crash scene exacted a huge mental and physical toll. The brittle aluminum walls of the plane had shattered making it like diving in a "sea of razor blades."

221

TWISTED WRECKAGE OF THE QUEBEC BRIDGE, AUGUST 29, 1907

In ten seconds, the bridge buckled and collapsed, dragging workmen with it. The fall was so powerful that people in Quebec City thought they had felt an earthquake.

A CANTILEVER CRUMBLES

Collapse of the Quebec Bridge, Quebec City

AUGUST 29, 1907

Another sweltering day of construction on the Quebec Bridge was drawing to a close. The south arm of the huge cantilever structure stretched out to grasp the centre span, high above the St. Lawrence River. Eighty-six workers laboured in the summer heat. Some were Americans, but many were local Caughnawagi Indians, skillful and proud to be a part of building the largest span bridge in the world. Over three years they had pieced together more than eighteen thousand tons of steel, meticulously shaped and measured, in a design that spoke of romance, grandeur and endurance.

Theodore Cooper, the New York engineer, had never seen the setting sun gild the steel web of his dream. Nor had he seen a single part of the bridge's progress. Nearly seventy years old, his poor health had confined him to his desk. He would have to supervise construction from New York City.

On Cooper's advice, the Phoenix Bridge Company in Phoenixville, with the lowest bid, won the contract to build the superstructure of the bridge. Once construction began, it progessed rapidly and smoothly.

Cooper's right-hand man was Peter Szlapka, a German-trained engineer with more than twenty years of experience designing bridges. Szlapka ensured strict adherence to Cooper's specifications, and he visited the site on several occasions. Though he had Cooper's ultimate faith, Szlapka, was little more than a desk engineer, with little experience in the actual erection of a bridge. It never occurred to Szlapka that his respected boss, the most famous bridge engineer in North America, could miss something crucial.

It would take a third party, a young Princeton graduate named McLure, to find a potential problem. On hand at the site for technical advice, McLure wrote to Cooper explaining that some of the steel web plates were buckling

THEODORE COOPER
The New York engineer ultimately found responsible for the collapse of the Quebec Bridge.

THE IMMENSE GIRDERS

A guard stands at the base of the south span. His size puts into perspective the immensity of the bridge.

COLLAPSED SPAN

(Opposite page) Although Cooper had examined and approved the bridge designs, he never accepted fault. (Inset) The ring worn today by engineers is made of steel to symbolize the structure of the Quebec Bridge. It is a reminder of human fallibility, and the importance of double-checking all calculations.

more than two inches. Alone with his designs in New York, Cooper was disturbed by this news. He demanded an explanation from Szlapka, who could offer none. Over the next three weeks, the buckling worsened.

On August 28, Cooper wired the contractor in Phoenixville: *"Place no more load on Quebec bridge until all facts considered."* He did not specifically order all men off the bridge, and his telegram was not picked up until the following day. Young McLure, arriving in New York on the 28th, assured Cooper that construction had been halted. But communication had at best been foggy, and McLure was mistaken.

And so on August 29, at 5:30 p.m., while Cooper and McLure discussed the matter in New York, a normal workday was ending in Quebec. The eighty-six workmen had tromped all day over the stressed components of the bridge. Forty-nine metres (160 ft.) below them, the wide waters of the St. Lawrence slid by.

M. Beauvais laboured on until the last minute. He had been wedged inside a compression chord driving rivets, when he came across a broken one. He'd put the rivet in just an hour before, and now it was snapped clean in two. Nearby, his workmate pointed out another one. Beauvais was baffled. He showed the rivets to his foreman, Mr. Meredith, also pointing out that the supporting ribs down the side of the bridge seemed to be bending inwards. Meredith leaned out to check, and noticed a slight curve to the ribs.

He turned back to address Beauvais when suddenly, with a deafening crack and the roar of tearing metal, the entire, huge south arm crumbled downwards. *"The bridge is falling!,"* came the screams. Those who were able, belted for the shore. It took no more than ten seconds for the structure to collapse. Time-keeper Huot, about to sound the end of workday whistle, heard the first rip of disaster and ran seventy-five feet to safety. As he moved, the deck dropped away under his feet. Once over land, he turned to see his workmates grabbed and crushed by twisted metal.

The thunderous collapse shook buildings in Quebec City, where inhabitants believed it was an earthquake. Beauvais remembered nothing.

Stuck inside the falling compression chord, he broke his leg and nose. Once regaining consciousness, he managed to wriggle free from the wreckage. Many of his colleagues were already dead, but others, injured and ensnared in the metal, still cried for help. There was nothing to be done for them and, as night fell, distraught but helpless crowds waited on the banks as the screams drowned in the river.

Investigations that ensued placed blame squarely on the shoulders of engineer Cooper and his colleague, Szlapka. Szlapka had designed inadequate compression chords. And Cooper, having ultimate responsibility, had examined and approved the designs. The investigating commissioners spoke of the two men's *"lack of common professional knowledge,"* *"neglect of duty"* and too strong a *"desire to economize."* In contrast, the media and other professional engineering organizations were charitable to the point of deference. The *Montreal Gazette* suggested *"pity for the designers,"* and *Engineering News* asked for *"suspension of judgment"* in light of Cooper's age and ill health.

Cooper's own statement to the inquiry was shockingly inadequate: *"I should have been glad to have had the physical strength and the time allowed me to have given further study to many parts of this structure, but in my physical condition I have been compelled to rely to some extent upon others."* He was relieved of any further involvement with the Quebec Bridge project.

THE ACTUAL FALL, SEPTEMBER 11, 1916

The centre span of the second Quebec Bridge as it was falling.

CROWDS WATCH AS SURVIVORS ARE BROUGHT TO THE MAINLAND

As the span plummeted, the cantilever arms reverberated violently, hurling workers into the river. Of those pulled from the water, twelve were dead and fourteen injured.

THE PLUMMETING SPAN

Second Quebec Bridge Disaster

SEPTEMBER 11, 1916

It took two years to clear the wreck of steel on the south shore of the St. Lawrence River after the first Quebec Bridge disaster in 1907. During that time, shocked engineers around the world reconsidered their theories of bridge design, recalculating stress loads and investigating construction sites with rapt attention. Meanwhile, the Quebec Bridge was still a necessary project, and it was handed over to the Canadian Government.

This time, a vast new cantilever was begun, swarming with an army of engineers, equipped with the latest scientific research. By September 1916, the cantilever arms stretched out towards the centre of the river, heavier, stronger and uglier than the earlier designs. Economy and strength had won out over aesthetic consideration. The span, 195 metres (640 ft.) long and weighing over 4550 tonnes (5000 tons), had been built on the shore, and on September 11, it was floated on pontoons, to be hoisted up 40 metres (130 ft.) into position. At dawn, thousands of spectators gathered on the banks and on the decks of boats ready to cheer as the hydraulic jacks began the task.

Progress was slow, just a few feet per hour. The spectators chatted, ate breakfast, some turned for home. Suddenly, a casting at one corner of the span broke, and the great dangling structure slipped downwards, broke its back and plunged into the water. The cantilever arms, relieved of the span's weight, reverberated violently, hurling workers into the river. Some leapt voluntarily, fearing another collapse. Flying debris tore clothes from men's backs. Twelve died. Fourteen were injured.

The cantilever arms were immediately suspect, and spectators suggested to reporters that the steel had buckled first. But the worries proved unfounded. A new span was built and hoisted into place a year later. Theodore Cooper, the original designer of misfortune, died a month before the bridge was finally complete.

COMPLETED BRIDGE
A new span was built and hoisted into place in 1917, a year after the accident.

THE DES JARDINES BRIDGE GIVES WAY

A Great Western Train derails and breaks through the rotting timbers of the bridge onto the ice below.

DES JARDINES CANAL TRAIN WRECK

Near Hamilton, Ontario

MARCH 17, 1857

The old, wooden swing bridge across the outlet to the Des Jardines Canal was known to be in bad repair. But it turned out to be, in fact, completely rotten. On March 17, 1857, a Great Western train, carrying ninety passengers and traveling at moderate speed, was on the bridge when it collapsed.

The engine and tender plunged into the canal, through 61 centimetres (2 ft.) of ice and into the water. The baggage car skidded sideways, smashing up against the shore, and two passenger cars plummeted into the twenty-metre (65-ft.) chasm. The first car, filled with people, hit the ice and broke partway through into the freezing water. Most of its occupants died on impact. The second car landed on end, and stayed that way. Ten of its passengers were killed and many others badly injured.

Scores of volunteers from Hamilton worked through the night in the gruesome and freezing wreck, lit by locomotive lamp and torchlight. They would rescue only thirty people. Sixty were already dead.

NEWS ILLUSTRATIONS OF THE EVENT

(Left) There were no survivors in the first passenger car. (Below) The conductor and two passengers jump from the last car as it tumbles over the precipice. (Bottom right) As many as sixty bodies were laid out in the temporary morgue.

CATASTROPHE ON THE RICHELIEU RIVER

The train, packed with immigrants, was already on the swing bridge when the engineer realized that the bridge was open. The engine and several cars crashed down onto a grain barge passing underneath.

TRAIN PLUNGE AT RICHELIEU RIVER

St. Hilaire, Quebec

JUNE 29, 1864

A driver for only eleven days, Engineer William Burney had never travelled on this section of track. He was apprehensive as the "Immigrant Special" chugged through the night on its way east to Montreal.

A large train for its day, the Special had eleven coaches—actually windowless grain cars—roughly fitted with wooden benches and buckets of water. More than 450 German, Polish and Czech immigrants were squeezed aboard.

The engine gained momentum on a decline towards the Richelieu River before beginning to cross a swing bridge. Suddenly, Engineer Burney saw that the bridge was open, with barges passing through, and that a small red lantern was waving frantically. The emergency brakes began to squeal but it was too late and the heavy locomotive lumbered off the bridge onto a grain barge below, dragging its coaches behind it.

Clinging to the engine, Burney was one of the first to be hauled from the water, unharmed, but 97 of his passengers died, along with two crew members. Many of the broken, crushed survivors underwent crude emergency surgery in a nearby shed. The following morning, a second train doubling as a moving hospital took the victims to Montreal.

An inquest was held, with the scales of justice plunging to one side. William Burney was assumed guilty from the start. He was not allowed to speak, nor to have legal representation. The Grand Trunk Railway, on the other hand, marched in a platoon of eloquent lawyers and managers eager to testify against him.

What came to light was that the corporation had no formal training program for their drivers. Experienced and competent firemen naturally graduated to the post of engineer, whether or not they knew the routes and signals. Was Burney even aware that there was a swing bridge on the tracks? His foreman, Thomas King, wasn't sure. "*I never asked him*," he told the jury. Nevertheless, Burney was accused of gross negligence. And the Grand Trunk Railway escaped the disaster unscathed.

MANGLED REMAINS
Whole families died together in Canada's worst train disaster.

Viewing the Destruction

Two ships collided in the harbour causing a highly volatile cargo to explode, and levelling everything within 800 metres (2600 ft.). People's homes and personal effects lay strewn out in a tangled mess. Until the nuclear bombs of World War II, the explosion in Halifax Harbour was the worst blast in terms of force and range of destruction.

Explosion in Halifax Harbour

Halifax, Nova Scotia

December 6, 1917

It was the morning of December 6, 1917 and Halifax Harbour was bustling with wartime zeal. It was a port of great excitement, of ships awaiting convoys across the Atlantic, of foreign uniforms, patrolling soldiers, and of rash speculation of German invasion.

A Norwegian vessel seconded for Belgian relief, the *Imo*, was just leaving the Harbour bound for New York. At the same time, the *Mont Blanc*, a French munitions ship, was heading through the Narrows to wait for a convoy. Vessels littered the busy port. The *Imo* manoeuvred through them, and began to pick up speed, only to find herself directly in the *Mont Blanc*'s path. A confused series of whistles sounded as the pilots tried communicating with each another. As they drew closer, the *Mont Blanc* turned hard to port in a last desperate effort to avoid collision. At the same time, the *Imo* threw her engines into reverse. Her bow swung starboard, slowly ripping a huge gash in the *Mont Blanc*'s side. Sparks flew as metal scraped metal, and the cargo on deck was ignited.

The *Mont Blanc* was tightly packed with a deadly load: her forward hold filled with highly explosive picric acid; gun cotton in the centre; and in the aft hold, trinitrotoluene (TNT). Her top deck was laden with barrels of volatile benzol that burned as it spilled from the broken containers, and was impossible to contain. Black smoke billowed upwards.

For the next twenty minutes, the *Mont Blanc*'s blaze was an awesome spectacle, drawing a fascinated crowd. In the harbour and on the docks, sailors, workmen, and tugboat crews stopped to watch the scene. The flat-roofed buildings on the waterfront, like the Acadia Sugar Refinery, offered unobstructed views for the swarms of people gathering to watch. The *Mont Blanc* drifted slowly towards Pier 6, unleashing furious fireballs through a tower of smoke.

In Richmond, the residential area nearest the pier, children saw the fire on their way to school and ran towards the harbour, fascinated by the sparks bursting upwards in the smoke. Children who were still at home raced upstairs for a better view, their little faces pressed against the glass.

SMOKE FROM THE *MONT BLANC*

Spectators who were drawn to the harbour by the column of smoke fell victim to the subsequent violent explosion.

IMO

The Imo (right) was hurled to the far side of the Narrows by the force of the blast.

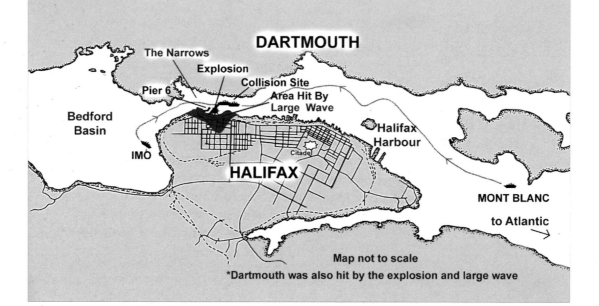

The Narrows
Explosion
Collision Site
Pier 6
Area Hit By Large Wave

DARTMOUTH

Bedford Basin

IMO

Citadel

HALIFAX

Halifax Harbour

MONT BLANC

to Atlantic

Map not to scale

*Dartmouth was also hit by the explosion and large wave

BEFORE AND AFTER

(Left) Halifax, 1902. (Right) The explosion levelled the city's early waterfront.

In the harbour, crews of the surrounding ships became alarmed and charged across the harbour to help douse the blaze. With all their might they laced a watery spray into the oily flames. Some men were instructed to attach a tow line to pull the ship away from the wharves. There were those who braved the heat and began to climb the Jacob's ladder onto the *Mont Blanc*.

Just one group of men had resisted the fire's magnetism, fleeing in the opposite direction. Just after the collision, Captain Le Médec and the crew of the *Mont Blanc* were seen diving into lifeboats, rowing madly towards the Dartmouth shore.

SURVIVORS OF THE MONT BLANC

The fire on board out of control, the Mont Blanc's *crew took to the lifeboats, racing to the Dartmouth shore. When they landed, they tried to warn people to run. They grabbed a woman and her child before diving for cover in the trees. Fortunate to survive, the woman the crew had saved gave important testimony at the inquest.*

The *Mont Blanc* was drifting dangerously towards the Halifax shore and no one could stop it. It rammed Pier 6 and ignited the pier's wooden pilings. It was nine o'clock by now, and a fire alarm was sounded for the first time. The Halifax Fire Department responded with Patricia, the only motorized fire engine in the city. Its crew of five hurtled through the wintry streets of Halifax towards the furnace. Behind Patricia, the Fire Chief Edward Condon and his deputy tried to keep up in a separate car.

In the rail yards at Richmond Station near Pier 6, telegraph operator Vincent Coleman was one of very few to realize the magnitude of the impending disaster. He could have fled, but instead he stayed to send out his last telegraphed message at 9:04 a.m., a warning to incoming trains: *"Munitions ship on fire in the harbour. Heading for Pier 6. Good-bye."* Thirty-five seconds later, the *Mont Blanc* exploded.

CRUSHED HOUSE

The force that shredded houses was felt 322 kilometres (200 mi.) away.

235

There was a split second of confusion while, according to the *Halifax Herald*, "*a tremendous, majestic and beautiful cloud of pearl-grey smoke columned to the sky from the wrecked ship.*"

Until the nuclear bombs of World War II, the Halifax explosion was considered the largest in terms of force and range of devastation. Its methods of destruction were many and extreme. A blast of air shot through the city like a steel fist, flattening everything within 800 metres (2600 ft.), and causing damage to everything within 1.6 kilometres (1 mi.). Halifax's south end was spared by Fort Needham and Citadel Hill which acted as shields, deflecting the blast upwards. White-hot shards of ship fell to the earth amidst an oily, sooty rain.

The blast's energy—thousands of atmospheres of pressure at its centre—blew outwards in a tremendous shock wave that shook the ironstone foundations of the city like an earthquake. "Infrasound"—energy travelling through

the air—was felt 100 kilometres (62 mi.) away in Truro, where a clock was hurled from a wall, and 322 kilometres (200 mi.) away in Sydney, where houses trembled.

At the explosion's core, the temperature was about 5000 degrees Celsius (9000 degrees F.), and the waters surrounding the ship vapourized immediately. The rest of the water in the harbour was displaced, exposing the sea bed, 18.3 metres (60 ft.) below. Rocks were thrown onto the city, and an enormous wave washed over the piers and through the streets of both Halifax and Dartmouth. Many people were swept into the harbour where they drowned.

Fallen stoves ignited the shattered wooden houses, starting fires all over Richmond. And the fire department was effectively wiped out. The motorized engine, Patricia, was wrecked, and all her crew but one was killed. The fire chief and his deputy also died in the blast. The tsunami, literally boiling with hot metal fragments, flooded the streets more than six metres (20 ft.) above the sea and, catching a few remaining firemen, swept them to the harbour.

Those terrifying minutes left 1963 people dead, 9000 injured and 25 000 homeless. All of the brave sailors who were closest to the *Mont Blanc* when it exploded were killed instantly, and their ships driven aground or flung from the water. Spectators—many children among them—watched as the fiery ship exploded. Shrapnel and flying glass slashed their eyes and faces.

The blast of air was unpredictable. Third Officer J.C. Meyers told his story to the *Halifax Herald*:

> At the time of the explosion, I was not 100 feet [30m] away. When the first puff came from the Benzol aboard the Mont Blanc *the first officer called, 'Look out!' That was the last thing I knew until I found myself on top of a hill, which I found later was Fort Needham. I had no clothes on when I came to except my boots.*

He'd been hurled one and a half kilometres (1 mi.) through the air.

The military took charge, trying to fight the fires and rescue trapped victims. When they discovered a powder magazine ablaze at Wellington Barracks, the soldiers tore through the streets in military trucks, shouting through megaphones for everyone to head for open ground. The shaken, injured people gave up digging through houses for relatives and hurried into parks and open lots until the army brought the fire at the barracks under control, sparing Halifax another huge explosion.

VICTIMS
(above) This photograph was published in 1918 in a book entitled, Heart Throbs of the Halifax Horror.

RESCUE WORKERS
(opposite page, top) Sailors, shown with picks and shovels, assisted in the rescue effort.

RELIEF STATION
(opposite page, bottom) Within three hours of the disaster, the relief effort had begun.

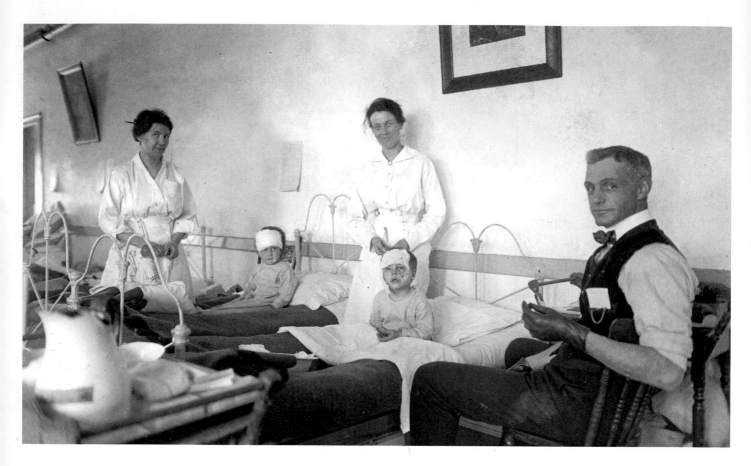

These young patients were fortunate. In some hospitals, up to five children were placed in a single bed.

The following day, with thousands still picking through the ruins of their homes in search of loved ones, a gruelling six-day blizzard began—one of the worst on record.

Wartime suspicion gripped the shattered city. It must have been the Germans' doing. There must have been spies aboard the Norwegian ship. Within four days, headlines proclaimed the arrest of all Germans in Halifax. People with German-sounding names were chased in the streets.

What was more remarkable was the people's heroism. Within three hours, a relief committee formed to conjure order from the chaos. With expropriated vehicles, the armed forces began to transport the injured to hospital. The hospitals, with their broken windows, crumbling plaster and damaged ceilings, turned nobody away. Mutilated, dying people filled every bed, the floors, the halls, the offices. In some hospitals, there were up to five children in each bed. Blown out windows were boarded up and the medical staff worked without rest in appalling, ill-lit conditions until they sometimes fainted from exhaustion. They set fractures, amputated limbs, repaired lacerations, and, most of all, they removed damaged eyes. Some survivors, badly injured and bleeding, were so stunned by post-traumatic shock that they simply wandered away.

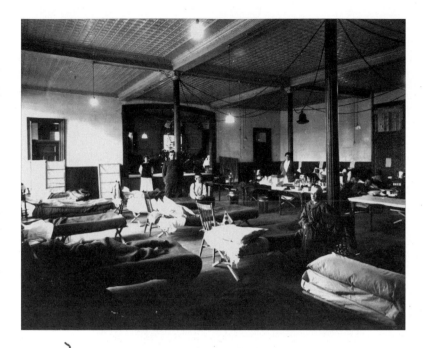

9000 INJURED

(Far left) Temporary hospitals sprang up to treat the victims. (Above right) This patient allowed photo-journalist William James to document the severity of her burns. (Left) Many children were watching from windows when the ship exploded.

Invaluable relief of all kinds soon flooded in from across the country and the United States. On his first visit to the ravaged area, a much shaken Prime Minister Robert Borden said: *"From many parts of the world and especially from the people of this continent, sympathy has poured forth to the afflicted population of Halifax... With such manifestations of sympathy and affection, the ties of kinship and comradeship have grown stronger than ever."*

But Haligonians wanted blood. As none of the Kaiser's minions could be pinned with the blame, the French *Mont Blanc* became the scapegoat. Canada had recently passed the Military Service Act, an act of conscription, to which Quebec had objected strongly, fuelling anti-French sentiment elsewhere in the country. The inquiry began just seven days after the blast, with the Honourable Arthur Drysdale presiding. The courthouse windows, blown out by the blast, had been boarded up, and there was no power. Two dim oil lamps shone on the dark proceedings.

The lawyer for the *Imo* was C.J. Burchell, who, according to writer Donald Kerr in the book *Ground Zero*, repeatedly *"browbeat and misled the witnesses"* while feeding insinuations to a culprit-hungry press. Disadvantaged by the deaths of the captain and pilot of the *Imo*—his key witnesses—Burchell attacked the French crew's testimonies. He was clearly aided by the judge who did not bother to hide his own anti-French bias.

In early February, Judge Drysdale filed his one-page decision on the cause of the world's largest explosion. He mentioned nothing of the *Imo*'s voyage down the wrong side of the Narrows, finding the *Mont Blanc*'s Captain Aimé Le Médec and Pilot Francis Mackey solely responsible. The two were arrested and charged with manslaughter. The pilot of the *Imo*, William Hayes, was named as the specific "man slaughtered."

The case for damages was brought first to the Exchequer Court of Canada in Halifax where the same Judge Drysdale heard the claims and (not surprisingly) rendered the same decision against the *Mont Blanc*. Upon appeal, the case was brought to the Supreme Court of Canada. Three of the five Supreme Court judges were suspicious of an obvious anti-French prejudice in the lower courts. Two of the three were French-Canadian. The judges decided to "apportion the responsibility equally," a decision the Privy Council in England later agreed with. Pilot Mackey was suspended for a short time before he was reinstated as a harbour pilot. Captain Le Médec emerged unscathed, and commanded French vessels for many years to come.

In 1942, the *Trongate*, a military transport ship packed with explosives also caught fire in the harbour, and Halifax faced the terrifying risk of an even greater explosion. To avert the catastrophe, Navy officials rushed to sink the *Trongate*. It littered the harbour floor with shells and cordite, and created a massive depression in the mud, but this time, the city was spared.

HALIFAX MOURNS
Large and small coffins lined up in front of the Chebucto Road School. Nearly 100 unidentified dead were buried together.

POINT ELLICE BRIDGE COLLAPSE

Victoria, British Columbia

MAY 26, 1896

In her namesake city, Queen Victoria's birthday celebrations lasted several days. As part of the festivities, a mock naval battle was being staged at the nearby Esquimalt Naval Base. People crowded onto electric streetcars to make the journey there. On Car No.16, even the outer platforms were full. Designed to seat 34, the car was carrying about 140 people.

As the streetcar neared the Point Ellice Bridge, it slowed to let other heavy traffic finish crossing first. The iron truss bridge, built in 1885, was shaky. In fact, three years earlier, it had suddenly sagged one metre (3 ft.) while a streetcar was on it. Despite repairs, horse-drawn carriages were advised to cross slowly to reduce vibrations.

The No.16 began to cross. Suddenly there was a loud crack, a jolt, then a tearing sound as the centre span gave way. The streetcar fell, turning on its right side, down into the water. Those seated on the left side struggled through the open windows. Those on the right were doomed. Onlookers pulled 55 bodies out into the bright sun. It was, and remains, the largest loss of life in a streetcar accident ever recorded in North America.

THE WORST STREETCAR DISASTER

Victoria's Point Ellice Bridge gave way when an overloaded streetcar lumbered onto the rotting beams. Fifty-five people lost their lives.

RESCUE DIVERS SEARCH THE BRIDGE

Divers search the wreckage for 18 men who were killed when the Second Narrows Bridge collapsed. The nineteenth fatality was diver Leonard K. Mot, a stunt man in the film Twenty Thousand Leagues Under the Sea. *One of the rescue divers when the bridge collapsed, he was swept to his death by Burrard Inlet's riptide.*

TWISTED WRECKAGE OF SECOND NARROWS BRIDGE

9000 Injured

(Far left) Temporary hospitals sprang up to treat the victims. (Above right) This patient allowed photo-journalist William James to document the severity of her burns. (Left) Many children were watching from windows when the ship exploded.

Invaluable relief of all kinds soon flooded in from across the country and the United States. On his first visit to the ravaged area, a much shaken Prime Minister Robert Borden said: "*From many parts of the world and especially from the people of this continent, sympathy has poured forth to the afflicted population of Halifax... With such manifestations of sympathy and affection, the ties of kinship and comradeship have grown stronger than ever.*"

But Haligonians wanted blood. As none of the Kaiser's minions could be pinned with the blame, the French *Mont Blanc* became the scapegoat. Canada had recently passed the Military Service Act, an act of conscription, to which Quebec had objected strongly, fuelling anti-French sentiment elsewhere in the country. The inquiry began just seven days after the blast, with the Honourable Arthur Drysdale presiding. The courthouse windows, blown out by the blast, had been boarded up, and there was no power. Two dim oil lamps shone on the dark proceedings.

The lawyer for the *Imo* was C.J. Burchell, who, according to writer Donald Kerr in the book *Ground Zero*, repeatedly "*browbeat and misled the witnesses*" while feeding insinuations to a culprit-hungry press. Disadvantaged by the deaths of the captain and pilot of the *Imo*—his key witnesses—Burchell attacked the French crew's testimonies. He was clearly aided by the judge who did not bother to hide his own anti-French bias.

In early February, Judge Drysdale filed his one-page decision on the cause of the world's largest explosion. He mentioned nothing of the *Imo*'s voyage down the wrong side of the Narrows, finding the *Mont Blanc*'s Captain Aimé Le Médec and Pilot Francis Mackey solely responsible. The two were arrested and charged with manslaughter. The pilot of the *Imo*, William Hayes, was named as the specific "man slaughtered."

The case for damages was brought first to the Exchequer Court of Canada in Halifax where the same Judge Drysdale heard the claims and (not surprisingly) rendered the same decision against the *Mont Blanc*. Upon appeal, the case was brought to the Supreme Court of Canada. Three of the five Supreme Court judges were suspicious of an obvious anti-French prejudice in the lower courts. Two of the three were French-Canadian. The judges decided to "apportion the responsibility equally," a decision the Privy Council in England later agreed with. Pilot Mackey was suspended for a short time before he was reinstated as a harbour pilot. Captain Le Médec emerged unscathed, and commanded French vessels for many years to come.

In 1942, the *Trongate*, a military transport ship packed with explosives also caught fire in the harbour, and Halifax faced the terrifying risk of an even greater explosion. To avert the catastrophe, Navy officials rushed to sink the *Trongate*. It littered the harbour floor with shells and cordite, and created a massive depression in the mud, but this time, the city was spared.

HALIFAX MOURNS

Large and small coffins lined up in front of the Chebucto Road School. Nearly 100 unidentified dead were buried together.

Second Narrows Bridge Collapse

Burrard Inlet, Vancouver, British Columbia

June 17, 1958

The first bridge to span Burrard Inlet's Second Narrows was knocked out by a freighter in 1930. This was no surprise to some, as Native lore spoke of evil spirits dwelling on a small islet located where the bridge crossed. (The islet had been removed during construction.)

By June of 1958, workers had begun on a new bridge. It was designed with several spans, six lanes for traffic and two sidewalks. Span Five already reached out across the water, resting on a temporary anchor of steel legs. And on that span were two railway trucks with a diesel locomotive, a huge Traveller crane, over 330 tonnes (300 tons) of equipment, and 59 workers.

Suddenly and without warning, the span's front end drooped downwards, paused, then plunged into the water with a deafening crack. About twenty men managed to run to safety, some were thrown into the water, and others were dragged down in the mess of steel. Mutilated bodies in torn, yellow life vests swirled in the bloodied waters. The fifth span's temporary support wasn't strong enough—a miscalculation by two engineers who died in the accident.

Eighteen men lost their lives. High steelworkers went on strike in response to the catastrophe but were ordered back to secure the unanchored span. When they refused, seven were arrested. Other unions—painters, pulp and sulphite workers, loggers and salmon fishers—rallied in support, demanding a safety review. The massive strike bogged the city down for fifty days. Since it was resolved that safety regulations were in effect during construction, the steelworkers settled for a pay increase and went back to work finishing the bridge.

Eighteen Men Killed

The "M"-shaped wrecks of Spans 4 and 5 killed 18 men. In honour of the men who died, the bridge is now called The Steelworkers Memorial Bridge.

STE. THÉRÈSE AIR CRASH

Near Ste. Thérèse de Blainville, Quebec

NOVEMBER 29, 1963

It was a routine evening run from Montreal to Toronto. Popular with business passengers, Air Canada's Flight 831 carried 111 mostly young and middle-aged men.

Before it even reached the provincial border, routine took an unexpected turn. The pilots applied an "Aircraft Nose Down" trim—to the maximum degree possible—a move which sent the plane into an acute, irreversible dive. It screamed out of the heavy skies, tearing an enormous crater into a swamp.

The worst airline catastrophe to that date, it provoked an extensive investigation. Fifteen hundred people sifted through the crash site. Three quarters of the aircraft was recovered. The analysis produced three explanations for the fatal dive, leaving the reason for the crash forever hazy.

One explanation was ice on the "pitot system"—used to determine speed. Another possibility was the failure of the "vertical gyro," the system that indicates up and down movement. Finally, the aircraft may have automatically compensated for some pitch, moving the nose into an upwards position which the pilot overcorrected by pointing the nose down. Whatever the reason for the dive, the plane's low altitude allowed for no possible reversal.

The destruction of the aircraft and all lives aboard was absolute. Seven crewmembers died with the passengers, bringing the death toll to 118. One hundred and fifty children would be left fatherless. Eighty widows were left wondering about the last moments of the deadly flight.

FATAL DIVE

For unknown reasons, the pilot of Air Canada's DC-8 sent the aircraft into an extreme and fatal dive. It crashed into a swamp near Ste. Thérèse, Quebec.

SECOND NARROWS BRIDGE COLLAPSE

Burrard Inlet, Vancouver, British Columbia

JUNE 17, 1958

The first bridge to span Burrard Inlet's Second Narrows was knocked out by a freighter in 1930. This was no surprise to some, as Native lore spoke of evil spirits dwelling on a small islet located where the bridge crossed. (The islet had been removed during construction.)

By June of 1958, workers had begun on a new bridge. It was designed with several spans, six lanes for traffic and two sidewalks. Span Five already reached out across the water, resting on a temporary anchor of steel legs. And on that span were two railway trucks with a diesel locomotive, a huge Traveller crane, over 330 tonnes (300 tons) of equipment, and 59 workers.

Suddenly and without warning, the span's front end drooped downwards, paused, then plunged into the water with a deafening crack. About twenty men managed to run to safety, some were thrown into the water, and others were dragged down in the mess of steel. Mutilated bodies in torn, yellow life vests swirled in the bloodied waters. The fifth span's temporary support wasn't strong enough—a miscalculation by two engineers who died in the accident.

Eighteen men lost their lives. High steelworkers went on strike in response to the catastrophe but were ordered back to secure the unanchored span. When they refused, seven were arrested. Other unions—painters, pulp and sulphite workers, loggers and salmon fishers—rallied in support, demanding a safety review. The massive strike bogged the city down for fifty days. Since it was resolved that safety regulations were in effect during construction, the steelworkers settled for a pay increase and went back to work finishing the bridge.

EIGHTEEN MEN KILLED
The "M"-shaped wrecks of Spans 4 and 5 killed 18 men. In honour of the men who died, the bridge is now called The Steelworkers Memorial Bridge.

STE. THÉRÈSE AIR CRASH

Near Ste. Thérèse de Blainville, Quebec

NOVEMBER 29, 1963

It was a routine evening run from Montreal to Toronto. Popular with business passengers, Air Canada's Flight 831 carried 111 mostly young and middle-aged men.

Before it even reached the provincial border, routine took an unexpected turn. The pilots applied an "Aircraft Nose Down" trim—to the maximum degree possible—a move which sent the plane into an acute, irreversible dive. It screamed out of the heavy skies, tearing an enormous crater into a swamp.

The worst airline catastrophe to that date, it provoked an extensive investigation. Fifteen hundred people sifted through the crash site. Three quarters of the aircraft was recovered. The analysis produced three explanations for the fatal dive, leaving the reason for the crash forever hazy.

One explanation was ice on the "pitot system"—used to determine speed. Another possibility was the failure of the "vertical gyro," the system that indicates up and down movement. Finally, the aircraft may have automatically compensated for some pitch, moving the nose into an upwards position which the pilot overcorrected by pointing the nose down. Whatever the reason for the dive, the plane's low altitude allowed for no possible reversal.

The destruction of the aircraft and all lives aboard was absolute. Seven crewmembers died with the passengers, bringing the death toll to 118. One hundred and fifty children would be left fatherless. Eighty widows were left wondering about the last moments of the deadly flight.

FATAL DIVE

For unknown reasons, the pilot of Air Canada's DC-8 sent the aircraft into an extreme and fatal dive. It crashed into a swamp near Ste. Thérèse, Quebec.

FINAL APPROACH

Toronto International Airport, Malton, Ontario

JULY 5, 1970

Captain Hamilton and his co-pilot disagreed. Hamilton, a 49-year-old veteran bomber pilot, always wanted to arm the jet spoilers—wing slats used to brake jets—while still in flight. This was an unconventional approach about which they'd had previous arguments. Co-pilot Rowland preferred to simply deploy the spoilers once the aircraft was on the ground. The same lever was used in a slightly different way both to arm and to deploy.

As their Air Canada DC-8-63 from Montreal to Los Angeles made its final approach to Toronto for a routine layover, Hamilton and Rowland reached a new compromise—they would arm the spoilers at eighteen metres (60 ft.). Rowland reached for the lever, lifting it into place. But he had made a desperate error. Rather than arming the spoilers, he had deployed them.

Braking in the air, the aircraft sank rapidly. Hamilton could not regain control. The plane struck the runway heavily before being catapulted back up into the air. The No. 4 engine fell onto the runway, and escaping fuel lit a trail of fire behind the plane. Veering right, Hamilton told controllers he could circle and attempt another landing. Before he had the chance, there were three explosions —one in the right wing, one as the No. 3 engine ripped free, and a third as the plane broke up and plunged into a field. One hundred passengers and nine crewmembers were killed at once.

The subsequent inquiry found a serious design flaw in wing spoilers that could be deployed while the aircraft was in flight, and that used the same lever for the two functions. The inquiry also cited Air Canada's negligence in failing to provide a clear policy regarding the spoiler's use.

**TORONTO AIR DISASTER
BLEAK SALVAGE**
The co-pilot was later heard on the in-flight recorder apologizing for a mistake that caused the aircraft to hit the runway, lose an engine and explode in the air.

245

MIRACLE DERAILMENT

Mississauga, Ontario

NOVEMBER 10, 1979

Canadian Pacific Freight Train No. 54 was pulling a poisonous, explosive load. Among its 106 cars were tankers of liquid chlorine, caustic soda, propane, chlorine, styrene and toluene. Near midnight on November 10, the train snaked through Mississauga. One of its wheel bearings began to heat until the axle snapped. A set of wheels flew off into someone's backyard. The car's undercarriage dragged along the tracks, showered sparks, and then derailed. One by one, 22 railway cars slipped off the tracks and crashed into each other. Some of the tankers burst into flames, followed by a massive blast that shook the ground and woke up most of the city.

"*When I arrived just before midnight, I thought many of us would not live through the night,*" firefighter Cyril Hare told *The Toronto Star*. Firefighters and residents had arrived to witness a spectacular fire that mounted 1500 metres (5000 ft.) into the air. A second explosion knocked the crowd to the ground. Pieces of metal spun through the air. A few minutes later, a third explosion sent a propane tank flying 700 metres (2300 ft.) into a field.

The chlorine tanker was the biggest worry. If it had exploded, it would have suffocated residents. Police began evacuating the nearest 3500 residents and the 1400 patients in surrounding hospitals. To avoid further explosions, the tankers were cooled and the escaping gases allowed to burn under control for the next three days.

After the derailment, hazardous cargoes faced new legislation: the use of devices to detect overheating components on the rails; reduced speed through populated areas; and safer arrangements of cars according to their contents. Miraculously, no one was killed in the spectacular disaster, although one cameraman fell and broke his leg, and eight firefighters were treated for chlorine inhalation. Residents were permitted to return home six days later.

UGLY DERAILMENT

The potential for disaster was intense when 106 railway cars carrying poisonous and flammable substances crashed, ignited and burned for days. More than 200 000 residents were evacuated from the area.

GANDER AIR DISASTER

Gander, Newfoundland

DECEMBER 12, 1985

Posted amid the decorations and the tinsel, the signs at Ft. Campbell, Kentucky said "Welcome Home" and "Merry Christmas." Two hundred and forty-eight soldiers were expected. Part of a multinational peacekeeping force in the Sinai Desert, they were beginning the last leg of their journey home. Setting off from Cairo, they had stopped in Bologne, and then again in Gander. The plane prepared for takeoff in a drizzly, Newfoundland dawn.

At 6:54 a.m., on December 12, 1985, the DC-8 lifted off the Gander runway, faltered, then crashed into the trees. A massive fireball lit up the sky. Racing to the scene, emergency teams found a trail of burning debris that stretched 1.5 kilometres (1 mi.) into the woods. Parts of the plane were hanging in the trees. All 248 soldiers with the eight crewmembers were killed making this the worst ever aircraft accident on Canadian soil.

Owned by Arrow Airlines of Miami, Florida, and under charter to the United States Defense Department, the McDonnell Douglas "stretch" DC-8 had flown thousands of U.S. military personnel all over the globe. Its 16-year history was not without blemish. Twice in 1985, the aircraft was forced to abort takeoff for different reasons, and the year before, Arrow Airlines had been fined for faulty record-keeping and maintenance procedures. After the crash, a majority of the Canadian Aviation Safety Board was convinced the crash was accidental.

For some, however, evidence of an in-flight detonation and fire led them to suspect an act of terrorism. Unfortunately, the efficient disposal of the wreckage rendered it impossible to consider physical evidence of a bomb, and to verify these concerns.

The Canadian Aviation Safety Board's report on the event mentions that the day after the disaster the Board received an anonymous call from Lebanon. The caller alleged that the Islamic Jihad was responsible for the crash.

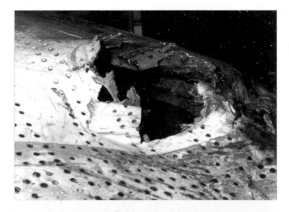

HINTON TRAIN DISASTER

East of Hinton, Alberta

FEBRUARY 8, 1986

Via Rail's Supercontinental was en route from Vancouver to Montreal, carrying 120 passengers. By 8:30 on the morning of February 8, some people had settled into the dining car for breakfast. Others were in the domed observation car. As they rounded a smooth bend, the train ploughed head-long into a monstrous freight train speeding towards them on the same track.

Canadian National's (CN) No. 413 freight train weighed 11 million kilograms (25 million lbs.). Its three powerful engines pulled 109 cars of grain, sewage pipe, sulphur, caustic soda and ethylene dichloride. It had been travelling full speed when the two trains collided.

PASSENGER AND FREIGHT TRAIN MEET
(Below) Some victims of the crash burned to death in the wreck. (Bottom) Surveying the mess.

While the passenger train was stopped cold, the freight's locomotives lumbered up and over its front cars, splitting them open. Fuel exploded into a 15-metre (50-ft.) fireball, grain cars jack-knifed forward, sewage pipes flew and sulphur coated the whole mess in yellow. A total of 76 cars were derailed.

Incredibly, there were survivors at the front of the Supercontinental, who spoke later of the horrifying noise and destruction. One man in the dining car was seared by the fireball then smothered with grain before he clambered out. All around him people were mutilated terribly. Twenty-three people died. Another 82 were injured.

CN swore categorically that their signals on the track had been working. The three-man team on the freight train should have seen a cautionary signal to slow the train, and then a signal to stop. A bent rod later proved that the freight train had forced itself through a switch and into the path of the passenger train. Popular speculation had both the freight's front-man and engineer asleep at the wheel. The men themselves could not be questioned. Their bodies were extracted from the wreckage one week later.

SUBWAY FATALITIES

Toronto, Ontario

AUGUST 11, 1995

Signals along the Spadina subway line had been checked that morning, but when a train approaching Dupont Station ran two red stop signals, an emergency-braking device on the tracks failed. The train rounded a sweeping bend and rammed into another train that was stopped in the tunnel.

Passengers at the outside ends of the trains felt a jolt and heard what sounded like an explosion. Those at the colliding ends were in no doubt as to what had happened. The moving train burrowed underneath the other, creating a mashed and twisted overlap of 5-6 metres (16-20 ft.). Lights went out soon afterwards, and there was a short period of darkness before the emergency lighting came into effect. Toronto Transit Commission (TTC) workers arrived at the scene to lead the 250 people, many anguished and confused, to the evacuation tunnel.

Rescue workers—from the TTC and emergency services—who descended the thirty metres (100 ft.) to the crash were shocked by the extent of the damage. Pieces of wrecked train pushed up to the ceiling and out to the tunnel walls. The scene was obscured by dust, dirt and gnarled metal.

After the crash, the TTC had cut power as a precaution. Without the ventilation system, temperatures climbed to forty degrees Celsius (104 degrees Farenheit). Rescuers could work for only short periods in the debilitating heat. Surgeons brought in to help free trapped victims struggled for hours in the furnace-like crash site to amputate one woman's leg in order to free her from the wreck. The woman died in hospital that night, bringing the death toll to three.

The component at fault in the accident was a trip arm, designed to deploy emergency brakes in any train passing through red signals. Many factors happened to be in place, contributing to the device's failure: it was too close to the running rails which were worn down; the wheels on the train were also worn down; and the train shifted sideways on the bend. The TTC quickly ran checks on the 879 other trip arms and began to work on modifications. Sustaining severe injuries on this, only his second day on the job, the driver would not return to driving subway trains.

SMASHED TRAIN
(Below) The remains of the front of the train at fault. (Bottom) A winch and chain hold the stopped train together for the investigation.

SWISSAIR RECONSTRUCTION
The Transportation Safety Board began a meticulous reconstruction of Swissair's MD-11 cockpit in a hanger at the Canadian Forces Base in Shearwater.

Flight 111 Crash

Off Peggy's Cove, Nova Scotia

September 2, 1998

En route from New York to Geneva, Swissair Flight 111 cruised into Canadian airspace at an altitude of 10 000 metres (33 000 ft.) and well above the clouds. At the helm was Urs Zimmerman, a Swissair pilot for 27 years and captain for eleven. Aboard the flight were UN staff, scientists, business travellers and vacationers from around the world.

It was 10:12 p.m., almost an hour into the flight, when Zimmerman contacted Moncton's Air Traffic Control:

Swissair 111 heavy is declaring Pan Pan Pan. We have smoke in the cockpit.

"Heavy" is code for "wide-bodied jet" while "pan pan pan" signifies something urgent, but not an emergency. Zimmerman asked Control if he could alter his flight path and head for Boston. The air traffic controller suggested Halifax, which was actually closer. Zimmerman agreed, started his descent, and announced the unscheduled landing to his passengers.

Within moments, the situation grew serious for the captain and his co-pilot, Stephan Loëw. Both in oxygen masks, they were racing through a long checklist—a "smoke in the cockpit" procedure—turning electrical components off and on, while trying to decide what to do with the plane. It was too heavy and too high to land safely at Halifax. They decided to dump fuel first, heading south over the Atlantic Ocean.

Air Traffic Control at Halifax International Airport had taken over from Moncton and responded, *"Roger. Advise me when you are ready to dump."* As the large aircraft wheeled over St. Margaret's Bay, dropping several thousand feet in altitude, passengers in the cabin would have been in darkness, all non-

PRESTIGIOUS FLIGHT

Renowned for excellence in service, Swissair's Flight 111 flew a popular route from New York City to Geneva.

essential power turned off. The crew, calling through a bullhorn, would have explained emergency procedures, stowing half-finished dinner trays by flashlight. There may have been little to indicate the feverish panic in the cockpit as the smoke and heat intensified, and the plane's electrical systems began to fail.

At 10:24 p.m., twelve minutes after the initial communication, together the pilots blurted out a message:

"We are declaring an emergency... We are starting vent now. We have to land immediately."

"Swissair 111, just a couple more miles," said the Halifax controller. *"I'll be right with you."*

"Roger... And we are declaring emergency now. Swissair 111."

Seconds later the controller informed them, *"Swissair 111, you are cleared to commence your fuel dump on that track and advise me when the dump is completed."* Then again, *"Swissair 111 you are cleared to start fuel dump."* But the pilots did not respond. A low thunder rumbled across St. Margaret's Bay.

Air Traffic Control had alerted staff at the Rescue Coordination Centre (RCC) in Halifax at the first sign of trouble. The moment the plane disappeared from radar, the RCC leapt into action. A Hercules aircraft and a Labrador helicopter were dispatched at once to the plane's last known location. Emergency staff were called in and immediately assigned their duties. It was the jolting start of a disaster response that was awesome both in its speed and magnitude. Navy supply ship, the HMCS *Preserver*, raced into the bay along with the Coast Guard and many volunteer rescue vessels. The region's largest hospital, the Queen Elizabeth II Health Sciences Centre, began to clear emergency rooms, preparing for an inundation. Ambulances, fire trucks and media vans sped to points around the bay. The RCC's phone lines were already buzzing with calls from journalists around the world.

Boat crews, guided in the night by brilliant yellow flares, floated through the crash site—thousands of tiny bits and pieces of debris. The powerful stench of jet fuel was hanging in the air. The rescuers searched the water for survivors. A fishing boat snagged the body of a woman. It would be the only body found intact.

CBC journalist Rob Gordon paid a fisherman to take him and his camera-man to the scene. Using the bright light of the camera, they too scanned the water for signs of life before Gordon, the only reporter in the action, delivered his live report of the horrifying scene to CBC's Newsworld.

As the hours wore on, it became obvious that no one would be rescued. Before dawn broke on the site, Swissair's head of communications in Zurich had announced that survivors were not expected, CNN had broadcast the message globally, and medical staff had been thanked and sent home.

Despite the horrifying prospect of there being no survivors, the response to the disaster was intense. Extra telephone lines and communication sites were needed at Peggy's Cove and Shearwater. A temporary morgue would be required, refrigeration trucks for the bodies, portable laboratory equipment for identifying remains. It was the overwhelming task of Nova Scotia's Emergency Measures Organization to search for and coordinate all of the resources.

On the morning of September 4, thirty-six hours after the crash, Rear Admiral Dusty Miller, Commander of Halifax Search and Rescue, issued a news release. The mission had shifted from "search and rescue" to "search and recovery." *"We did everything which could possibly be done to find survivors,"* he said. *"Our hearts go out to the families of these 229 souls...."* The ultimate responsibility for investigation and retrieval of the crash could now be passed on to the Canadian Transportation Safety Board (TSB), the RCMP, and the Canadian Navy.

EXAMINING THE PIECES

(Above) The engine awaits inspection. (Left) The complex, multi-faceted investigation into the cause of the fire would ultimately cost over $47 million.

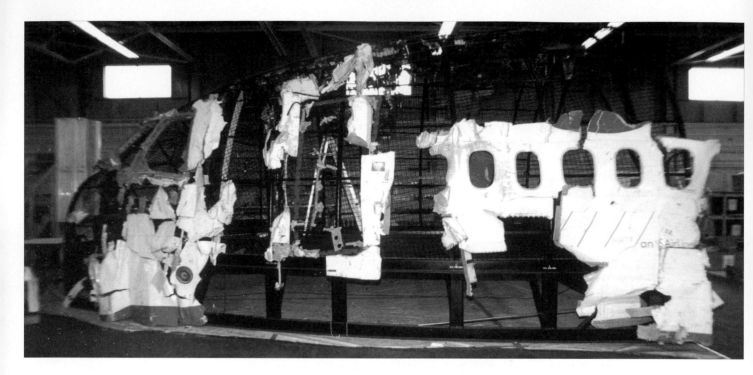

**EXTENSIVE
INVESTIGATION**

*Using evidence retrieved
from the ocean floor, the
flight's last few minutes are
gradually reconstructed.*

Navy personnel had, in fact, already been diving at the site. Arriving the morning after the crash aboard the HMCS *Sechelt*, four teams of two dove each day. They were later joined by diveship HMCS *Granby*. The wreck lay 55 metres (180 ft.) down on a bed of rock. The waters of the Atlantic were pitch black, but each diver's helmet had a powerful light and a small camera, sending images of the scene to dive coordinators on the surface. The plane covered a surprisingly small area on the ocean floor, having telescoped in on itself. Its brittle aluminum walls had shattered like glass, leaving a swamp of scarcely recognizable fragments in a sea of razor blades. Navy diver Josh Boisvert recalls stumbling upon the delicate, intact wheel of a vintage car within the carnage—just one piece of Flight 111's 13.7 tonnes (15 tons) of extraordinary freight. But Boisvert's first priority was retrieving human remains, a ghastly duty for which he believes there could have been no adequate training or mental preparation.

The divers were tethered to the world above by a thick "umbilical" cord, containing sources of light and gas, communication cables, depth gauge, and heated water to course through their dive suits. They breathed a helium-oxygen mixture for the 30-40 minutes they picked through the debris, then surfaced for an hour of recompression in the ships' dry chambers. Though the divers were well-trained for working at this depth and length, the crash scene itself exacted a great mental and physical toll.

On September 6, the *Sechelt*'s crew found the Flight Data Recorder. Then, on September 11, divers on the *Granby* discovered the Cockpit Voice Recorder. The last few minutes of the aircraft's flight could now be deciphered. Vic

254

Gerden, TSB's lead investigator, officially thanked Canadian Navy divers for their perseverance and dedication. The USS *Grapple* had arrived, a large and well-equipped American dive ship, dwarfing the Canadian vessels at the crash site. Together Canadian and American teams continued the intensive salvaging.

The human remains presented the ultimate challenge in identification. The giant plane had plummeted its last 300 metres (1000 ft.) at over 640 kilometres (400 mi.) per hour, probably spiralling as it fell. Nose first, it slammed into the water, which at that velocity would be a surface as forgiving as cement. No one on board Flight 111 could possibly have been conscious when the plane was ripped to shreds on impact.

Nova Scotia's Chief Medical Examiner, John Butt, grouped the human fragments into those that could be distinguished, and those that could not. Grieving relatives were asked for DNA samples to link with the remains, and thereby confirm everyone on board. The first victim identified was the woman whose body was the only one to be found intact. After five days of photographing, fingerprinting, X-raying, analyzing DNA and extensive information from families, the second victim was given a name.

The investigating team of forensic pathologists, working flat out, found no cataloguing system capable of handling the glut of information. A new program had to be developed to sift the details, a task that fell to the computer experts at the RCMP. Within a few sleepless days and nights, they had created one. In just over three months, every victim would have positive identification.

The Transportation Safety Board, meanwhile, had been piecing the shards of plane into one enormous puzzle, rebuilding the aircraft in an effort to solve its tragic mystery. Twenty samples of wiring from the forward area of the plane have revealed heat distress and electrical arcing, which may have caused, or been caused by the fire. Some of it is Kapton wiring which, in tests conducted by the U.S. Navy, has shown a tendency to explode and burn if its insulation is degraded. It has since been removed from long-range, armed forces aircraft. But wiring was not the only possible culprit. The small halogen reading lights on either side of the cockpit have been shown to overheat their casings. Almost two years and $47 million later, the investigation continues.

Whatever the cause of the smoke, questions regarding the pilots' role still linger. Could Zimmerman and Loëw possibly have landed the plane in time? Some MD-11 pilots claim they could

DIVER BEING MOVED TO RECOMPRESSION CHAMBER

Divers had approximately six minutes to remove their diving equipment and be transferred into recompression chambers. Taking longer would run them the risk of contracting the "bends"—a serious decompression illness that can cause paralysis and other complications.

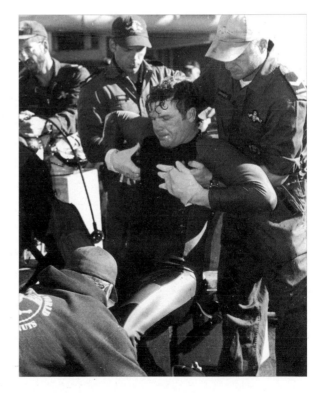

RAISING THE PLANE
Recovered landing gear is lifted onto the Canadian Coast Guard vessel. Co-operation between various governmental agencies provided valuable expertise.

have, with some *"good old American cowboy instinct."* Swissair's *"smoke in the cockpit"* checklist, with its 208 steps, was longer than the list of other airlines. Instead of sending them to the nearest landing strip, the strict discipline and training of the Swissair pilots took them diligently through their company's policy. Part of the checklist required rotating a selector switch, turning one third of the electrical circuits off at a time, a step which may have made things worse, creating an electrical surge in the already-damaged wiring. According to aviation attorney Arthur Wolk, the pilots were not trained or equipped to fight the fire. After much deliberation, Swissair has altered its policy, admitting that an emergency descent and landing is the best procedure possible.

The book is still open on the Flight 111 disaster. Families continue to follow a rocky course to settlement, although their work has been greatly assisted by pioneers in the field: families of victims of Korean Airlines Flight 007, Pan Am Flight 103, and TWA Flight 800. Hauntingly beautiful Peggy's Cove, from where the victims' families looked out across the water, became the backdrop to their tragedy.

At the Lord Nelson Hotel in Halifax, which housed many of the bereaved, someone placed an unsigned, printed message in each guest room, addressed to the families and friends of Flight 111's victims. It read that the people of Nova Scotia pledged to take care of those waters around Peggy's Cove on behalf of the families,

...for they have become part of your lives, just as they are a part of ours.

It went on to say,

Our hearts go out to you, and we will never forget. We are tied to you in sorrow and in friendship. We hope that one day you will feel strong enough to return to our province and that you will always feel that you are coming home.

REMEMBERING THOSE ON FLIGHT 111
Family members of victims embrace as they pay respects on the deck of HMCS Goose Bay.

INDEX

PICTURE CREDITS

d'Aragon, Jacques 210

Archives of Ontario 31(l), 102(b), 104, 110, 116, 119(lr), 120, 121, 181(bl), 200, 203(t), 208(tb), 209

British Columbia Archives 204-205, 206(r), 207, 241

Bruce County Museum & Archives 158(b)

Hatfield, Pearl (Brushett) 186

Canada Steamship Lines Archives 137, 142(t)

Canadian Press 149(t) Martin Chamberland, 177 Tom Hanson, 178 Jeff McIntosh, 179(bl)Wayne Glowacki,179(br, t), 212(tlr), 213 Fred Chartrand, 214 Suzanne Bird, 215 Robert Galbraith, 247(b) Jeff De Booy, 257 Andrew Vaughan, 264, 265(b), 268

Canadian Red Cross 255

Centre For Newfoundland Studies Archives 16-17, 20, 22, 23(tb), 24, 25,188, 189

Chagon,Yves Jean 52-53, 94, 95(tb), 96

City of Ottawa Archives 103(b), 112, 113(l)

City of St. John's Archives 26

City of Toronto Archives 106(tb), 107, 109(t), 166(b), 232, 235(b), 236(tb), 238, 239(all), 240, 265 (t)

City of Vancouver Archives 130, 131, 242(t)

Confederation Centre Art Gallery & Museum 163(l)

County Grey Museum and Archives 5, 13(r)

Crowsnest Museum 73

Dalhousie University Archives 220(b)

Department of Defence 92

Emergency Preparedness Canada 57(b), 171, 182, 183

Environment Canada 147

Filotas, Les 221(t), 247(t)

Glenbow Archives, Calgary, Alberta 54, 76, 77, 78, 79, 84, 86, 89, 144-145, 168, 169(b), 181(tlr), 218

Hallimand Press 143(lr)

Hamilton Public Library 228, 229(all)

Hartigh, Robert den 170

Hibernia Management and Development Company 48

Historical Collection of the Great Lakes, Bowling Green State University 156, 161(b)

Huronia Museum 7(b)

Lanken, Dane, *Montreal's Movie Palaces* 132, 134

La Presse 244

Lynx Images Inc. 70(t), 225(inset), 234(c), 215(c)

Manitoba Provincial Archives 174, 175, 176(tb), 148

Maritime Forces Atlantic Public Affairs 221(b), 255, 256

Maritime History Archive, Memorial University of Newfoundland 185

Maritime History Archives 21

Maritime Museum of British Columbia 40

Matheson Public Library 118

Metropolitan Toronto Reference Library v, vi, 4, 6(tlr), 8, 9(tb), 10, 11(tb), 12, 14, 15, 28, 36, 38, 39, 42, 46(tcb), 47, 57(t), 71, 72, 81, 87, 88, 90(tlr,blr), 98-99, 100, 101(tb), 102, 105, 108, 109(b), 122(lr), 124(tb), 125, 135, 138, 139(lr), 140, 141,142(b),151(b), 163(r), 165, 169(t), 172, 184, 192(t), 195(t), 198, 201, 202(tb),203(b), 220(t), 223, 224. 227, 235(t), 237

Milwaukee Public Library 158(t)

Ministry of Natural Resources Canada (map) xiv, xv, xvi

National Archives of Canada x, 3, 18, 19(b), 43, 44, 60, 61, 62, 74, 80, 82(tb), 83, 91, 103(t), 113(r), 114(tb), 115(tb), 123, 126, 129(tb), 149(b), 150, 160(l), 162, 166(t), 180(tb), 181(br), 193, 196(t), 197, 206(l), 222, 225, 226(tb), 230, 231, 234(tl, blr), 246, 248(tb)

National Library of Canada 58, 74

National Museum of Health and Medicine 167

Newfoundland Public Archives 27, 127, 128, 187

Nova Scotia Museum 151(t)

Prov. Archives of Newfoundland & Labrador 234(tr)

Royal Canadian Mounted Police 57(c), 97(tb)

Saskatchewan Archives Board 152-3, 154, 155(tb), 190, 192(b), 194, 195(b), 196(b)

Saskatoon Public Library 146

Scotland Yard Archives 32(b)

Seawolf Communications, Cris Kohl 158(c), 160(r), 161(t)

Springhill Miners Museum 55, 56(lr), 63(tb), 64, 66, 67(tb), 68(tb), 69, 70(b)

St. John's Telegram 51

Swissair Corporate Communications 252

The Museum At Campbell River 7(tc)

The Salvation Army 33, 267

Thunder Bay Historical Society 6(b)

Toronto Star, B. Spremo, C. M. 245

Traffic Investigations Unit 249(tb)

Tragic Story of the Empress of Ireland, Logan Marshall, L. T. Myers 30(tb), 31 (trl,b), 32(trl), 34, 35(tb), 37

Transportation Safety Board 250, 253(tb), 254

Vancouver Public Library 45, 216, 217, 242(b), 243

Winnipeg Free Press 164

Wright, Steven Lee 136

Selected Bibliography

Anderson, Frank W. *The Frank Slide Story*. Frontier Books, 1961

A Red River Rising. Winnipeg: Winnipeg Free Press, 1997

"Avalanche Accidents in Canada III: A Selection of Case Histories, 1978-1984," National Research Council Canada

Baehre, Rainer K., ed. *Outrageous Seas, Shipwreck and Survival in the Waters off Newfoundland*. Ottawa: Carleton University Press, 1999

Baird, Donald. *The Story of Firefighting in Canada*. Erin, Ontario: The Boston Mills Press, 1986

Bird, Michael, J. *The Town That Died*. Toronto: Ryerson Press, 1962

Brown, Cassie. *Death On The Ice: The Great Newfoundland Sealing Disaster of 1914*. Toronto: Doubleday Canada Ltd., 1974

Brown, Roger David. *Blood on the Coal: The Story of the Springhill Mining Disasters*. Nova Scotia: Lancelot Press Limited, 1976

Bumstead, J.M. *Floods of the Centuries: A History of Flood Disasters in the Red River Valley*. Great Plains Publications, 1997

Burden, Arnold. *Fifty Years of Emergencies*. Hantsport, Nova Scotia: Lancelot Press Limited, 1991

Campbell, Lyall. *Sable Island Shipwrecks*. Halifax, Nova Scotia: Nimbus Publishing Limited, 1994

Coates, Kenneth. *The Sinking of the* Princess Sophia. Toronto: Oxford University Press, 1990

Cornish, Shaun. *The Westray Tragedy*. Halifax, Nova Scotia: Fernwood Publishing, 1993

Craig, John. *The* Noronic *is Burning*. Don Mills, Ontario: General Publishing Co., 1976

Cranford, Garry, ed. *Not Too Long Ago*. St. John's, Newfoundland: Seniors Resource Centre, 1999

Dotto, Lydia. *Storm Warning: Gambling with the Climate of Our Planet*. Toronto: Doubleday Canada Limited, 1999

Dowson, William C.H. *The Matheson Forest and Field Fire—Ontario's Most Devastating Pioneer Fire*. Willowdale, Ontario, 1975

Drake, Earle G. *Regina: The Queen City*. Toronto: McClelland & Stewart Limited, 1955

Fitzgerald, Jack. *Newfoundland Disasters*. St. John's, Newfoundland: Jesperson Press, 1984

Gray, James, H. *Men Against The Desert*. Saskatoon, Saskatchewan: Fifth House Ltd., 1967

Halliday, Hugh, A. *Wreck! Canada's Worst Railway Accidents*. Toronto: Robin Brass Studio, 1997

Hemming, Robert, J. *Ships Gone Missing: The Great Lakes Storm of 1913*. Chicago: Contemporary Books, Inc., 1992

Hoeg, Judith Ryan. *Coal in Our Blood: 200 Years of Mining in Nova Scotia's Pictou County*. Halifax: Formac Publishing Co. Ltd., 1992

House, Douglas. *But Who Cares Now? The Tragedy of the* Ocean Ranger. St. John's, Newfoundland: Breakwater Books, 1987

Kennedy, Betty. *Hurricane Hazel*. Toronto: Macmillan of Canada, 1979

Kimber, Stephen. *Flight 111: The Tragedy of the Swissair Crash*. Toronto: Seal Books, 1999

Kitz, Janet F. *Survivors—The Children of the Halifax Explosion*. Halifax, Nova Scotia: Nimbus Publishing Limited, 1992

Lindsay, John. *Palaces of the Night: Canada's Grand Theatres*. Toronto: Lynx Images Inc., 1999

MacDonald, Jake and Shirley Sandrel. *Faces of the Flood*. Don Mills: Stoddart, 1997

Marshall, Logan. *The Tragic Story of the* Empress of Ireland, *and Other Great Sea Disasters*. L.T. Myers, 1914

McTaggart, Kenneth. *The Victoria Day Disaster*. McTaggart, 1978

O'Keefe, Betty and Ian MacDonald. *The Final Voyage of The* Princess Sophia. British Columbia: Heritage House Publishing Co. Ltd., 1998

Pethick, Derek. *British Columbia Disasters*. Toronto: Stagecoach Publishing Co. Ltd., 1978

Petroski, Henry. *Engineers of Dreams: Great Bridge Builders and the Spanning of America*. New York: Vintage Books, 1995

Pettigrew, Eileen. *The Silent Enemy: Canada and the Deadly Flu of 1918*. Saskatoon, Saskatchewan: Western Producer Prairie Books, 1983

Rawson, Nancy. *The Great Toronto Fire*. Erin, Ontario: The Boston Mills Press, 1984

Robinson, Ernest Fraser. *The Halifax Disaster, December 6, 1917*. St. Catherines, Ontario: Vanwell Publishing, 1987

Ruffman, Alan and Colin D. Howell, eds. *Ground Zero: A Reassessment of the 1917 Explosion in the Halifax Harbour*. Halifax, Nova Scotia: Gorsebrook Research Institute, Nimbus Publishing Limited, 1994

Ryan, Shannon. *The Ice Hunters*. St. John's, Newfoundland: Breakwater Books, 1994

Stephens, David E. *It Happened At Moose River*. Windsor, Nova Scotia: Lancelot Press Limited, 1974

Swayze, David. *Shipwreck! A Comprehensive Directory of Over 3,700 Shipwrecks on the Great Lakes*. Boyne City, MI: Harbor House, 1992

Varkaris, Jane and Lucile Finsten. *Fire On Parliament Hill*. Erin, Ontario: The Boston Mills Press, 1988

Watson, Lyall. *Heaven's Breath: A Natural History of the Wind*. London: Hodder & Stoughton, 1984

Wood, Herbert, P. *Till We Meet Again: The Sinking of the* Empress of Ireland. Toronto: Image Publishing Inc., 1982

Zeni, David. *Forgotten Empress*: The Empress of Ireland *Story*. New Brunswick: Goose Lane Editions, 1998

ACKNOWLEDGEMENTS

This book could not have been compiled without the assistance of the following individuals and institutions. While many people have contributed to the project, any errors or omissions found in the text are mine alone. I would like to extend a special thanks to those who shared their personal experiences with me, to those who graciously allowed me to draw on their published material, and to the project's sponsors—each distinctly connected with Canadian disasters. My gratitude also goes to all others who helped with research, fact-checking and picture gathering:

Jacques d'Aragon
Serge Blondin, City of Ottawa Archives
Marilyn Bolton, Toronto Transit Commission
Josh Boisvert, Canadian Navy
Mike Bonin, Maritime Forces Atlantic Public Affairs
Annemarie Bourassa, Musée de la Mer
Gary Branford, Burin
Jean-Yves Chagnon
Barbara D. and R.W. Chisholm
Maria Coletta MacLean and F. E. Jordan
William Laurier Courville
Robert den Hartigh
Richard Dubois, Hydro-Québec
Ron Eamer, Cornwall Electric
Debera Earl, Hamilton Public Library
Ruby Ewen
Les Filotas, Gander Air Crash
Nils Floren
Bob Hall, Haldeman Press
Pearl (Brushett) Hatfield
Paul Ho
Wayne Hollett
Douglas House
Janet Kitz
Cris Kohl, Seawolf Communications
Eric Kramers, Natural Resources Canada
Karl Larson, Salvation Army
John Lindsay
Linda Lougheed, Matheson Public Library
Yan Michaud and Andre Lamalice, Emergency Preparedness Canada

Roberta MacMaster, Springhill Mining Museum
Diane Mann, Natural Resources Canada
Pat Molesky, Glenbow Museum and Archives
Peter Mumford
Eddy Nishida
Betty O'Keefe
Jacqueline Pash, Swissair
Ron Poling and Andrea Morton, Canadian Press
Lynn Marie Richard, Maritime Museum of the Atlantic
Janelle Reynolds, Manitoba Provincial Archives
Sargeant Ferguson Reynolds, Metro Toronto Police
Scott Robson, Nova Scotia Museum
Alan Ruffman, Geomarine Associates
Gary Shutlack, Nova Scotia Provincial Archives
Heather Wareham, Maritime History Archives
Julie Warren, Pan Productions
Gail Weir, Centre for Newfoundland Studies
Steve Wright

British Columbia Archives
Canadian Broadcasting Corporation
Golden Museum
National Archives of Canada
Regina City Archives
Saskatoon Public Library
Vancouver Public Library

I would especially like to thank the Lynx Images partners: Russell Floren for spearheading the project and for listening to the gnashing of teeth; Andrea Gutsche for visual talents and a life-saving spirit; and Barbara Chisholm for clear and meticulous thinking. Thank you Deborah Wise Harris for your excellent editing; George Hart and Cameron Taylor for all your researching; and Ginny Chau, Susan Lee and Beth Yarzab for picking up so many threads. Thank you Steve Gamester for passionate ideas and tireless help and support. Thank you to my family and friends for having faith in me. And thank you Maria Coletta MacLean, Collette Yvonne, Bryna Wasserman and the M.G. for sharing all the joy and pain, and contributing so much.

CANADIAN PRESS

T he Canadian Press started life during a disaster and, 80 years later, the news agency is still the first to give Canadians bad news.

That doesn't mean that the many reporters and editors who have worked for The Canadian Press since it formed in 1917 look forward to that call in the night signalling tragedy. But Canada's national news service does know what to do when the call comes.

The training started Dec. 6, 1917, when the agency, cooperatively owned by Canada's daily newspapers, was only three months old. An explosion of a munitions ship in Halifax Harbour flattened the city and left some 2,000 people dead and dying. Telegraph and phone lines were knocked out and CP's own Halifax office, plus those of the Halifax newspapers were silenced by the blast. Yet the agency's descriptive reports dominated worldwide coverage the next day, thanks to A.R. Coffin, publisher of the *Truro News*. He and a driver skidded over icy roads for three hours to get to the outskirts of Halifax and gather information. Coffin's efforts to get the news to the other members of the cooperative were warmly received and the concept of newspapers sharing news became an important cornerstone of CP.

**CANADIAN PRESS
WAR CORRESPONDENT
ROSS MUNRO**

Munro took Benzedrine pills to keep himself awake while covering the disastrous Allied raid on Dieppe.

Unfortunately, CP's expertise at covering disastrous events is often called upon. During the Second World War, CP war correspondent Ross Munro's graphic first-person account on the disastrous Allied raid on Dieppe—written under the worst conditions imaginable—gave readers their first close-up look at Canadian troops in combat. Based in London, Munro had joined the troops at Dieppe, close enough to the action that he had the blood from wounded soldiers on his battle-dress shirt. He barely slept for three days, keeping awake with Benzedrine pills and cigarettes, while he covered the story.

Lack of sleep is often a hazard for reporters on such assignments. Ian Donaldson, who covered the Springhill mine disaster in 1958, recalls he grabbed catnaps on a desktop in a mine office for 10 days while the story unfolded. Donaldson and Harry Calnek, both of them greenhorn reporters, filed copy, first by phone and then by direct tele-type connection, from the mine day after day. Day Six brought the electrifying news that 12 men had been found alive. "We were punching out bulletins, running for more quotes, tearing to the pithead to see the miracle miners, shouting questions, struggling not to bawl, and running back through the mine yard muck to punch and punch and punch (out news bulletins)," Donaldson recalled later.

That year, for the first time in history, the National Newspaper Award for spot news coverage went to a team, Donaldson and his

VOLUNTEERS SEARCHING THROUGH DEBRIS HALIFAX EXPLOSION, 1917

CP, cooperatively owned by Canada's daily newspapers, was only three months old when its first international story broke with the Halifax explosion in 1917.

colleagues in the Halifax bureau of CP. It was not the last time. CP teams have also won for coverage of the train derailment in Mississauga, Ont., in 1979; the crash of Swissair Flight 111 off Nova Scotia in 1998; and the avalanche in northern Quebec that crushed a school gym on New Year's Day 1999, killing nine.

Although the technology of newsgathering has changed in mind-boggling ways, with reporters and photographers able to file from almost every corner of the earth via e-mail or wireless technology, today's CP reporters still deal with many of the same problems faced by those who covered the big disasters of years ago.

CP desker Steve MacLeod, working the Halifax desk by himself the night Swissair Flight 111 went down, faced the same problem as A.R. Coffin during the Halifax explosion in 1917: a vacuum of information. One of CP's Atlantic contacts phoned MacLeod to say he had just heard reports of a jet crash over a police scanner. MacLeod used CD-ROM phone lists to confirm with residents near the site that a major search-and-rescue effort was going on off the coast. But emergency officials would not confirm anything.

Just like Coffin, MacLeod hurried out to the site to see what he could see, and then tell Canadians about it.

And the sleep-deprived Munro, Donaldson and Calnek would have felt right at home working alongside CP Halifax Bureau Chief Dean Beeby and News Editor Judy Monchuk who went without sleep for 40 hours while they directed CP's coverage of the crash.

SWISSAIR DISASTER, 1998 A VICTIM IS REMOVED

CP Halifax Bureau Chief Dean Beeby and News Editor Judy Monchuk who went without sleep for 40 hours while they directed CP's coverage of the crash.

Coverage of such tragic events must be reliable, accurate and fast. CP's information is everywhere: on hundreds of newspaper pages every day; on Internet news sites; on radio and television throughout the country. Reports are picked up by other news agencies that rely on CP to cover Canada for the world.

It is a responsibility that CP's journalists, putting together hundreds of stories a day from their desks in bureaus across Canada, take very seriously.

RED CROSS

✚

Canadian Red Cross

Most Canadians don't think disasters happen to them but in recent years, disasters have forced more than four million Canadians from their homes and caused billions of dollars in damage. Payments by governments and insurers have doubled every five to 10 years. Though the type and magnitude of disasters in Canada can vary greatly, one thing remains constant: people affected can count on help from the Canadian Red Cross.

Many Canadians are aware of the essential role that the Canadian Red Cross played during both World Wars. People may be less aware of other similar life-saving services provided when disasters occurred throughout Canada's history. In response to the Halifax Explosion (1917), the Influenza Epidemic (1918), the Prairie Drought (1936), the Winnipeg Flood (1950), Hurricane Hazel (1954) and many other disasters, the Canadian Red Cross led the voluntary relief effort providing essential services to those in need.

During the Pine Lake tornado (2000), ice storms in Eastern Canada (1998), Manitoba flood (1997) and Saguenay flood (1996), the Canadian Red Cross mobilized thousands of volunteers and raised millions of dollars to provide food, clothing and shelter. When Swiss Air flight 111 crashed off the coast of Nova Scotia (1998), hundreds of Canadian Red Cross volunteers comforted those grieving the loss of loved ones.

Each year, the Canadian Red Cross helps thousands of Canadians in crises ranging from house fires and chemical spills to large-scale disasters such as floods and forest fires. Long after these disasters fade from the headlines, the Canadian Red Cross continues to provide support, helping people return to their homes and rebuild their lives.

RED CROSS EMERGENCY TRUCK PUSHES THROUGH ICE STORM, 1998

(Right) More than 1000 power transmission towers collapsed in the Ice Storm. A month later, 700 000 people were still without power. (Above) Red Cross worker helps with emergency sand bagging during Red River Floods, 1998.

SALVATION ARMY

From the moment that William Booth, founder of The Salvation Army, saw the needs of the destitute in London, England, and said to his son, Bramwell, "Do something!" The Salvation Army has been active as a social relief agency. An early extension of this work was into emergency and disaster relief.

The two World Wars saw this work develop rapidly. All around the world The Salvation Army is now recognized as a major relief agency, active in natural disaster relief and in assisting those in crisis because of political unrest.

In Canada, The Salvation Army has been at the scene of the greatest disasters, as well as those that haven't hit the headlines. From major floods in Manitoba to a house fire in Georgina; from an air disaster off Nova Scotia to a major traffic accident on the 401, wherever tragedy has struck, Salvation Army officers, members and volunteers have responded to people in need, offering a comforting word, help with finding a place to sleep, and replacements for the goods they have lost. They are there, too, to support the workers of the emergency services, and those who are helping them, listening as they unburden themselves and giving them encouragement and counsel, usually accompanied by a hot drink and sandwiches.

In recent years the work of The Salvation Army in emergency and disaster relief has expanded. Emergency response plans are in place around the country, and members stand ready to answer the call of need at a moment's notice, wherever it is. Working in partnership with other agencies, The Salvation Army is able to bring its unique capabilities to any situation where people are hurting or where disaster has struck. Truly it can be said, "Where there is a need, there is The Salvation Army!"

SALVATION ARMY IN ACTION
(Bottom left) Salvation Army volunteers move sand bags in the Red River Flood, 1997. (Bottom right) Relief trucks bring aid during the Ice Storm of 1998. (Below) Canvassing to assess people's needs after the Barrie, Ontario Tornado, 1985.

WEATHER NETWORK/MÉTÉOMÉDIA

The employees of The Weather Network/MétéoMédia are well aware of the powerful and sometimes destructive results of natural disasters. By watching The Weather Network viewers across the country have immediate access to disaster-related information, in conjunction with weather forecasts and reports. Also, The Weather Network/MétéoMédia brings Canadians valuable public service information regarding disaster preparedness.

Each week, more than 9.4 million Canadians rely on The Weather Network and MétéoMédia, 24-hour weather-related national specialty television networks broadcasting coast to coast both in English and French, for up-to-the minute accurate weather forecasts. Pelmorex Inc. operates the Weather Network, MétéoMédia and their respective web sites, theweathernetwork.com and meteomedia.com.

The Weather Network/MétéoMédia transmits a local forecast to over 1000 Canadian communities simultaneously. This is possible due to patented technology, which allows different content and information to be delivered to local markets. Thanks to one of the most advanced computer forecasting systems in the world, the Pelmorex Forecasting Engine (PFE), The Weather Network/MétéoMédia broadcasts detailed and extensive weather forecasts, geared specifically to Canadians whose activities depend on the weather. For example, through seasonal programming grids, viewers receive ski and road reports in the winter, and UV forecasts, and pollen counts for allergy sufferers in the summer. Local, national and long range forecasts ensure that The Weather Network is Canada's #1 source of weather information.

By accessing theweathernetwork.com /meteomedia.com, visitors make this web site the most visited Canadian weather information site. The Weather Network also distributes weather information to Canadians through radio, newspaper, telephone and wireless communication services.

The Weather Network – depend on us!

Through its television, radio, newspapers, phone Internet services and The Weather Network/MétéoMédia, Pelmorex is Canada's leading private sector weather information provider.

RED RIVER FLOOD 1998

While men in foreground move bags of sand by boat, a family in the background is covering their furniture with a giant tarp.

MYSTERIOUS ISLANDS
FORGOTTEN TALES OF THE GREAT LAKES

Mysterious Islands is an adventurous historical journey to islands found within the vast basin of the five Great Lakes. Standing removed and alone, islands have been central to some of the most important, outrageous, and tragic events in Great Lakes history, from a decisive and bloody naval battle in the War of 1812, to Prohibition rumrunning, to harrowing tales of shipwreck and rescue. The waves of time have left many islands behind, but remnants of the past still mark their shores—burial grounds, grand hotels, abandoned quarries, lighthouses, strategic forts, and even a castle.

THE BOOK includes over 100 stories and over 500 rare photographs and helpful maps. **THE VIDEO** takes viewers to beautiful and intriguing places through remarkable cinematography and compelling archival footage and images.

Silver Screen Award, U.S. Int'l Film and Video Festival, 1999

> "...the book is vividly illustrated and skillfully written... the video is enchanting... It takes your breath away, because it's so all-encompassing and so beautifully done."
> —Linda Turk, *Chronicle Journal*

ISBN 1-894073-12-6	Book/Video	$49.95
ISBN 1-894073-10-X	Video	$29.95
ISBN 1-894073-11-8	Book	$24.95

MORE GREAT LAKES HISTORY WITH LYNX IMAGES...

Since 1988, Lynx Images has been exploring and documenting vanishing pieces of Great Lakes history. Our filmmakers and writers search out fascinating stories, characters and photographs—clues to the Great Lakes' rich and dramatic past.

SUPERIOR: Under the Shadow of the Gods
(book and film)
ALONE IN THE NIGHT: Lighthouses of Georgian Bay
(book and film)
THE NORTH CHANNEL AND ST. MARY'S RIVER
(book)
GHOSTS OF THE BAY:
The Forgotten History of Georgian Bay
(book and film)

For a full catalogue, log on to our web site: www.lynximages.com

LYNX ∞ TIME...

LYNX ∞ PLACE...

LYNX ∞ IMAGES

Lynx Images is a unique Canadian company that creates books and films filled with engaging stories and dramatic images from Canada's history.

Lynx projects are journeys of discovery, expeditions to sites where the past still resonates.

The company is comprised of a small, dedicated group of writers and filmmakers who believe that history is something for all of us to explore.

CANADIAN AUTHORS   CANADIAN STORIES

JANET LOOKER

Lynx Images seeks out authors who tell Canadian stories in an engaging way. Our talented researchers and writers have created several bestselling books and award-winning films.

Joining the Lynx Images team for *Disaster Canada* is first-time Canadian author, Janet Looker. A native of Zimbabwe, Looker lives in Toronto and enjoys exploring the northern landscape and fascinating history of her adopted country.

JOIN THE ADVENTURE!

We are searching out powerful archival photographs, film footage, knowledgeable contacts, and stories from Canada's past for our future projects, *Childhood Canada* and *The Rock: Newfoundland.* We welcome your input and comments. Please mail, fax, or e-mail us at input@lynximages.com

---

LYNX
IMAGES∞

COMMITTED TO A FUTURE OF BRINGING YOU MORE OF THE PAST

Thank you for your support
—Russell Floren, Barbara Chisholm, Andrea Gutsche

PO Box 5961, Station 'A' Toronto, Ont. M5W 1P4
www.lynximages.com